MORE THAN
just the
STROKES

To Jance,
I hope this keeps you
on the path to personal best
tanis.
All the best.

Joh
2006
NVe

MORE THAN
just the
STROKES

Personal Best Tennis in Clubland and Beyond

JAK BEARDSWORTH

Ivy House
Publishing Group

www.ivyhousebooks.com

PUBLISHED BY IVY HOUSE PUBLISHING GROUP
5122 Bur Oak Circle, Raleigh, NC 27612
United States of America
919-782-0281
www.ivyhousebooks.com

ISBN: 1-57197-434-2
Library of Congress Control Number: 2004109105

Printed in the United States of America

Praise for *More Than Just the Strokes*

"More Than Just the Strokes is the perfect book for club players who seek to improve their competitive skills. Jak distills more than 25 years of successful coaching into concrete, practical strategies for enhancing competitive success."

—Jim Loehr, Ed.D., best selling author, including *The Power of Full Engagement* and *Toughness Training for Sports*, developer of the Corporate Athlete Training System, coach of dozens of world class athletes and Grand Slam winners Monica Seles, Jim Courier and Gabriella Sabatini, columnist for *World Tennis* and *Tennis Magazine*

"A treasury of wisdom and insight. Years of experience on the court in a bottle. A must read for all those who play the game. Fun, sometimes hilarious."

—Don Henson, USPTA Master Professional, senior tester of aspiring pros

"The most make sense, easy to apply on court tennis book I've ever read. Its many lessons actually did convert into achieving my most satisfying, personal best tennis to date. If tennis is in your blood, treat yourself and your game!"

—Trevor Lavelle, Head/Penn Racquet Sports

"Jak Beardsworth explains what no other instructor or instruction book has ever attempted—how to really understand the tennis game."

—Peter Eipeldauer, Austrian National Coach, coach of former world #10 Barbara Paulus

"A very engaging and insightful primer that has captivated my MIT varsity tennis players. This compilation of tennis articles is thoughtful, humorous, and enlightening. Beardsworth creates a unique blend of anecdote and tennis wisdom—a good match and enjoyable read for players of all levels."

—Jeff Hamilton, Associate Professor/MIT Men's Tennis Coach, Nike Tennis Camp Director

"I have been coached by many individuals, but none as able to identify innate talent, develop physical skills and communicate the non-tangible aspects of a sport as Jak Beardsworth. In the sessions we spent cross-training, I learned not only the game of tennis, but also what truly makes an athlete a competitor. *More Than Just the Strokes* captures the essence of what makes Jak a stellar coach and is the next best thing to having him on the court beside you."

—Cameron Myler, four-time U.S.A. Olympian, flagbearer at 1994 Opening Ceremonies, seven-time luge national champion

In Memoriam to my Mother,
Helen McGowan Beardsworth, who unfailingly provided
me with the very best rackets, gut, and sneakers, which she could
ill afford, when I was just starting out and
embracing the game.
And to my Grandfather,
Fred Beardsworth, a Soccer Hall of Famer,
whose mere presence first inspired me as a young lad,
and continues to do so today.

Acknowledgments

There are many individuals, past and present, who ultimately have had a part in the writing of this book. I am eternally indebted to them all. Notably Jerry Aillery, who gave me, along with a number of kids looking for their sport, my start in tennis. My high school coach, Walter Bonner, a Harvard man no less, who taught me how to play fair, compete to the best of my ability, and make every effort to always conduct myself with class. Fellow pro Don Henson, who not only shared his exceptional knowledge of, and love for, the game, but who has also always encouraged me to aspire higher. And mental toughness innovator and guru, Jim Loehr, who showed me, day-in and day-out, that there was indeed much more to playing, teaching, and coaching tennis than just stroking the ball.

I also want to thank the thousands of students and players, young and old, players extraordinaire and recreationalists alike, that I have worked with on and off court over a forty-year span—I have learned something from every single one of you, and continue to do so daily.

Special thanks to Hal Adams, who has not only represented me but has also been a loyal friend over the years. And to Linda Huber, without whose enthusiastic organizational skills and encouragement this book never would have come to fruition.

Finally, much gratitude to all the fine people at Ivy House Publishing Group, notably Janet Evans, Benjamin Kay, Michelle Dewitt, Christine McTaggart, Amy Eudy, and Tami Stoy for their professionalism and support.

Table of Contents

Introduction

As the title suggests, there is so much more to the great game of tennis than simply striking a ball. The intangibles that enable consistent winners, both on tour and at clubs around the world, are vital in a multi-faceted sport like tennis—a sport that requires not only physical, technical, and tactical skills, but also emotional and mental ones as well. The latter two have, thankfully, steadily evolved into an identifiable and coachable component, one that not so long ago was a complete mystery to most in that you either "had it" or you didn't, and that was that. Of course, it's a given that highly developed mechanical and physical skills are necessary to excel on the tennis court. However, what's not a given for so many is developing an equally high level of mental and emotional control—especially for those moments when under extreme pressure. This is not only what makes the difference in players otherwise comparable in their ability with the racket, but also what's ultimately essential in realizing one's true game within . . . win or lose.

Regarding those mechanics, trust me, all the six-frame sequential shot-making photography in the world is never going to be the end-all to honing your ball-striking ability. Nor are any diagrammed multi-shot patterns going to readily translate into a big plus in one's match management skills. And you will not find any of the aforementioned in the body of work to follow. This is not *Tennis for Dummies.* Sorry, it's just not that easy—especially in a day and age in which we are constantly conditioned to expect immediate gratification. So, you'd better start getting used to the fact that you're going to need a coach to fully grasp all that's needed—even the world's best are subject to misperceptions and player's block—to eventually consistently play to the limit of your given talent.

In the spirit of the late Jack Barnaby, whose career as a player, coach, and athletic advisor at Harvard University spanned seven decades—if you're looking for a system of playing you will not find one in the ensuing pages. When asked at the height of his success what "system" he utilized, Barnaby stated that his goal was to "avoid all systems like the plague" and "adapt to the individual." Further, the famed martial artist, teacher, and visionary, Bruce Lee, put a viable Eastern slant on the topic with, "I cannot teach you; only help you explore yourself. Nothing more."

This guide does, however, take dead aim at those of you who have been playing the game for a while, paid some dues, and continue to be motivated to improve. Those that have maintained a reasonable fitness level, learned to handle the stick reasonably well—steadily learning the myriad grip changes and the accompanying variations in stroking paths for every shot—and who have, on occasion, been able to impress their sometimes skeptical selves with patches of outstanding shot-making, represent the heart and soul of tennis in clubs and at public parks around the world.

Amazingly, far too many of these passionately-committed-to-the-game players are too often not progressing—worse yet, they are completely stuck on a "plateau," as it's politely known—at a rate that's perceived to be both significant and satisfying. This is precisely when the going gets especially tough, and why the spirit and drive within has to always strive to make sensible solutions.

The real stumbling block in the average club player's tennis world is manifested daily in the fact that they are often blatant victims of their own lack of consistency. Then, cumulatively and predictably, the players domino into a state of self-doubt, unleashing the usual stream of well-intentioned yet undermining over-thinking. Sometimes—perhaps even more than just sometimes—you lose to players that you *know* you're better than. Of even greater concern is the haunting sense that you're without crystal clear solutions regarding how to regularly go about playing the personal best tennis that, deep down, you know you can play and have previously played, but never more than intermittently.

All that you're going to need to be a mechanically solid player is addressed in the very first of six chapters. Unfortunately, some still stubbornly cling to the belief that all that's really necessary to play the game well is made possible through good technique, and that's *it*. Certainly, in the instance of dedicated club players, one must continually strive to not only offset the realities of aging through the daily pursuit of shot-making improvement, but also to keep pace with the game's ever present raising of the bar. Nonetheless, it is still, and always will be, the individual mastery over the management of one's accumulated physical and technical ability that not only embodies the primary message presented within—a distillation of over forty years experiencing the game at every level—but which also ultimately makes *the* difference.

To be sure, tennis is a very physical endeavor, not meant for the physically fragile or lazy. You're running, jumping, reaching, reversing directions, and required to be at the exact right place at the exact right time in order to connect successfully with a relatively small ball flying through the air at constantly differing speeds—along with various spins as well. But, all things being relatively equal, it is the total development and possession of other powers, emotional and mental ones—along with a working knowledge of sound tactics—that separate the big dogs from the pack in any league. Surprisingly to many, these skills are also, in the end, instrumental in equipping players to consistently be able to take full advantage of their hard-earned ball-striking prowess. After all, it's the unforced errors, the ones that you know all too well—the completely unnecessary ones that absolutely should not be happening—that drive club players in particular completely crazy, and that are always the most accurate and revealing statistic of one's true playing ability at any level.

Always being able to play at, or at least play close to, your existing potential makes for an incredibly satisfying off-the-scale tennis experience. That developed ability is especially reinforcing, and confidence building, when compared to the wildly fluctuating up and down days that so many not only endure on a regular basis, but have subjected themselves to for years on end without any relief in sight.

Along with developing a common sense brand of conditioned response shot selection in singles and especially doubles, you'll know that you've arrived when there is little or no thinking involved. Improving one's sleight of hand with the racket, of course, never ends, is constantly evolving, and is very much a lifetime pursuit. Yet all the technical wizardry in the world will only take you so far if you do not possess the capacity to consistently manage that capability on a regular basis, particularly on the big points and big occasions. Regardless of the venue, you must always be able to raise your level of play, or at least right yourself, when the going gets tough, doubt enters into the equation, and you find yourself breaking down—*above* the neck.

The very best in the world—let's say the top one hundred on the Association of Tennis Professionals (ATP) tour and the top fifty Women's Tennis Association (WTA) players—are unquestionably more than able to strike all their shots with exceptional technical expertise and authority. Some, notably those with an especially explosive weapon, are at an advantage, but otherwise all operate with a similar set of tools. But the best of the best possess something more, something that's recognizably extra—referred to lately as the X-factor. You can actually sense it from across the net, even at times through the limitations of television. This most often represents the difference between winning and losing, and always, at the very least, equates to the number one result—performing well regardless of the outcome.

A potentially championship football team featuring top players at every position, but without an outstanding quarterback to call the right plays, that makes the right split second decisions, stays cool under the gun, and adeptly takes full advantage of the talent and physicality at hand, will not only be consistently inconsistent, but mediocre at best.

If you have a fairly solid all-around game, often feeling like a million bucks when just hitting or practicing, but just as often feeling far less successful in producing the same mindset and results under the pressure of match play, you'll be inconsistent and mediocre too. Sadly, you will, as a result, typically underachieve what is in reality actually possible for you right now—today!

The mercurial career of Andre Agassi has clearly illustrated, more than once, how important having your head in the right place really is. When Agassi is totally focused and committed, when he has that unmistakable look in his eye, he can be devastating and at times completely unstoppable—the derivation of his tour moniker, the "A-Train." He can dominate from start to finish. He can even come from way behind, seemingly out of it, to win a Grand Slam. Yet when distracted for whatever reason, and unable or unwilling to quarterback himself well with conviction, his more than formidable arsenal can not only unravel—illustrated in his loss of composure in the fifth set versus Patrick Rafter in their 2001 Wimbledon semi-final showdown triggered by an overzealous warning from the chair over an alleged profanity Agassi had muttered to himself—but then also completely disappear altogether, right along with the match. In Agassi's less focused times opponents with far lesser reputations, and game for that matter, often appeared apologetic in upset victory with comments like: "It's good to get the win, but Andre was way off his game today; he was missing shots he normally doesn't miss."

When working with motivated players, especially when deep in the heart of club or junior land, I always remain cognizant of the rather large responsibility to consistently demonstrate, by example, every phase of the game as well as I possibly can. Although not very sophisticated at first glance, it's always, in large part, monkey see, monkey do! Beware of those who, while providing solicited instruction for a handsome fee, attempt to explain away their somewhat less than impressive shot-making demonstrations—typically the result of a questionable work ethic or a suspect background—with the "do as I say, not as I do" excuse. You need to seek out much better than that when it's your nickel—you deserve it.

In the mid-'90s, I found myself assisting the team of the now-retired Austrian number one, Barbara Paulus, for a couple of years in her determined and incredible comeback from carpal tunnel surgery on *both* wrists—ultimately resulting in her reaching number ten in the world at the end of '96. Early in our relationship, her superb coach, the affable Peter Eipeldauer, was totally surprised to find that I could actually play. He came to this conclusion upon seeing me change gears from my normal club role to filling in adequately for one of Barbara's usual, and more youthful, sparring partners. In retrospect, it seemed that my somewhat overzealous habit of always offering the best possible playing example for my everyday students on an adjacent court had led him—used to exclusively working with tour players—to believe that it was all I could do to keep up with decent club level players when involved in any "live" one-ball-in-play drills or when playing practice points.

Those teaching and coaching the game must always be constantly aware of another important responsibility: communicating to players, since everyone learns somewhat differently, on *their* own wavelength. It's totally up to the teacher/coach to find the "right" way to explain how one's true abilities can actually be realized in order for them to seldom experience being way off *their* game. Knowing that you're able to gather yourself when you're sputtering, or to stay the course when you're humming right along—by methodically acquiring the mental and emotional tools, as well as the technical, physical, and tactical ones—is instrumental in creating a strong sense of self-belief and confidence.

And, above all else, being able to combine it all into the development of superior match management skills, to the extent that you are nearly never—remember, perfection is not attainable—a victim of your own self is a huge accomplishment.

Nonetheless, the realities of the game are such that you will always remain vulnerable to a more talented or more experienced player, and could simply get outgunned and outclassed. More importantly, however, you *can* become good enough to eliminate losing—which is not the same as getting beaten—mostly because of complacently committing dozens of unforced errors against relative equals, or even worse, playing clearly less skilled, less experienced, and generally less capable opponents.

In the offerings inside, you'll recognize an occasional cross-referencing of key reoccurring themes necessary in fully appreciating the formidable challenge of such an athletic, deeply layered, intertwined, repetitive, and remarkably cumulative game like tennis. You'll also benefit from the enduring images and thoughts of a number of the game's very best—icons, established names, and rising stars—utilized throughout and often as examples of how the game should, and in certain instances shouldn't, be played. And a few crossover bytes, citing accomplished athletes in other sports, along with a sprinkling of notables from other relevant fields, contribute to the work's underlying message as well.

As your commitment to improvement strengthens, you will hopefully become increasingly aware of the fact that a personal coach will indeed *always* be a necessary part of the journey, and that you'll never get it *all* from any book—including this one—despite the usual representations that you can. It's always the little things that ultimately create the biggest possibilities.

Look no further than a great champion like Pete Sampras, who, in the twilight of his career, recognized more than ever the need to enlist help. First Sampras teamed up with former Davis Cup Captain Tom Gullikson—twin brother of Tim Gullikson who, more than anyone, first harnessed Sampras' awesome potential—as 2001 came to close and his longtime coach Paul Annacone signed on with USA High Performance Tennis. Then, still looking for answers to his steadily declining loss of form, Sampras joined forces with Jose Higueras in early 2002. And finally—thankfully as it turned out—Sampras went back to

Annacone, leading up to his incredible and unthinkable U.S. Open triumph as a "washed up" seventeenth seed.

Coincidentally, at about the same time Pete began his odyssey, Andre Agassi (whom he vanquished in that final) and Brad Gilbert parted ways, also after a long relationship. Shortly thereafter, the Aussie, Darren Cahill, the very one who brought Lleyton Hewitt along so beautifully to the very top of the game only to then be dismissed, was immediately retained to fill Agassi's void. Most recently, beginning in June 2003, Gilbert took on a somewhat stalled Andy Roddick (who possessed a 25-11 won-loss record under boyhood coach Tarik Benhabiles). "A-rod," as he is called, immediately ignited and went on a summer tear that led to a U.S. Open title in three short months, followed by a number-one world ranking at year's end, and a 47-8 match record during that run. Yes, coaches at any level, most especially yours, are vital and can make *the* difference.

Obviously, you'll need to follow suit in order to be able to fill in the blanks, and I guarantee there will be areas of your game that you will be completely unable to sort out on your own. Players at every level, and especially at the club level, misperceive aspects of both their strategic and tactical play right along with the nuts and bolts of their ball-striking. An experienced, knowledgeable teacher will not only keep you on the straight and narrow of realistic goal setting, both overall and with regard to shot selection specifically, but also distinguish the all-important and routinely misunderstood differences between symptoms and causes. After all, it is pointless to focus—as so many do—on a withered branch if it is the tree trunk itself that is diseased.

The good teachers also will never cavalierly patronize you with false praise, or whatever it is that some players think they want, or need, to hear. Unless you're clearly uncoachable and they've got kids in college, a sizeable home mortgage, car payments, and credit card debt, the reality of that approach would enable you to most likely succeed in perfecting inefficiencies with all sorts of negative long-term consequences. Your teacher will, however, doggedly interpret and integrate the nuances of the sport, *including* the above-the-neck mental and emotional issues—the ones that underachieving players always fail to fully comprehend—while factoring in the student's signature ability, personality, personal preferences, and idiosyncrasies. And, all the while, simultaneously considering the short-, mid-, and long-term potential that *anyone* who is totally into tennis brings to the court.

In the end it is indeed about much more than just the strokes if you're going to realize the true path to your own personal best tennis. Hopefully, the pages that follow will be instrumental in showing you the way.

SHOTMAKING

Getting a Grip

Let's get this straight from the start—there is no such thing as the "right grip." Gripping the racket in a self-customized, biomechanically efficient position—which is really what is at the heart of the matter—continues to be one of the most misunderstood and misperceived aspects of the game.

Too many instructional books, past and present, predictably illustrate generic hand-on-grip positions that do not tell the whole story and, for the most part, have little resemblance to what you see the players you're aspiring to using on tour. To make things more nebulous, no two tour players use the exact same grips anyway. Although similarities exist, grips are a very individualized component of striking the ball with both authority and control. Some are choked up. Some are way down on the butt cap. Some are identified by an extreme trigger finger. Some are noteworthy for a distinct lack of a trigger finger. Some are especially idiosyncratic while others are more mainstream, all aimed at closing, opening, or keeping the racket face right on edge.

Far and away, the most important reference point in realizing your best grip fit is the distinct arm-racket configuration that directly results in creating an optimal position of leverage and strength at the point of impact—something seldom addressed, but inescapably important.

Although I wouldn't impress anyone in the weight room, when striking a forehand my power can, at times, still be considerable. With a naturally segmented upper arm, lower arm, and wrist position, I'm able to strike the ball well in front, resulting in my legs and entire body being solidly and literally behind the shot. My exact hand placement on the handle is a byproduct of this leveraged alignment, a position of efficiency and personal comfort at the ball-on-racket moment.

Has the ball ever ripped the racket practically out of your hand? Your answer is probably "yes." You might have thought you were not holding the racket tightly enough, right? Or have you ever thought that you have a weak wrist? More than a few will answer with another "yes." In either instance, a faulty grip actually prevented you from meeting the ball in both a neutral and natural position of power, which *everyone*, all sizes and shapes, possesses to one degree or another.

For example, specific to the "well-armed" forehand grip referenced above, go ahead and place your hitting arm in the position you would use to prevent a falling wall from collapsing on top of you. You'll find that you have laid your wrist back at a comfortable angle, about 45 degrees, in combination with a slightly bent elbow. Bingo—a position of tremendous strength and power that utilizes the hand, wrist, and arm in a linked position through the impact zone.

With racket in hand, go ahead and use the same configuration while posing in the forehand ball-striking position at an ideal point of impact—well in front of your body with the racket face on edge. If I were to push aggressively against your racket face in this position, you would happily discover that you would quite easily and comfortably be able to resist even a considerable force. Wherever your hand now ends up being positioned on the handle—adjust if necessary to attain the best possible leveraged position—is *your* natural forehand grip. You'll also see that it's a long way from the tired old advice that's still given to beginners to "shake hands" with the racket without much, if any, attention given to optimal arm-racket form.

Experienced players respond to an array of ground stroke opportunities with altered grips and configurations on both forehand and backhand designed to generate varying degrees of topspin, underspin, and any accompanying sidespin that could also be part of the mix. It's the same when playing the net, approaching, zeroing in on an overhead, lobbing, serving, or receiving. These changes can be slight variations on the theme or major departures, but all have an obvious effect on the racket face position both during the take back and the follow-through and, although mostly invisible to the human eye, at the crucial moment of impact as well.

Professional golfers can carry up to fourteen clubs in their bag—

featuring widely differing club face angles and thicknesses along with differences in overall shaft length—all designed for a specific shot situation. Tennis players face the considerable task of creating their own "bag" of sticks through a variety of grip and positional changes—large and small, applied to a single racke—that are tailored to swing path alterations to best deal with the specific challenge presented by the approaching ball. Physically supporting your shot selection with such a core component of sound biomechanics *always* instills confidence—a nice combination once you've evolved to the point where you can fully realize it.

Factors that also come into play, besides type of shot and desired spin, are hand size; grip size preference (absolutely use the largest grip you comfortably can by experimenting with thin overgrips); swing speed; string tension; open stance; closed stance; and, of course, physicality. Ultimately, your chosen grips will be the end result of learning those combinations that best enable you, with your signature mechanical nuances, to strike shots in powerfully leveraged positions that are anatomically right on the money for *your* style of play. And that's what achieving *your* best "right" grips should be about.

Wimbledon titleholder Roger Federer, near illusionist, all-around shotmaker, and clearly the most gifted player on any surface on planet earth at the conclusion of the 2003 season, differs noticeably in stroking paths and the grips that go along with them than former world number one, clay court grinder Gustavo Kuerten.

It's rare that one doesn't need help from a good pro in getting this sorted out on all of your shots—an entire book in itself if fully addressed—and I highly recommend that you get it! Inefficient hitting positions, if left unattended, cannot only severely limit your continued improvement and lead to injury—especially long-term—but also become so entrenched in muscle memory that reprogramming becomes increasingly difficult and anxiety-ridden due to a methodically developed false sense of security.

In fact, grips are of such a vital importance early on in a player's development that a master tactician like Brad Gilbert—author of *Winning Ugly* and the architect of Andre Agassi's late career transformation, as well as Andy Roddick's rise to number one in the world at 2003's end—made it clear that he thought they should be left to the stroke coaches when he said, "I don't do grips."

Smooth Operator

Knowing that you can step out on the court and hold your own with just about anyone in clubland—first by diffusing pace and then controlling it in the initial feeling-out process of a trading baseline rally—always leads to another level of play and confidence. At the same time, despite the nature of a game like tennis, one that thankfully allows for a great deal of individuality in ball-striking style, there is nonetheless, underneath it all, absolutely no way around being fundamentally rock solid in order to have a fighting chance to dictate play. When this kind of strength becomes an everyday given—as is clearly visible among the very best club players anywhere, and of course a necessary staple for survival and humiliation avoidance at the professional level—these clearly personalized approaches to shot-making can be especially viable in producing, at will and completely by design, a variety of potent combinations of pace, spin, trajectory, and bounce. Being extremely reliable from the back of the court has always been such a seminal part of the club game and, to an increasingly large extent, the modern power baseline pro game as well.

The most underestimated nitty-gritty component of groundie mechanics, and definitely the most important for players coming up somewhat short when compared to the off-the-scale raw athletic skill of professional players, is the "take back." The timing inherent in preparing the racket for the approaching ball is almost always misperceived as not being all that critical in creating the opportunity for an unhurried, effortless, smooth-as-silk well struck shot. A very bad call, since it absolutely is.

An important rule of thumb next step, even more significant than exactly how and where you take the racket back, is to complete that take back at least by the time the opponent's shot bounces on your side, *regardless* of your court position at the time. Note I am definitely not suggesting that you should "run with the racket back" since that's not exactly it and is generally a bad cue. Hopefully, that approach has not been suggested to you previously since it tends to conjure a less than useful image and interpretation, and could, if strictly followed, lead to an awkward and out of balance feeling when in pursuit of the ball. No matter the speed of the approaching ball, the racket should arrive in striking position in a singular uninterrupted movement. Leave the hitches and any last second loops at home—reminiscent of the bewildering inefficient, but incredibly still lethal Steffi Graf forehand—or to the current crop of young and flexible tour professionals with, like Graf, impeccable timing, superior athleticism, and an extremely high level of physical strength.

Many players unknowingly bring the racket back twice. First, approximately half to three-quarters of the way to their preferred start point, then, at the very last moment, a second movement back, a reload if you will, just prior to launching the shot. This undermining bad habit results in uncontrollable, last second ball-striking, not to mention muscular stress and high potential for joint injuries to the wrist, elbow, shoulder, and even the lower back for anyone, especially anyone over forty.

Last-second preparation results in underachievement in any and all walks of life. Yet, along comes a Monica Seles, hitting two-handed off both sides, and windshield wiping her arms back and forth while running the ball down, and succeeding. Somehow Seles still managed to get the racket ready just in the nick of time, launching her racket into the ball without being played by the ball, while always working at producing the best possible footwork for uncanny positioning despite the absence of exceptional foot speed. But for weekend warriors, the athletic and physical management of that sort of shot timing, practiced by a former world number one, is totally out of reach.

When focused intensely on an approaching ball, the racket remains peripherally in sight through the first stage of the take back. Once it

reaches a position just out of your visual field, but still not fully prepared, there is a debilitating tendency to mistakenly believe that you
actually have readied yourself to hit the shot—you playing the ball—
which is arguably the biggest misperception among club players everywhere.

The take back is of vital importance and must be executed with soft
hands (relaxed grip), low upper body muscle tension, and in a generally smooth, easy fashion. Accompanying hip and shoulder rotation—the
crucial "unit turn" that gets everything in motion and initiates preparation, working in concert with the necessary arm/racket movement—is
also an essential ingredient in getting ready not only early but also
effortlessly for any shot. And speaking of soft hands, they should remain
just that in between shots by gently gripping the racket, not strangling
it, prior to preparing for the next ball.

Some players take the racket directly back, which I recommend as
a very positive neutral zone since most will naturally produce an easily
manageable small- to medium-size so-called "C-loop" on their own.
Large loopy take backs, popularized in the Borg era and normally fea-
sible for only very advanced players, create a higher difficulty of timing
for most since they can take valuable extra time to complete. Jimmy
Connors and John McEnroe remain etched in our minds as incredible
players who were, and still are, great models for club players because of
their economy, efficiency, and effectiveness in being essentially
"straight" take-backers. Today, the Williams sisters (whether they're playing full-time or not), and Roger Federer (the absolute best tennis player on the planet)—unlike Seles—exemplify preparing the racket early
and economically without any visible frills. It's the lean, clean, hitting
machine.

The "off-arm" for the one-hander plays an important role in work-
able preparation on the backhand side. The left hand, for the right-
handed player, should be placed as high as possible around the throat of
the racket in the ready position. This technique not only creates a
greater feel for the location of the racket head in relation to your body,
but should also be instrumental in pulling it back into position while
the grip/arm/racket position change is simultaneously occurring during the accompanying shoulder turn.

The top hand, not only dominant in striking the ball with the two-
handed backhand, is also, like the one-hander, instrumental in perform-

ing the same take back function since two-fisted players need to adjust their bottom hand as well. As a result, the left hand should always be slightly dominant in the ready position—for either the one- or two-handed player—to consistently benefit preparation on the backhand side.

Preparing early will allow you to take your time, squeeze off your shot smoothly, get as big a piece of the ball as possible, and result in the opportunity for a gradual, easy-on-the-arm deceleration of the racket during follow-through. You will also perceive, and this is a striking revelation to all at first experience, that the approaching ball is not coming so fast after all. And, of course, perception then becomes reality.

As noted photographer Greg Ross liked to repeat during his training sessions with me, "Don't poke it, s-t-r-o-k-e it."

Evolving Beyond Flat

Give me just one good reason why you shouldn't be using topspin, especially on the forehand side or with the two-handed backhand. Striking the ball with "top" is not only the safest approach, but also, at the same time, the most naturally aggressive approach to hitting big groundies. This is a nice combination, and easily learned by anyone with a little patience and some motivation.

Unlike flat shots, topspin allows for a very forgiving passage over the net because of its looping rainbow-like trajectory. Not only can you hit higher over the net and still bring the ball back into the court with great depth in baseline rallies, but you also can "bend" returns sharply down at an attacking player's feet. A club player that I have been working with intermittently for a few years, upon beginning to transform his forehand into a real weapon, said to me with a renewed excitement for his possibilities, "Oh, so topspin takes the net out of play." Perfect! And, the meticulous American poet Robert Frost said, in his criticism of those looking for a less demanding approach, "Writing free verse is like playing tennis with the net down." Playing with topspin would have made Frost cry foul.

Utilizing topspin is also an effective tool in eliminating tentativeness or, more specifically, steering the ball when under pressure. Although there can be an acceptable loss of some pace—compared to hitting relatively flat where ball compression at impact is greater—topspin players can swing the stick uninhibitedly with so much more room for error with such safer margins to the net. Conversely, knowing that you're going to have to thread the needle with flat shots, especially in crunch time, can put you on very thin ice.

The considerable forward rotation on the ball results in the air pressure above the ball exceeding the pressure below the ball, causing it to drop much more rapidly than a ball hit with very little or no topspin. This rotation, at times slightly tilted to the side as well, in combination with gravity, will allow you the opportunity to pack a big wallop without losing control. And, as an added bonus, due to the accompanying steep angle of descent with a topspin shot, the ball will also bounce sharply up and into opponents, potentially making them late if well executed, especially if they have a suspect take back.

In soccer, the very same technique is employed, especially on free kicks with a wall of defenders a mere ten yards away from the kicker, and very much in the way of the goal only nineteen yards behind that "wall"—sharply up, over, immediately back down, and in.

The technique involved is much less demanding than many club players initially perceive it to be, and there are many signature approaches to the shot even at the tour level. The key components include: 1) a "closed" racket face—angled downward and closer to parallel to the court surface versus perpendicular or "on edge"—along with a laid-back wrist position and the resulting grip adjustment in the take back position; 2) an exaggerated low-to-high stroking path that approaches the ball with above average racket speed from well below the projected point of impact and then brushes up its back side; and 3) a follow through that feels and appears as if you have rolled the racket face directly over the top of the ball. Typically, your elbow will "fly" a bit on the forehand—which is characteristic, and it will end up pointing somewhat upward through a downward descending follow-through at the stroke's finish. Additionally, if properly relaxed, your wrist will be very much involved in the "roll" at the very end of the kinetic chain— the transfer of ball-striking force beginning in the legs, then traveling into the hips, trunk, shoulder, arm, and out the wrist. Exactly where this follow-through ends up is of little consequence. It's simply a byproduct of the stroking path, particularly in comparison with any classic old schooler's low-to-high posed finish, still unfortunately embraced by those whose games have stood still and not kept pace with the equipment revolution.

An adjustment in one's margin to the net visualization, often initially accompanied by a little overcompensation until the brain circuit-ry adjusts, is always a necessity for flat hitters previously used to launch-ing laser beams with precious little net clearance.

Particularly inviting balls arriving in your "wheelhouse," knee to mid-thigh high, are made to order for very aggressive ball-striking with topspin. You can really hammer these babies and effectively penetrate an opponent even from the baseline, at times without the usual necessity of exceptional depth, due to a best-of-all-worlds margin to the net—not too high, not too low—that can be readily dialed in. The result becomes shots that really go through the court, coupled with a rein-forcing feeling of security that comes with the accompanying level of shot safety and forgiveness.

Generating topspin is also particularly applicable to low bouncing, short, and mid-court approach shot opportunities that can be difficult considering the closer you move toward the net, the greater, or "taller," a barrier it becomes. To clear the net both safely and aggressively, with-out sending the shot beyond the baseline into the weeds, topspin is an absolute necessity. Again, both the forehand and two-handed backhand are very predisposed to developing this technique, which, in this instance, is as an acute roll-over follow-through as there is.

Keep in mind that there's nothing "wrong" with aggressively hitting relatively flat trajectory shots with less ball rotation—if you actually have the skill to consistently get it done—that will travel from point A to point B somewhat sooner. Why was Jimmy Connors able to play his groundies mostly flat? Because he could! However, flattened-out shots demand much greater precision with a comparatively smaller margin to the net, resulting in little room for error. Underspin, particularly on the one-handed backhand, and on the about-to-bounce-twice, well in front, low approach, also has its uses. That difficult forehand, the one that even the great Connors struggled with at times in his career, can be safely lifted over an imposing net in close proximity by going under the ball.

On the backhand wing, a well-carved slice will not only change the tempo in a rally, but will also keep the ball in the air longer for the one-hander needing to buy some time. With the air pressure now being greater under the ball, being stretched out in the back of the court and still needing to maintain depth off the ground is very doable. It can also make passing shots more difficult for the bad guys when you're approaching since the ball can be made to stay very low to the court, along with a disrupting skidding action on any surface.

That stated, it is definitely the development of topspin—ultimately off both sides, including the one-handed backhand—that will eventually round out your game. You'll raise the level of your play by becoming simultaneously more consistent *and* aggressive, as well as develop the ability to take control of the points, and even finish them off on occasion when opportunities present themselves.

Just say "yes" and begin the process today.

Right Place, Right Time, Right Shot

You have timed your split step perfectly and, in recognizing that the approaching ball is to your backhand side, you lean into your turn and begin to run the ball down. Hopefully, you're also instantly aware of much more than simply which side the shot will be played from since the real deal is: are you going to play the ball, or are you going to allow the ball to play you?

Ideally, not only are you reading the line, pace, and spin of approaching shots, but also the all-important trajectory. Even players who lack a great deal of experience are readily able to accurately judge the appropriate lateral spacing to the ball. Lateral position to the ball varies little from shot to shot with even marginal footwork, and can even be tweaked while in the midst of hitting whenever necessary— witness Jennifer Capriati's at times somewhat acrobatic approach to playing groundies. Yet many players commonly do not recognize the necessary forward-back positioning adjustments required to play varying incoming shots both proactively and efficiently.

Whether you're hitting topspin, underspin, or relatively flat, there are three distinct ways to play the ball on a groundstroke: 1) as it's descending; 2) at the top of the bounce; or 3) on the rise. Although there can be variations on this theme, or 'tweeners, you must recognize immediately—precisely what you should be "watching"—how you intend to play every ball in order to then be in the right place at the right time.

Everyone is most comfortable striking the ball as it descends into his or her wheelhouse. Opponent's shots that approach with a fairly flat trajectory, clear the net with little margin and, as a result, land not particularly deep are tailor-made for this version. Hitting in this striking zone is anatomically neutral, allowing the entire body to easily get into the act and produce a very powerful stroke that's relatively effortless.

Unfortunately, either by design or otherwise, opponents are most often an uncooperative lot when it comes to placing the ball right where you like it. They also deliver shots that approach with high looping trajectories accompanied by a steep angle of descent. These balls—often unnecessarily perplexing to even fairly accomplished club players—can be a direct result of pronounced topspin, or simply be a poorly hit floater with a 3.0 or less player stamp on it. Compared to those beauties right in your optimum zone, they should be played in dramatically different fashion in order to hopefully gain an advantage, at least be handled without any difficulty, and without ending up in a disadvantaged position for the next shot.

Instead of allowing these balls to descend, as so many club players are in the habit of doing, they should be played well in front of the body, as always, and struck at the ball's highest point, or right at the "top," give or take a little, after bouncing. This more aggressive *and* less physically demanding approach eliminates the need to be continually backing up well behind the baseline toward the windscreen, attempting to allow these high bouncing shots to drop all the way back down into that more familiar lower but one-dimensional strike zone. Not only is this practice a huge waste of energy, but it also opens up greater angles of attack to better opponents, especially in doubles with the alley in play, which will be impossible to defend—not to mention the disadvantage of firing bombs from long range in a hand-to-hand combat sport.

Playing the ball at its apex does require particular attention to footwork. Staying busy and energized, while anticipating the optimum moment to pounce in order to be balanced and well positioned at impact, is vital. It is not uncommon for skilled players to literally jump up and into this shot, turning loose the athlete inside, particularly on the higher ones. Some players also close their racket face slightly more than normal, producing additional topspin for added control on the forehand and two-handed backhand. Most one-handed backhanders, faced with a comparatively more difficult topspin task, typically go to the slice, or the chip, and carve the ball instead of going over it, which is by no means a bad idea. Keep in mind that you should take the racket back proportionately higher on this shot in order to get more behind this elevated ball.

The third option, or necessity to be more precise, is familiar to most. Hitting on the rise involves handling an opponent's best stuff—shots delivered with exceptional pace and depth that are very penetrating as a result. Controlling this shot begins with an especially early recognition—there's that word again—in order to avoid any panic or overreaction. Since there is precious little time available, and because this ball will explode off the court after landing, it must be played immediately after bouncing, or short-hopping it, as much in front and low as possible. This is what being aggressive is all about—you get it before it gets you. The result of "taking the ball on" *before* it penetrates your strike zone will allow you to play the ball far more comfortably just as it begins to come off the court. It's much like a half volley—in this instance shin- to knee-high at most—but with a longer follow-through for added length of shot. Besides preparing immediately—without which you'll have no chance—always soften up your grip hand(s) in order to absorb the increased weight of the ball on the racket face, put the fire out, and keep the ball in play. Also, definitely avoid any foolish and misguided urges to whack these balls back faster than they arrived.

At the 2000 Masters in Lisbon, Andre Agassi, the master of the baseline half-volley, acknowledged he enjoys an exceptionally "broad strike zone" that enables him to not only play the ball the "three ways" addressed here, but also anywhere in between with, in his case, considerable authority. It's the key element in his ability to dominate even the very best from the back of the court. This is something to strive for to say the least, even if you didn't start playing tennis at age two.

At a bare minimum, you'll be able to play your shots not just proactively, but more easily. You'll also prevent all but the very toughest balls from playing you. And you'll completely eliminate any ill-advised previous habit of always attempting to play the exact same type of shot off the ground—specifically chasing the ball all over creation in order to wait for it to descend into the narrowest possible strike zone.

The Knife

Although topspin is the technique of choice among one hundred percent of touring pros on the forehand side—hopefully yours too now—it is not unusual to see the same players opting for underspin, some more often than not, on the one-handed backhand. Penetrating shots can be hit in *both* instances, not just with topspin as is commonly thought among club players, but also with the slice backhand. Referred to as "the knife" by Jim Courier after using it to fend off a teenage Marat Safin in the Davis Cup late in his career, whenever well executed, it can be extremely effective. The slice not only can take the form of a sneaky "penetrator," but can also be delivered as a waffling knuckleball that seems to stay in the air forever before landing deep in the court—a nightmare change of pace for one-speed rhythm players with suspect footwork.

The legendary Aussie Ken Rosewall is generally recognized as the model for the power slice. Another great player, Steffi Graf, came over very few backhands in her entire career, not because she was unable to produce formidable topspin, which she often demonstrated on the practice court, but because she had so much more confidence, and proven success, with her own version of underspin. Martina Navratilova was still featuring it when she won the 2003 Wimbledon mixed title at age forty-six. Former world number one, Ivan Lendl, started on the tour ripping topspin backhands almost exclusively, but later evolved into employing the knife on a regular basis once under the tutorage of Tony Roche, a world top-tenner of an earlier era. Aggressive players like retired Wimbledon champion, Jana Novotna, and other more recent net climbers—a rapidly dying breed—such as Pete Sampras, Patrick Rafter, or a still-active Tim Henman, are well-known for their effective use of the shot in keeping the ball low when approaching the net to make the passing shot a much more difficult proposition. It can also be used effectively in the backcourt to negate incoming blasts, perfectly exemplified by one of those classic Rafter-Agassi repeated crosscourt backhand exchanges—two-handed topspin bullets answered with one-handed pace absorbing, tempo-changing slices, and by Justine Henin-Hardenne versus anyone when pushed out on the wing in order to but time to recover. And, let's not underestimate the reach advantage of the one-hander when pulled out wide versus a strict two-handed player without one in the same predicament.

The versatility of Henin-Hardenne and Roger Federer's one-handed backhands had the television commentators gushing with repeated praise during their triumphs at the 2004 Australian Open. Notably, this praise was not so much for their obvious ability to rip the ball with topspin, but because of their facility to use the slice to manipulate and generally control the tempo of the backcourt exchanges, and play defense when necessary.

There are a gazillion club level players who have never fully appreciated the potential of underspin and believe that it's a liability since *their* backhand slices often end up floating back weakly and setting up for opponents to jump all over. These players do not yet understand the key components needed to hit under the ball and still be able to generate enough power and ball action to challenge the other player.

It can never be stressed enough that an early and full preparation— "full" meaning as far back as comfortably possible, versus those who have been led to believe that shortening up one's take back is some kind of cure all—is essential in getting enough stick on the ball. Without it you're dead. You will not be able to get enough racket on the ball, and eventually you'll be thinking about switching to two hands.

The off-hand, the left hand for righties, is initially dominant and especially responsible for pulling the racket back into a slightly opened face position while the comparatively relaxed grip hand adjusts simultaneously. The racket is positioned roughly shoulder high in the full take back position, the wrist on the grip hand is a bit cocked in a mostly fixed position, and the shoulders are fully turned, slightly beyond sideways to the net, with the chin and hitting shoulder in close proximity.

As the stroke is launched, the racket moves from its high starting position down through the backside of the ball, "carving" it with an extended follow-through that then travels aggressively up, out, and away from the body—not mostly around like a topspin forehand—after impact. Had a ball been lodged in your hitting armpit while taking the racket back, it would drop completely out during the stroke's finish.

The power component is triggered by lowering your center of gravity substantially, also referred to as "sitting down" on the shot, by bending your knees as the ball is being struck and then staying low through the end of the follow-through. This moves the point of impact well in front—never the case with the typically weak club player slice—allowing for some surprising pop on the shot. Floating underspin backhands are always struck late, causing these players to lean back, stand up at impact, push the ball back into play (at best), and end up having little depth or weight of shot. Apprehensive players, so conditioned to being late, lean back at first sight of an approaching deep shot, setting the late hitting cycle in motion by inviting the ball to play them.

Staying sideways during the entire shot, by keeping your weight on the front leg and by leaving the off-arm behind as an anchor once the racket is released, will keep you balanced and prevent you from coming weakly across the ball versus directly through it with authority. It will also eliminate those embarrassing mis-hits off the end of the frame when opening up prematurely and "coming off" the shot. You can naturally rotate right out of a forehand during the follow-through, or even somewhat before when utilizing an open stance. Not so on the one-handed backhand where you must complete the follow-through before rotating out to recover position, resulting in a necessary but completely manageable delay, compared to the forehand, with no court coverage downside because of the pace-slowing underspin.

When hitting down the line, carve under the *inside* of the ball with the racket head down; when going crosscourt, go under the ball but on its *outside* surface by getting down really low to keep the racket head up and somewhat elevated at impact. In either instance, the resulting shot will not only skid explosively upon landing, but will also fade away from the player in pursuit. In doubles, the deuce court player can also strike the ball on the inside to produce the "off crosscourt" backhand slice—especially on the return—a shot rarely needed in singles but essential in the doubles game at any level.

Naturally, if you're going to get what you expect out of the knife, you'll also have to visualize the appropriate shot trajectory, one that passes relatively low over the net yet still delivers the ball deep in the court. Again, since underspin keeps the ball in the air longer than a typical topspin or flat shot, you'll have ample time to recover position. By gaining both time and depth, you'll be able to keep your opponent pinned—handcuffed by the heaviness and skidding action of your ball, or put off by a pace-changing flutter ball so perfectly exemplified in the Rafter-Agassi match-up—and hard pressed to counter effectively.

Combine the ability to vary the trajectory and degree of topspin on the forehand, at will, along with the skill to rip a topspin backhand whenever the ball is right in your zone, and you've really got something: a complete arsenal of groundies—all the answers—to be reckoned with.

Eliminating the Bounce

Taking the ball cleanly in the air consistently from any place on the court is no easy proposition. Yet, the attraction lies in the fact that the advantage of volleying reliably is absolutely essential in playing really good doubles, and nice to have at your disposal in singles as well. Whether it's being able to move in confidently behind a mid-court approach shot, denying a down-the-line pass, or making a quick poaching move in doubles, the ability to volley skillfully can provide you with the flexibility and freedom to play shots from anywhere.

Since club players often struggle with transition volleys in particular, usually because it's so tempting to over swing, it's not a bad idea to get solid by taking a page from the Patrick Rafter book—Volley 101. The very first image of the classic Rafter volley that comes to mind is that of the Aussie getting way down in order to play those tough low ones as close to eye level as possible. Balls that are already up in the strike zone, the ones that can be easily volleyed eye-high without the necessity of a great deal of knee bend, are of course the easiest to execute. Rafter's commitment to taking every volley around eye level is a major part of the reason that he was recognized as the best pure volleyer in the game, and also a very accomplished serve-and-volley player before retiring. His skill was all the more remarkable since the sport has steadily morphed into points involving balls being bludgeoned back and forth almost exclusively from the back of the court. The two-time U.S. Open champion's model low center of gravity, matched to the height of the ball, creates not only an excellent opportunity to strike volleys well in front with superior leverage, but also, as a direct result, allows one to see the ball extremely well. Rafter's resolve and commitment to physically getting down resulted in his exceptional ability to consistently spank and carve balls simultaneously, including the difficult low ones, with authority *and* control.

Every volley, whether you're on the way to the net or already in, needs to be preceded by a well-timed split step that's landed at the exact moment the opponent is striking the ball. Without it, you will never own a solid volley. Where you are positioned at their moment of impact is irrelevant—there is no "right" place to split step—although the closer in, the better. This technique results in the ability to explode quickly to the ball, to the right or left, and forward on the diagonal as well. Then, remaining relatively still during the moment of impact—especially important when still in transition and farther away from the net than you'd like to be—will allow you to control these difficult approach volleys more than you thought was ever possible. The necessary passage through no-man's land on your way in—perceived by so many as precarious at best—will become a considerably more attractive task.

Never run through approach volleys because you're in a hurry to get to the net. Some players have been conditioned to get in as fast as they can—usually at the expense of controlling the shot itself—as their top priority. It's not a track meet. You've also got this stick in hand and there's a ball sailing through the air that must be struck on the fly. (Ever notice how world-class track athletes can inexplicably drop the baton in relays during the hand-off?) This run-away-train mentality most often results in a failure to execute a well-timed split step, a wild swing while still on the move, and a predictable unforced error. Even more frustrating at the point's end is the realization, as it most often turns out, that ultimately there was no resulting opportunity at the net to close in for anyway.

When in any volleying situation, contrary to anticipating a groundie, keep the racket face elevated well above the wrist in the ready position. Players who do not adjust a normally lower racket ready position also often end up triggering unwieldy take backs that result in roundhouse volley attempts resembling groundstrokes. In the same vein, those groundie grips will also need to be adjusted in the ready position, while closing, toward a more continental position in order to be able to get under the ball and play it with underspin.

Solid volley technique mostly involves moving the racket head as little as possible, both on the take back and in the actual striking of the ball. Did anyone ever move the racket head as little as John McEnroe? Many metaphors are utilized to trigger an effective response; especially the typical "punch it" or "block it." Fair enough, but I've always preferred "spank it" since the act of spanking—either gently (as in touch) or forcefully (as in pace)—is something that just about everyone can readily relate to. Punching and blocking are not only less familiar to many, but are also technically less accurate for club players since (as cues) they typically raise both grip and arm muscle tension unnecessarily. In Mac's case, even the seemingly softest of volleys in his prime were, and often still are today, sufficient to generate enough power to get the job done through the superior timing of such an understated technique.

Unlike just about every shot in the game where hitting completely through the ball is at a premium, volleying skill involves the technique of hitting more at the ball while still striving to lay the racket fully on the ball—to get as much of it as possible—but then immediately pulling back into a ready position after a small follow-through. A term not used much anymore to describe this skill, but still analogous, is "stop volley."

Once, while working with former U.S. Davis Cup captain Tom Gorman at a corporate clinic for—would you believe—the Mars candy bar people, it didn't take long to recognize that, although enthusiastic, our particular group was not made up of tennis players in any way, shape, or form. Tom gave them the basics at the net and I put them through a simple drill with some very ugly results, even for beginners. Our group wasn't very athletic, either. Tom, patient as a saint, then picked a few "volunteers." One by one, standing behind them in close proximity, he held their racket hand in his, asked them to relax (ha!), positioned their racket in an ideal strike zone (eye-high), and directed me to feed the ball right onto their racket face. Then, with the former world-class performer's hand leading the way, they began to get the feeling of a short spanking movement on the forehand volley as opposed to the wild, panicked attempts these rookies were previously taking, despite what we both thought was a perfectly good demonstration of what the shot should look like.

Regarding the previously alluded to degree of grip tension necessary to volley effectively, let's clear up any myths. The only instance in which you should ever be aware of an extremely tight grip, whether it's on the volley or any other shot for that matter, is when you have inadvertently allowed the ball to play you. The ball-racket collision occurs in the wrong place at the wrong time, spontaneously triggering a last moment death grip in attempting to fight the ball off.

In a well-timed shot, when you are playing ball and not vice versa, the racket dominates the ball—right place, right time—and a well-struck shot is produced with comparatively nominal grip tension, *especially with today's large head, high tech sticks*. The racket does the work very nicely, thank you; stay out of it as much as possible. You're absolutely going to instinctively "grip it up" a bit anyway, so just relax.

The role of the wrist in playing the net is equally misunderstood. Imagine for a moment that your wrist is completely fused, that it is totally immobilized. Now try to take the ball in the air. It doesn't get any more awkward and inefficient. You can't help but take a big, stiff, labored swing at the ball with the total elimination of the wrist. Obviously, you wouldn't want a full range of wrist motion either, but some—albeit only slight—should be incorporated into the shot in order to realize a classic volley technique to the fullest.

Getting back to the earlier "carving" reference regarding the Rafter model, almost all volleys—with the exception of the now commonplace swinging mid-court topspin forehand volley (first popularized by a few back court specialists in the early 1990s), or any sitters right at the net that can also be aggressively struck relatively flat from either side—are played with measured underspin. But they are also produced with a bit of sidespin as well, either inside or outside of the ball, in order to maximize control of the shot in an anatomically neutral position. Balls that are "away"—ones that have to be stretched for—and higher in the strike zone are gone "around" to a degree. Balls that are "in"—ones that are close to the body—and low are played on the "inside."

While on the subject of balls on the inside, a rule of thumb, particularly regarding handling shots that are right at you, is this: balls chest-high and above should be played with the forehand; balls stomach-high and below should be played with the backhand. Any last-second movement to the side to create additional hitting space, especially on the higher forehand where you can really get jammed, will make the shot substantially easier to play.

Grips are also the subject of much confusion at the club level, notably because so many players have been told they do not have time to change their grip. *What?* This belief is one of the biggest myths in the game. There is plenty of time to execute a slight change, all that's necessary in order to open the racket face for the desired carving opportunity. The degree of change isn't nearly as great an adjustment, for example, as the one necessary to switch from a Western forehand groundie to an equally closed racket face on a topspin backhand, one or two-handed. In fact, the change in grip, or, more accurately, the change in the arm-racket hitting position, is considerably less by comparison.

Picture our model, Patrick Rafter, at the moment of impact on the forehand side—the racket face leading, the wrist laid back, the elbow slightly bent, all in order to create a segmented positioned of leverage and strength. Would that exact position be functional while reaching across your body for a backhand volley? Of course not—no way! What you would have would be an arm-racket configuration without any strength or leverage, and a complete inability to strike the ball well in front of the body. You absolutely have to make an adjustment of some kind. Those who actually believe they do not have time to change positions are typically players who watch the ball poorly, and who, as a result, are both startled and at times even threatened at the last moment by a harmlessly approaching ball that might have a little extra pace.

When already well positioned at the net, a key component of volleying confidently is constantly stimulating your feet in synch with what's happening on the other side, as opposed to standing flat-footed while waiting for the opponent to strike their shot. Keeping your "motor" going will actually keep your eyes connected to the ball, trigger the absolutely essential split step, and provide plenty of time to change arm/racket/grip positions as necessary in order to make an unhurried, crisp volley.

You'll never be able to play legitimate doubles until you're able to confidently eliminate the bounce whenever the opportunity presents itself. And, you will always be a one-dimensional baseliner in singles with no options when losing from the back of the court, or when you should be taking advantage of short balls–in either game–that your penetrating baseline shots have set up for you.

Start getting both your technique and physical self down *now*. It's not as difficult as you might think. Do not allow yourself to be overcome with fear by any perceived pressure. And never foolishly believe that every single ball taken in the air should be a winner—an unrealistic goal that even an incredibly skilled volleyer like Rafter, always exceedingly aggressive yet stubbornly patient at the very same time, never even came close to sharing.

Bending It In

Developing an aggressive serve with spin is recognized by tennis coaches as both the most challenging and important shot to learn among those players seeking to have a truly serious game. Unfortunately, since it is the most essential component in not only being an all-around server, but a complete player as well, it's all too often the last addressed, if ever. Players, even fairly good players, who are limited to flat serves—especially tentative, "patty cake" second serves—are in big trouble against otherwise relative equals who *can* routinely spin serves in with confidence and authority, especially under pressure, and who can also take advantage on the return of serve versus those who cannot. That being the case, the match is over before it starts.

Take Elena Dementieva's shockingly poor service performance in her completely one-sided loss to fellow Russian Anastasiya Myskina in the 2004 French Open final. After prevailing over sixty-three of the world's best in her half of the draw, the ninth-ranked player in the world not only made an over-the-limit number of errors off the ground, but also double faulted ten times while winning precious few second serve points behind her less-than-professional delivery. At the post-match press conference, a tearful Dementieva first confessed, "I hate my serve," then incredulously added, "I don't know how to serve."

The key benefit of the "bender"—the particular type of spin serve that will dramatically change your station among your peers—is a looping trajectory that's generated by both a slight change of grip and an adjustment in the toss compared to what's utilized on relatively flat serves. The resulting ball path will allow the serve to clear the net—a formidable three foot-plus barrier—with a very safe margin for error while still landing in a box measuring only twenty-one feet long by thirteen-and-one-half feet wide from thirty-nine feet away.

By tossing the ball closer to your body, you'll be able to naturally hit "up" on the ball and "over it," ideally with a relaxed wrist to produce an optimal combination of sidespin *and* topspin. It is positioned nearly above your head, and slightly left of the usual flat power toss that's typically placed directly in front and in alignment with your forward moving hitting shoulder. Some players benefit from picturing themselves striking the ball at an approximate one o'clock location. The resulting rainbow-like ball trajectory passes high over the net, with minimal right to left movement for the right-handed player, and then dips sharply downward at the last moment due to the effect of the heavy rotation on the ball. This serve is particularly effective when serving up the "T" from the deuce court, and when serving out wide in the ad court, to confront an opponent's backhand return.

Before continuing, I have a few words to share on tossing technique. Ideally, it involves a soft, relaxed, full-range-of-motion movement. Once one's startup ritual is complete, it ultimately begins its upward path from just in front of the forward positioned leg's thigh. The weight and momentum of a neutrally positioned tossing arm (the very position it would naturally assume hanging by your side, as opposed to palm up or palm down) is sufficient to get the ball in the air to the desired strike point. Do not rush the toss and fling it up like a hot potato. Guide it up while gently holding it in your fingertips—not surrounded in the palm of your hand—and release it with as little spin as possible upon reaching a *fully* extended position. Although not "wrong" to begin with the connected tossing and hitting arms extended well in front of the body, most players can avoid flipping or "hooking" the ball too far backward—*the* common error—by beginning in a position closer to the body with the elbows comfortably "in." This will allow for better ball control, regardless of chosen toss location, and trigger the full extension already noted during release.

With a new awareness of their tossing technique, some will ask, "Then what do I do with my arm after hitting the serve?" A nice improvement in one's service motion can also be gained by allowing the tossing arm to naturally "fold" into the abdominal area during impact and throughout the follow-through.

Coupled with the tossing change needed to bend it in, you'll also need a corresponding adjustment in your grip towards a traditional one-handed eastern backhand position—learned most easily in very small, cautious, gradual increments (one sixteenth of an inch at a time) until you've got just the right position and feel. The racket face will then be favorably altered into a more closed, spin-imparting position during impact. In principle, it's very much akin to the mechanics necessary to produce topspin on a groundstroke, but with the grip change in reverse, if you will.

Since you are "brushing" up on the ball and coming in contact with only a small portion of its surface, ball speed will be reduced. To offset this, racket head speed on any spin serve *must* be at least equal to, and at times can and could actually be greater than, the speed of swing on a relatively flat power serve. Once a comfort level is reached you will no longer feel the urge to slow the racket head down and tentatively steer the ball in, especially in those second serve situations that can make or break you at any level of the game. Eventually, as you become adept at generating spin, you will develop the ability, and the nerve, to routinely swing more aggressively in second serve situations.

Introduce "the bender" into match play only after experiencing success and developing confidence by practicing on your own. Initially, use it on first serve only in friendly matches where nothing particularly important is at stake. The pressure *should* then be dramatically reduced. If it isn't, it's most certainly because you're still unwilling to take this step—c'mon, you can still fall back on your normal delivery if you fault—which will forever undermine your long-term growth in a game that you are most likely planning to play for life.

Those who mistakenly attempt to unveil their new spin serve in the pressure-packed second serve situation upon first learning the technique, without sufficient practice on their own, typically double fault themselves right out of the match. They often give up on learning the shot, never develop their serve fully as a result, and this most important part of their game stops growing. Over the years, I have observed numerous players—completely frustrated by their more motivated and patient peers' growth in this area compared to their own stagnation—eventually become, lamely, more interested in golf. In that game, one without any direct player interaction, weaker players are regularly afforded the opportunity to be matched with better players without any need for improving their own skills. Nice "work" if you can get it.

Once you have attained a fifty percent success rate bending in first serves, you can then graduate to the "two to make one" strategy—two chances to make one aggressive spin serve. Specifically, this means two opportunities at the *exact* same serve with no backing off on the second when necessary. Think about it, shouldn't you be able, with a little practice, to make at least one out of two in almost every instance? This represents a new level of play versus the previous dead-end pattern of a big first serve followed by a meek little "tap in," a great blueprint for getting discouraged with the game.

Upon reaching an even higher success rate on first serve—at least seventy percent—you can then experiment with going big-time. Now you'll be able to freely go after a big serve on occasion, perhaps with a touch of spin to bring it in, in order to win a free point every now and then when both the match and game score is favorable. Without any of the previous underlying apprehension, you'll automatically improve your big first serve percentage since you now possess a confident back-up—one delivered with a biting spin that jumps up at opponents who will, unlike the reality of your previous service game, have comparatively great difficulty taking advantage. The term "holding serve" will take on new meaning when you possess the goods to actually get it done.

The same scenario can also be followed in developing the "slider," or what's commonly referred to as a "slice" serve. By adjusting the grip back toward continental to reduce the angular arm-racket configuration necessary with the bender, and by moving the toss back out in front and slightly to the right of a standard toss, you'll be able to hit efficiently around the ball at about two-thirty on the dial. The looping trajectory of the bender will be mostly eliminated and replaced instead by a high degree of right-to-left action as the ball travels through the air and into the service box while moving away from a right-hander's forehand. The slider, although especially useful serving out wide in the deuce court and even up the "T" from the ad court, should, for the most part, represent an occasional variation on the bending-it-in main theme since it is somewhat less forgiving with its inherently lower net clearance.

Even at the tour level, an inability to consistently bend penetrating serves in, especially second serves, can cost players dearly. After beating both Pete Sampras and Marcelo Rios at the 2001 Ericsson Open in Key Biscayne, Florida, the then-meteoric American teen sensation Andy Roddick ran into big trouble while playing with a hand injury against the more seasoned Australian youngster Leyton Hewitt. "When I had to use a lot of wrist action on my serve, I couldn't do it," Roddick said, "so basically all I had was the hard one, and you are not going to serve a high percentage with that serve all the time."

It is never too late to learn these spin serve techniques by first getting some coaching, and then by putting in the practice time a couple of times a week. You'll not only develop all-around serving skills, but also simultaneously, have a positive effect on your overall level of play in a very big way since serving well is so validating.

The Eraser

So you want to deliver a legitimate first serve bomb and win a few free points every now and then. . . . Don't we all? Being able to really bring the heat—the eraser—is mostly about grip, toss, and relaxation synergy. To begin with, in order to achieve your maximum serving power potential, you'll want to strike the ball relatively flat with no appreciable spin. The often-used phrase, "flattening the ball out," couldn't be more applicable, *and* useable, because that is literally what takes place on a genuinely big serve, particularly in clubland where radar guns are mostly embarrassing. What better way to get the ball moving through the air as fast as possible while resisting gravity and still getting the ball in the box?

At the tour level, however, all the big boys, and more and more of the girls—a trend referred to by tennis commentator Mary Carillo as "big babe tennis"—are reaching speeds up to and well over one hundred and twenty miles per hour. In this realm, a little spin is still necessary to assist gravity and move these lasers slightly off line and down into the court.

Although similarities exist from player to player regarding the actual grip used, the traditional "shake hands with the racket with its face on edge," or some variation of this "continental" position, is anatomically a good place to start. Each individual must experiment to locate the exact hand position that naturally produces the optimal amount of racket-on-ball at impact. Very often, it's ultimately a product of a player's own unique evolution since it must feel reasonably comfortable as well.

Once armed and ready to grip and rip, the placement of the toss then comes very much into play. The power toss, once released, should remain no less than a full arm's length (tossing arm) in front. It should also be placed slightly to the right of your lead foot in order to be in an ideal strike zone alignment for the "whip"—the shoulder, arm, wrist, and racket in concert—to snap through. The ball could be positioned even further in front for more athletic servers who, like *all* professional players and better club players, jump up and into the shot. Leading with their front leg while simultaneously kicking the rear leg backward to create balance during the follow-through, they land well inside the baseline on that front foot after striking the ball.

The best height of this toss is much debated. Too low, anywhere below one's full extension, will put severe limitations on your natural range of motion and greatly inhibit the generation of racket speed, which of course equals power. No debate there. Too high, well above one's full extension, will make timing the serve, although not impossible, somewhat more difficult due to the necessity of having to wait momentarily for the ball to drop into the ideal striking position.

Most big servers keep it as efficient as possible by tossing the ball seemingly right at, or more specifically slightly above—approximately six inches—their perfect strike point. This skill was artfully demonstrated by Goran Ivanisevic while recording an all-time record number of aces during his title-capturing serving clinic at the 2001 Wimbledon Championships . . . the "good Goran!" Ivo's former coach, Australian Bob Brett, in evaluating his one-time pupil's sudden re-emergence, said, "At his best, he's a player who lets the racquet do the work. He doesn't really swing or hit that hard. Goran is all about timing."

In a previous era, Roscoe Tanner, armed with a puny PDP aluminum frame, captured the serving imagination of the 1970s tennis boom while winning numerous titles along the way. With his so-called, but badly misperceived, "low toss," he possessed the biggest serve of the day. In more recent times, Pete Sampras has been, and the Williams sisters have become, great models for delivering smart bombs and erasing opponents, not so coincidentally with their own economical and efficient tosses. After escaping with a five-set win over clay court specialist Juan Antonio Marin at the 1999 French Open, Sampras, in recognizing his match-saving serving prowess, said, "When I'm feeling it a little bit,

I thank God for my serve, I really do. It gives me some cheap points, some quick points. I can recover."

A widely effective cue for those striving to add bigger and better serving to their arsenal is focusing on striking the ball at its highest point, its apex, or precisely when it's hanging in mid-air versus attempting to hit a moving target. Hall of Famer Ivan Lendl, no small serving weenie by any means, lowered his toss considerably when he emerged as the best player on the planet for a few years in the eighties. In case you've forgotten, the transplanted Czech had a career winning record against the icons of the day: Mac, Jimmy, and Borg.

Conversely, a former top ten player like the excruciatingly mechanical Jana Novotna, who never veered from tossing the ball to the moon, suffered from serious bouts of inconsistency and sudden collapse triggered, in part, by the serving difficulty she experienced from the herky-jerky motion produced by such a toss. Golfing great Jack Nicklaus made the perfect analogy when he said, "When you're struggling with the putter, it just goes right through the bag and makes every other shot difficult." So too the serve in tennis.

Unfortunately, none of this is going to do you much good if you serve the ball as if you're simultaneously performing an isometric exercise. You gotta be looooose! So many club level servers have no chance because their take back, or first stage of their service motion, is not only tight and rigid but is also accompanied by a death grip on the racket. Instead, the take back, and the tossing arm as well, must initiate the serve in a slow, soft, and easy manner. Once coiled up, best triggered by considerable hip and shoulder rotation during the toss to fully load the racket and create natural knee flexion or leg drive, awesome racket speed—compared to any tin man attempt—can then be unleashed through the ball off of such a relaxed platform . . . bada-bing, bada-bang, bada-boom!

Early in my teaching career, a reoccurring embarrassment inadvertently taught me a wonderful lesson. When demonstrating some specific component of a student's serve that needed some work, and with no real pressure to get the ball in as a result, I would invariably deliver the ball right on the money. I was relaxed. Then, after making my technical point, I would proceed to show that student what a difference my advice would make for them. Under the considerable pressure of proving that point, and with my expertise on the line, the results were often less than spectacular. I was failing at maintaining the same relaxed approach.

Pete Sampras—back to him again (and why not?)—is as fluid a serving model as there ever was. Young Mr. Roddick, another "low" tosser, is no serving slouch himself, despite being far less than Pete's equal in the "thing of beauty" department. Sampras appears as if he's nonchalantly throwing the racket at and through the ball. He also finishes with a follow-through that effortlessly, almost lazily, decelerates back into the ready position. It's so incredibly free—no pushing, no steering, no forcing. In the same vein, I loved Jim Courier's comment on ESPN of "no hands on the handlebars" to describe the way in which new German hope Rainer Schuettler confidently served out his match—no easy task anytime, but especially when it represents an opportunity for a breakthrough victory—versus favored James Blake at the 2003 Australian Open.

Yet you'll have no real opportunity to emulate that level of relaxation and looseness if you underestimate the value of a clean, high friction grip to facilitate relaxation. Whether you prefer full replacement grips, thin overgrips, or even if you're a throwback who periodically has to have a brand new classic Fairway leather one, it must be free of dirt, grease, and grime. If not, you'll be unable to lose that counterproductive clench that always creeps in when playing with a slippery, worn out grip.

In your big serving quest, do not ever lose sight of the fact that warming up your serve slowly and incrementally is, and always will be, essential. Most importantly, it will eliminate much of the potentially debilitating stress on the shoulder—not nearly as resilient a joint as so many perceive it to be. It will also enable you to dial in the type of low muscle tension/pure timing approach that Ivanisevic exemplifies when at his best, and a proven coach like Bob Brett recognizes as an integral part of the big serving mix.

Returning the Bomb

After big serving Goran Ivanisevic's loss to a bigger serving Pete Sampras in the 1997 Wimbledon final, Ivo said, in deference to the Sampras bombs of that day, "I mean it was just 'Boom' and I couldn't even react. Even when I picked the right side, I couldn't reach it."

The good news is that you will not be facing the Sampras or Ivanisevic delivery any time soon, and you're probably not playing on a slick grass court at your club either. But being able to return truly big serves on any surface is one of the most challenging parts of the game. Opponents, particularly those with very good second serves, have an absolutely free shot at you with their first delivery. Unless you find yourself completely over-matched and out of your league, you must be able to handle those big first serves with returns that not only get you into the point but, hopefully, level the playing field as well.

Andy Roddick, again illustrating his savvy for the game, came up with another gem after being upset in the second round at the 2002 Key Biscayne stop when he analyzed his undoing this time by saying, "I didn't really get into my returns. That's kind of what separates me from playing well and not playing well."

Receiving rituals play a major role in becoming a confident and eager returner. At the tour level, no two players ready themselves for the return in exactly the same way. Some are more energized than others, yet you will observe every one of them shifting their weight rhythmically from foot to foot while rotating their upper body slightly side to side at the same time. This strictly adhered to routine both readies and relaxes the receiver leading up to their split step at the server's impact.

As the server begins their own ritual—ninety-nine percent of the time by bouncing the ball a few times—be sure to read their eyes. Would you believe that many players telegraph their intentions by looking right at their intended target just prior to serving? Then concentrate directly on the ball as their toss is released in order to get as early a "look" as possible since you must see the ball really well to have a good opportunity at a solid return.

Regardless of your eyesight, the lighting conditions, or the speed of the court, you will absolutely have to keep your head very still—perhaps *the* triggering component of consistently returning well—while simultaneously maintaining an aggressive forward posture. This posture is necessary in order to lean into the shot, without lunging, and be able to consistently and confidently connect cleanly with a—modest by tour standards, but it's all relative—ninety-plus mile per hour club level bomb. No bobble heading allowed! Any slight head movement, or exaggerated forward movement, will knock your eyes off the ball, resulting in a weak, late return, a mis-hit, or no return at all.

Sports specific eye researchers, Drs. Revien and Tieg, in creating their pioneering visual skill inventory for athletes, recognized that "spatial awareness—the ability to maintain good posture, balance and orientation while moving"—was a key component in allowing the eyes to work together to quickly blend stimuli (fast moving balls) into a clear three-dimensional image.

Visualizing your returns in advance, astonishingly practiced by so few club players, will create a considerably calmer emotional state as you enter the ritual stage. Differentiating your return placement in your mind's eye in advance, off both wings, crosscourt, down the line, or up the middle—especially *including* the applicable margin to the net—will eliminate undermining last second confusion and panic. You will feel an accompanying elevation in confidence knowing that you simply have to pay close attention to the ball and pull the trigger early.

Mechanically maintaining the relaxation initiated in the ritual right through the shot is another key element in both absorbing and controlling penetrating serves. Upon landing the split step, and recognizing the direction of the serve, the hip/shoulder turn and the accompanying take back (shortened only if necessary), must not only be extremely quick—the ball waits for no one—but most importantly, soft and easy at the same time. Relaxed muscles are fast and smart; tight muscles are slow and stupid and are *always* in direct conflict with successful muscle memory.

The goal in returning the bomb is to create sufficient time to swing through the ball as slowly as possible while still being able to take the ball well in front. Use the pace instead of fighting it. Put the fire out instead of inflaming it with a wild flail at the ball. This quick-to-slow technique is a difficult "gear change," much like having to shift your roadster's five speed from first gear directly into cruising overdrive while bypassing all the in-between gears that are normally a part of smooth ball-striking. But, with practice and commitment, the feeling of this technique will become familiar. Returning bombs, and other big shots as well, will grow into a welcome challenge instead of an exercise in fear and dread.

A troubling habit of many players is not always allowing sufficient time to set a clear visualization. Be well into your ritual prior to having to take on the serve. Many opponents—some opportunistic, some oblivious—serve before the receiver is ready and settled in. Do not accommodate them! Sure, as some announcers love to tell us when the game is televised, you must play to the server's tempo. This is true, but only if it's a reasonable tempo. Under normal circumstances, taking about fifteen seconds in between points should be enough time for anyone to gather themselves. But don't expect to be truly focused for the return in ten seconds or, worse yet, less. If you are being rushed into returning, put your hand up and wave the server off immediately. And absolutely do not attempt to return the ball if they ignore you or did not see your signal. Inform them that you were not ready and play two. In dealing with those who persist, always approach your actual receiving position from well behind the baseline—not a bad idea anytime—in order to take control and make the server wait until you have had a moment to get comfortable and focused.

When in situations against much lesser players, or even fairly good ones with underachieving serves, always move well inside the baseline to simulate returning bombs, and avoid a possible loss of return rhythm versus especially slow deliveries. Why would you stand in the same relative position that you would choose out of necessity against a big server? This tactic represents a great practice opportunity without compromising yourself or the outcome of a match you know you're going to win. And it's also a flat-out good idea when up against otherwise hard-hitting opponents who lack the same pace on their serves, especially the tentative second serve deliveries.

The Equalizer

Is there anything more frustrating and deflating than repeatedly getting beaten more times than you'd like to admit to by a damn drop shot? I don't think so. You can live with being aced. You can accept an out-of-reach winner. You can even handle a perfectly placed lucky lob every now and then. But I suspect that you have never quite liked the sinking feeling produced by a devious little drop, out of nowhere, that you cannot do anything about.

That stated, it seems like a good idea for everyone to have a reliable drop shot in their bag of tricks. Not only can it be an extremely effective offensive weapon, but it can also disrupt players who thrive on predictable pace and its resulting rhythm. In club tennis, it can even be useful in doubles since some opponents, unwilling or unable to engage you and your partner in a test of ball-striking skill, are often found clinging to the baseline for dear life and attempting to lob you to death. Bringing them into the net feels like quicksand to these limited yet bothersome "players."

While attending the 2001 Nuveen Senior Championships in Naples, Florida, I got the chance to see the acrobatic native of Cameroon, Yannick Noah, a French Open Champion, for the first time from just a few feet away. I fully expected to witness a game oozing with athleticism to the nth degree, which I got—and then some. What I didn't anticipate was the numerous slashing, swashbuckling drop shots from Noah that periodically diffused any attempts by another previous French Open champion, Andres Gomez, at a dueling game from the back of the court. The normally stoic Gomez was increasingly left shaking his head across the net and helplessly moving on to the next point.

In the world of tennis mortals, some of the very best drop shot proponents are very often senior circuit players who, lacking the power that they once possessed, embrace the tactic and take full advantage of any peers who are unable to run the court the way they once did.

Richard McMichael, a veteran Bethesda, Maryland-based club pro who attended a USTA Super Seniors (75s and 80s) men's singles (!) event at their Sanibel Island, Florida stop a few years ago, came up with a totally unique take on the scene, "Serve, return, drop shot."

I had to see for myself, so I took in the next circuit event and focused on two of these old warriors right at the start of their match. Upon falling behind 30-0, a victim of McMichael's scenario, the receiving player, clearly wanting to hang 'n' bang, announced to the server in a frustrated can't-beat-'em-join-'em tone of voice, "Okay, two can play that game, you know." From there, it proceeded to get really ugly— serve, drop shot.

Every summer in Lake Placid, New York I have the pleasure of putting Nancy Stout, one of the better USTA over-seventy players in the country, through her paces on a regular basis. Nancy, who covers the court extremely well, plays groundstrokes exclusively with underspin equally well off both wings. With a stealthy disguise off of the exact same take back, she can also consistently carve drop shots from even the back of the court for winners.

Hitting underneath the ball with a nice, light, delicate touch produces good drop shots. The take back is high, typical of any shot hit with underspin, and the racket is gripped to create a slightly open racket face. Balls that are knee-high and below are particularly well suited and will produce a stroking path that travels quite naturally from high to low and then back up to high in a sweeping motion.

There are a number of metaphors that can be used to describe this technique. I'm partial to, "Leave a bald spot on the bottom of the ball," which seems to be an effective cue for many players. In any event, coming down the backside of the ball, deftly brushing its bottom side, and then following through along a sharply upward path will create considerable backspin. If applied just right, the spin produced results in a ball-stopping bite that will especially leave less-fleet-of-foot club level opponents, much the same as Gomez versus Noah, totally helpless.

The shot should be attempted beginning in no man's land, particularly in and around the service lines when moving in to cover short replies, which at times present inviting low bounce opportunities. These balls are made to order for being dropped back over without any anticipation from an opponent expecting the usual attempts by attacking players at making deep, penetrating approaches.

The key to making the shot mechanically comfortable is understanding that you should not only be working the bottom of the ball, but also the inside of it, creating a touch of sidespin upon landing. Whether it's a forehand or backhand, this more biomechanical natural approach can be realized by dropping the racket head a bit while coming through the ball, and not expecting to be perfectly under the ball.

In visualizing the shot, picture it reaching the highest point of its acute trajectory relatively close to the net on *your* side. Players commonly place the ball much too deep with trajectory high points that are well into the opponent's court, leaving nice little sitters to be munched on by even heavy-footed slow pokes.

More advanced players with grips producing heavy topspin off both sides must deftly create disguise by setting up as usual and then, at the very last moment, switch their grip to a more continental position in order to carve the shot. A temporarily revived former world number one, Carlos Moya of Spain, found his form and gave the eager but outclassed Andy Roddick a lesson in clay court tennis at the 2002 Monte Carlo Open, in part, by periodically doing just that.

Making it a point to add a little variety to your game will serve you well in mixing it up a little when prudent. You will be able to bring poor net players in, disrupt happy baseliners, take the lob away from the misguided pushers of lower-rated club doubles, and generally be able to run players not only side to side, but forward as well on your terms.

A word of caution: despite the successes that you will hopefully achieve with your own equalizer, I strongly recommend leaving the baseline attempts—so attractive because of their potentially demoralizing effect—to Nancy and her friends.

Escape Shots

From a spectator's perspective the game is never more exciting than when you're watching it at the highest professional level. Better yet, seeing one of your favorites pulling off an incredible shot—from a seemingly impossible position to miraculously stay in the point and occasionally even turn one into a winner—is as good as it gets.

At first glance the "backfire," the "can opener," the "buggy whip," and the "'tweener"—tags first coined by the inimitable Bud Collins—might appear to be completely out of reach for the everyday club player. Regarding the 'tweener, first brought to notoriety by the wonderfully athletic Argentine bombshell, Gabriella Sabatini, and later elevated to a near art form by Andre Agassi in his flashier days, that's probably true. But the others *are* absolutely learnable for ambitious players with help from a good pro and a little practice. Most importantly, they are a necessary part of your game if you're going to possess the ability to regularly extricate yourself from serious trouble, versus essentially conceding points because you currently lack the tools to retrieve balls nearly out of reach.

The backfire is typically the most easily learned of the four, and is particularly useful in clubville, where players' inability to catch up to even mediocre lobs that initially appeared attainable, and play an overhead, is commonplace. A typical last moment response to these less-than-perfect lobs is, "yours" or "you" offered too late, or in singles simply "nice shot."

But with this shot at your disposal, it doesn't have to be that way since you can do an about face, chase the ball down, and actually do something with it. In doubles you'll be able to save surprised partners from any last second rescue attempts, and in singles comfortably stay in the point. With a topspin backhand grip in hand, *not* a forehand grip, you can hit around the outside of the ball over your opposite shoulder while in full flight with your back to the net—hence the label backfire. Since all but the best topspin lobs bounce relatively high and sit up a bit, this shot can be utilized to offensively drive the ball back into play in some instances. If it can be timed to be struck when the ball is positioned slightly lower than service toss high, and aligned opposite your non-hitting shoulder, you can get a pretty good whack at it. When the opportunity is less than ideal, because it's nearly out of reach or you're peeling it off the windscreen, you can still get just enough of the ball to lob it back defensively with the same basic technique. Since the shot can be played not only on the outside of the ball but also, in desperation, a good deal on its underside as well, it's still very make-able.

The can opener is practically a mirror image of the popular high backhand slice that's played off the forehand side instead. It is especially applicable in retrieving particularly well hit, deep shots out wide that are waist-high and above that have not only penetrated your preferred strike zone, but are also angling away. Balls nearly bouncing twice are also doable, but somewhat more difficult unless you can get down really low at the very last moment. A change of grip—once again toward the topspin backhand position along with a cocked, but very loose, wrist—will provide you with another opportunity to not only carve the outside of the ball, but to also move it through the air from right to left back into the court, usually crosscourt from the deuce side, to keep you in the point for another shot.

Another forehand wing 911 call comes in the form of the buggy whip. The incoming problem ball is again angling precariously away from your forehand and moving off the court either deep or short, but in this instance it's no more than waist-high and often lower with a reduced level of emergency. A grip change from your normal topspin-producing forehand position is usually not necessary since the *key* ingredient of the shot is to aggressively brush up the backside of the ball. By following through very sharply, this time over your hitting shoulder while in an open stance, with an accelerated flick of the wrist to not only get around it, but also to create enough lift and spin to get it over the net—hence the name buggy whip. At the same time, you'll be able to bend the shot back into the court—that's right to left again—at the very least down the line or, better yet, crosscourt if possible in singles or doubles.

Last, and without a doubt absolutely least, is the 'tweener, since club players are seldom fast enough to find themselves in position to even attempt this shot, never mind exhibit the timing and skill to actually make it. Nonetheless, this scenario finds you chasing down a very good lob that you legitimately had no overhead play on. If your foot speed is respectable, you're obviously not about to give up on it. Initially you intend to respond with a backfire, but this lob is too good and by the time you arrive within striking distance, the ball is too low and about to bounce twice. With the afterburners on and the backfire option gone, you once again switch to the topspin backhand grip and prepare the racket by placing your grip hand approximately head-high with the racket head up. At the very last moment, when positioned directly over the ball, now about six inches off the court, you reach down between your legs with a quick flick of the wrist and slap it back over the net—hence the name 'tweener. This shot can be especially risky for those of the male gender with questionable fine motor skills, and probably should not be tried initially unless at home and completely out of sight.

There you have it—four shots Houdini would have gladly included in his on-court repertoire. Three of these shots are very doable for club players and can keep you in the point in those frantic moments. The fourth shot, however, is probably better left to the pros. After taking the time to get a feel for these new tricks, by all means start attempting them in match play. Since there is no downside, you'll find an upside soon enough and develop the ability to turn what was previously certain defeat into more than just a stay of execution, and even a victory every now and then. And that's immediately a few more than you would have ever had otherwise.

The Why and When of the Lob

You're scrambling and you're in deep trouble. The only shot available, with your opponent tight on the net, is—at best—a totally defensive lob. There aren't going to be any opportunities for backfires, can openers, buggy whips, or especially 'tweeners. You've already calculated that all you're going to have, lacking Lleyton Hewitt's foot speed, is a desperate last-second stab at the ball, assuming that you actually do catch up to it in time. You're going to put it up high, really high, sixty-plus feet in the air, and hopefully deep, as well, to at least stay in the point. Maybe you'll even draw an error by an overhitting opponent intent on dusting you off, but more likely from one who simply chokes in the face of such height—it happens. And if they do take your successful effort and rocket an overhead faster than a speeding bullet by or through you, or angle it off completely out of reach, at least you made them finish and earn the point!

There are no worries here about technique. You're in all-out pursuit, giving it the gas, and in full stretch attempting to get underneath the ball, lift it with soft hands, and follow-through with just enough racket speed to get it into the stratosphere and foil their near winner.

Now, before you become obsessively interested in the idea of actually seeing that one particularly annoying player overhit your sky-high defensive gem into the windscreen or, better yet, completely gag and frame it into the next court, this is the *only* time that you're going to lob. That's right—unless of course your opponent has his nose over the net to close down your passing angles, is just asking to be victimized by an *offensive* lob, and you've got a good ball to hit.

When the opportunity for an aggressive lob is there, especially in doubles, it's ideally executed with topspin, which makes for a very difficult read by a net man who's in tight, intent on poaching, or already has poached more than once. As an effective counter measure, it must begin with disguise by coiling up and preparing the racket just as you always would. Then, by allowing the ball to enter a little further than normal into your hitting zone, you can effectively "hold the shot" for that deceiving extra moment. By brushing up the backside of the ball with a little extra racket head speed, and following through sharply over your hitting shoulder behind your head, you'll be able to catch them completely unprepared. The shot, conjured up in an instant with an altered visualization, is much the same as a buggy whip, but with substantially more lift to get the ball over the net man. Upon striking the court, after completely disarming an opponent of any possible chance at an overhead, the ball explodes and runs away from any futile attempt at pursuit as a result of the exceptional "forward" spin.

In this day and age of lively tennis balls, and extreme "muscle" rackets with two-inch beams made of space-age materials featuring hitting areas approaching twice the size of the wooden rackets that I grew up with, today's playing style is a product of the evolution of equipment. Almost anyone at club level, even a self-proclaimed weakling, can learn to hit the ball with at least some power with an up-to-date stick strung to match their stroking profile.

So other than the two scenarios described above, if you have a hittable ball in front of you, go ahead and *hit it.* I'm begging you to give it a try. You'll soon develop a greater appreciation for the heart and soul of the game—striking the ball well and with authority—and you'll also really enjoy it when you periodically happen to time a shot just right and please the heck out of yourself. First it's one, then it becomes a couple of good ones, and eventually more often than not on a regular basis, if you really want it. Now that's playing tennis!

However, if you were initially optimistic about getting something out of this book, but your idea of playing the game is still not going to budge one iota from anchoring yourself to the baseline and indiscriminately putting up lob after lob after lob, then give it to a friend and surrender your racket to the Salvation Army. You can always take up horseshoes, which is perfectly predisposed to incessant one-dimensional lobbing.

I'll never forget sitting next to super senior player Joe Rissi a few years ago—always an aggressive ball-striker when he took the court—watching four of his contemporaries playing doubles. I could sense a growing irritation in Joe's demeanor over the repeated lobbing that was taking place for no apparent reason. Finally, Joe exploded out of his seat as the reigning older guy and yelled over to his contemporaries in a lecturing tone of voice, "Damn it, hit the damn ball, that's what they make 'em for!"

If that's not enough to get you to at least attempt to mostly play the game the way it was intended to be played, the subject was recently addressed in Nike's print ad campaign, "Ask Mac." "Libby the Lobster" writes, "I love to lob. Sometimes even when my opponent is on the baseline, I lob. Or when I'm returning serve, I'll lob. I can't help it. I know I shouldn't lob all the time, but my passing shots are suspect. What should I do?" Mac responds, "If they arrested people for being annoying on the tennis court, you'd be looking at doing 15 to life."

Very much analogous to "get a life" is "get a game."

Not the Smash

The number one problem regarding the overhead is first making it an opportunity instead of the all-too-common exercise in avoidance. It is essential to put in perspective the constant references made by television commentators to it as the "smash," and to be realistic about your own goals for the shot when compared to the indelible image of tour players routinely playing the shot with total finality from any position on the court. At times, the talking heads, potentially at the very least, can unwittingly influence club players into unreal expectations. And, the overhead skills so clearly exhibited by tour players can also lead to shot-making visualizations that are also mostly an exercise in self-deception.

With these kinds of skewed goals, subliminal or otherwise, and so little practice time devoted to the overhead by the vast majority, it's little wonder that lobbing becomes so attractive to those playing club doubles whenever challenged by even a marginally penetrating incoming shot. Why bother to develop all-around shot-making skills when you can throw up lob after lob and watch inept opponents self-destruct under the pressure? After all, most are well aware of the fact that they've hit far fewer overheads versus forehands, for example, in their tennis lifetime, and, consciously *or* unconsciously, usually lack confidence in the shot.

It's always a good idea to keep in mind that the game being played by today's professionals hardly resembles what's generally being played at any club, anywhere worldwide. Well-known broadcast analyst and former player Mary Carillo—a 1977 French Open doubles champion with a Douglaston, New York neighbor by the name of John McEnroe—after covering a match at a 2001 WTA event, compared the tennis she was reporting to her own experience as a player: "They were playing a brand of tennis that I was totally unfamiliar with. The pounding was so concussive and the running back and forth so athletic—everything about that match was so much more ballistic than I could have scared up. I played another sport." The overhead, perhaps more than any other shot, exemplifies these huge differences when compared to the game being played at the club level.

In order to really develop your overhead, you must first remove your head from the sand and begin insisting on taking at least a dozen or so overheads in every pre-match warm-up, *before* declaring that you're ready. Avoiding the inevitable, as so many choose to do by asking for only a couple or none at all, couldn't possibly be more counterproductive—both short- and long-term—in light of the fact that a solid overhead can potentially represent such a huge advantage in the club game.

Technically, the overhead is little more than a half-serve with an exceptionally high toss. Think about it—it's not that big a deal. Learn to not fear it. The real challenge of the shot is to make your very best effort in getting into an advantageous position under any kind of lob—one that consistently puts the ball in front of you versus allowing it to descend right on top of you—in order to have a clean shot at the ball. Players with lousy overheads are *always* guilty of inadequate footwork and its resulting poor position. More time elapses between the moment an opponent launches a lob and the moment you're able to respond than in any other exchange. Yet players commonly exhibit less footwork in this instance than in any other, especially when they find themselves fairly well positioned early on. If there ever was a shot that requires non-stop stalking to get the ball right where you want it—constantly moving to continually adjust to the ever-changing flight of the ball, especially in the wind—it's the overhead.

A moderately high defensive lob should absolutely be a sitter for you. Reminding you that the feet and eyes must work totally in concert if you're going to have a chance at timing any shot well, energized footwork is key in staying completely focused on the flight of the ball without suffering any inopportune lapses.

Once the lob is read, getting coiled up and into a ball-striking pursuit position involves pivoting either toward the net or away from it—depending upon the lob's depth—and then continuing to move forward, backward, or holding position if already there. You should not only have turned sideways into a posture that's almost entirely identical to your initial serving position, but also readied and loaded the racket. By cocking it up behind you, with the racket pointing upward and the upper arm positioned parallel to the court, you're ready to plat the shot. Do not place your racket in the archaic and completely inefficient "scratch your back" position, a bad habit irresponsibly instilled in so many through previous unskilled coaching. Being in a balanced position to confidently strike an overhead ideally triggers a motor response to then always stalk a lob with serious intent. For those of you who have been led to believe that reaching up skyward with one's off arm and actually pointing your index finger at the ball is going to help you watch the ball—another beauty from the dark ages of the tennis teaching profession—think again.

There are three versions of the shot: 1) the grounded overhead where you're leading with your front foot; 2) the jump overhead (known as the "scissors kick" in times past) where you're leading with your back foot; and 3) the Pete Sampras signature "slam dunk."

Short lobs allow you the luxury of pivoting forward and hitting off your front foot, which can remain on the court, or grounded, through impact. The jump overhead is just that. The lob is a deep one, but not impossible to reach. You pivot backward in hot pursuit and, upon reaching striking distance, jump at the opportune moment off your back foot up and into the ball before it escapes your reach. You make this overhead while moving *away* from the net. You cannot move forward and into better lobs at the very last moment while simultaneously going backward, out of necessity, as some club players impossibly attempt.

For our extremely athletic and ambitious friends, probably those of a more youthful chronology, the "slam dunk" overhead is the ultimate exclamation point, one that the game has not quite seen before. While moving in for the kill, arms pumping to get there quickly in order to pounce on a juicy short lob that resembles a large piñata, go airborne in full stride. At the very top of your leap, suspended above the court and ready to uncoil, spike the ball with all the raw power at your disposal to bounce it over and/or through an opponent most likely ducking for cover. . . . Yeah, sure.

Regarding chasing these lobs down, there are two modes of lateral movement that can be utilized in order to gain a good striking position while still remaining poised with the racket loaded to make the shot. Basic lateral footwork involves simply side stepping, foot-to-foot, in order to move comfortably, forward or back, into a desirable position under an easily playable ball. A really good lob can require a somewhat more accelerated version requiring a crossover version. In this instance, the front foot steps across the body and slightly past the back foot while moving backward to cover more ground and catch up to the ball.

The overhead is one of the most aggressive shots in the game. The aggressive reference, however, is *not* about how hard the ball is hit—it never is. There's that "smash" misnomer again. It does refer specifically to really extending fully up and into the ball, versus allowing the ball to descend into you and completely tie you up. Simply, you must go up and get it before it comes down and gets you.

If all goes wrong and you realize at the very last moment that the lob is practically out of reach despite your best effort, you're just not going to have a good swing at it. In fact, if you do take a good poke at one that is too far behind your power zone, you'll send it well over the baseline every time. Instead, just try and stay in the point by flicking your wrist at the ball to at least maintain control with reduced pace. Pick your spots wisely and realistically—it doesn't necessarily have to be a winner to get the job done.

Making more time to practice your overhead in order to steadily gain on that typically far out-of-balance ratio of forehands to overheads, along with a little work on your movement for greater court coverage, will develop the shot into a weapon instead of a liability. And, as you improve, perhaps even one of those pro-like smashes on occasion.

In Julius D. Heldman's article, "The Style of Rod Laver," he insightfully addresses the vital importance of possessing a highly evolved overhead with, "There is not an Aussie net rusher who does not have a great overhead to back his attack. Otherwise he would get lobbed to death."

Playing Big

"He's really putting some stick on it." "She hits a very heavy ball." "Their ball explodes off the court." These are just a few of the phrases used to describe players that hit with exceptional power and play big.

Players who are routinely able to serve up aces and unreturnables, or knock off winners with their groundstrokes, display their power in no uncertain terms. Although less spectacular, they can also mix it up and win points by causing numerous forced errors with their ability to hit penetrating shots right at opponents. Some are advantaged in being big and strong, while others, although smaller in stature, use quickness and exceptional athleticism to their advantage. No matter—they are all utilizing the same ball-striking skills that make them big hitters.

Don Budge was the first player to ever win the Grand Slam, all four majors in the same year, in 1938. Only one other man has done it since—Rod "The Rocket" Laver, who, incredibly, did it twice! The first came in 1962 before joining the still-fledgling professional tour. The second took place in 1969 after being banned from "shamateur" tennis for seven long years in his absolute prime. That's pretty big playing. No one in the four-surface modern era of the game has been able to achieve the seemingly impossible, and probably never will. George Lott, a 1930s rival of Budge, commenting on the legend's ability to play big, said, "When you came in against Budge's backhand, he hit such a heavy ball, you'd swear you were volleying a piano."

Power is the direct result of a number of components working in concert. Utilizing the racket to the fullest as the hitting tool, not a stiff-as-a-board arm, is essential in generating controllable power.

Specifically, racket head speed in combination with maximum possible racket *and* hitting arm mass at the moment of impact equals power.

How fast you swing the racket through the ball is the obvious element. How much racket mass you achieve simultaneously—or better yet, *allow*—is the far more subtle but equally important element. Today's high-tech rackets range in actual weight from as low as seven-plus ounces upward to a still-modest top end of nearly twelve ounces unstrung. The latest highly maneuverable lightweight models, (most notably beginning with HEAD's breakthrough Titanium series a few years ago, continuing with the more recent and further evolved Intelligence and X versions featuring piezoelectric technology adapted from the aeronautical industry, and currently the LiquidMetal line) produce exceptional power *and* control without sounding like a tin can. They also feature an incredibly comfortable, soft, forgiving, and stable feel with considerably less stationary weight or the head heavy balance points that were previously necessary in less sophisticated racket designs. While on the subject of rackets, a model change should immediately enhance your existing game; you should never switch to a racket that requires you to make any major adjustments in your game—even if you do like the way it looks. Nonetheless, it's still the amount of "swing weight"—technically a racket's stationary weight in combination with its balance point and overall length—*generated by the player* wielding the racket that makes the difference. Dialing in your ideal degree of muscle tension—as little as possible in order to maximize a racket's capabilities—is still mostly responsible for playing big.

Virtuoso violinist Joshua Bell, an enthusiastic participant in both tennis and golf, offered the perfect analogy when comparing his artistry to that of striking a ball when he said, "Both require immense concentration and mental focus. Physically, when one draws a sound with the bow, relaxation is the key. Technique is more important than physical strength. Often, the harder you press, the less sound comes out."

Many players exert tremendous effort, but produce little real power. They actually make themselves weak at the core. Typically, they are gripping the racket far too tightly, creating ineffective muscle tension that radiates up their arm, first into their elbow, then the shoulder, and finally into the rest of their body, including the lower back. This results in a very "light" swing weight. Players who utilize a comparatively relaxed grip tension allow a then-unencumbered racket, and arm, to "freewheel" through the ball, and produce a considerably "heavier" swing weight that ideally peaks precisely at the point of impact.

The result of swinging a heavy stick is a longer impact time and greater ball compression. Granted, the maximum time the ball can sit in the string bed is commonly recognized as a mere 4/1000ths of a second, confirmed long ago through high-speed photography. Additionally, tennis balls are *made to deform* in a very particular range, between .220 and .290 inches. In any event, whether or not you can articulate the physics, you are the first to know that you have "gotten all of it." The unmistakable tactile feeling, along with the accompanying full sound of the ball being compressed, results in an explosive, penetrating shot that's launched effortlessly.

When you're trying too hard, and applying excessive muscle tension, you're negating the designed effectiveness of the racket on the ball. There is no feel, no booming sound, no shot penetration, and you end up getting very little of the ball. Big investment, small return—not an ideal scenario in any activity. Sooner or later, this approach to striking the ball could also very well lead to physical problems. In fact, you're asking for the always-dreaded bout with tennis elbow, which, incidentally, is never caused by lighter rackets as some club players, unable to adjust, typically conclude. Unfortunately, the affliction can appear fairly quickly because of *any* new racket/string type/string tension package that, regardless of its on-paper groundbreaking technological advance, does not fit your natural stroke length, speed of swing, and feel.

Concentrate on learning to relax more by lowering your grip tension as much as possible without feeling the risk of losing the racket. Once again, you'll find this exceedingly difficult if you're in the habit of playing with well-worn, greasy, slippery grips that always lead to overgripping. The racket does the hitting by allowing *it*, along with your arm, to accelerate through the appropriate stroking path. Avoid muscling the ball by staying out of the mix as much as possible.

Remember, when you're feeling like you're at your best, in your ideal tennis world, the ball leaves the racket face when it's good and ready, and no sooner. Ride it! You've got to *let* that happen to be able to play big.

Loose as a Goose

Whether you've always loved the game, are just beginning to feel a real passion for it, or you're experiencing a reawakening, every once in awhile you'll hit a shot that's right smack on the money. It couldn't have been hit much better by anyone on the planet at that precise place and time. You're world-class for a fleeting moment, and you thoroughly enjoy your "fifteen seconds" of fame.

For a truly devoted tennis player, there are few things that can surpass the experience and flat-out exhilaration of a perfectly struck ball—the ball deep into the string bed, the racket directing it right on line to a perfect destination, time standing still for the moment. You get a genuine taste of the athletic artistry, power, and touch on a level that's difficult to describe to non-subscribers. The feeling will be something special to behold; most will smile widely, whether it's on the inside or the outside.

In the final of the 1997 Paris Open Pete Sampras handled a patented Jonas Bjorkman sinking passing shot, one that the bottom dropped out of, with a silky half-volley, at full stretch, for a sharply angled, clean crosscourt winner. The normally tough-minded Swede was not only stunned, but also slack-jawed in awe. However, the unflappable Sampras, a force for so many years and on record as no mere mortal when it comes to shot-making magic, did not smile widely, but the subtle glint of joy in his eyes—in stark contrast to the completely unsportsmanlike in your face berating and showboating prevalent in certain team sports—revealed the recognition of, and pleasure in, his feat.

It's so easy to make mention of Pistol Pete since the consecutive six-time world number one exhibited a free flowing game that was unmatched during that span, and takes a back seat to no one who preceded him. Strangely, his genius, artistry, and all-around extraordinary abilities have often been criticized as "boring" by both an unappreciative media and an overly critical tennis audience—the millionaires will riot unless they get their free cookies. Sampras' own take on his ability explains, "I've watched tapes of me playing, and it looks easy. If people only knew how much hard work it took me to get there."

The reality is that his game at its best was something to behold, emulate, and aspire to. Recognize the difference in those, at the tour *and* club level alike, who not only appear to unnecessarily expend such prodigious physical effort, but who also simultaneously labor so dramatically. The latter is often exhibited by "against the true grain of the game" players with always-increasing shot-making contortions whenever in trouble and under duress, and with results ratcheting steadily downward.

I'm sure that it comes as no surprise when I remind you that tension and stress, in any setting, tend to physically manifest themselves in the upper back and neck. The resulting restriction in movement, loss of raw physical strength, and reduced overall range of motion is not a good thing. Some club players, especially when under the gun, tend to raise their shoulders and tighten the surrounding muscles while playing their shots. Needless to say, even with today's very lively tennis balls and high-tech rackets, you're still going to consistently deliver bricks with a frozen shoulder muscle group. And, constantly getting a bigger, fatter, stiffer, longer, and more loosely strung stick is not going to cure all of your mechanical ills.

It only gets worse when this manifestation of tension blocks appropriate trunk rotation, and radiates in the reverse direction—*down* into the forearm and hand—of that triggered by excessive grip tension, resulting in a battering ram approach to ball-striking that is the antithesis of the lithe Sampras model.

Working from the outside in: if a tightly clenched fist is a ten, and a totally limp hand is a one, it's your goal to try and operate as low as possible on the bottom end of the scale. This means not attempting to muscle or force the racket at the ball, but instead allowing the stick to flow freely *through* the ball . . . the proverbial hot knife through butter. But, without maintaining an appropriately relaxed upper back and neck, you'll remain stiff as a board, right down to practically leaving a hand-print in the handle of your racket.

As a kid still very new to the game, I witnessed the biggest match of my young tennis life one summer at the blacktop public courts in New Bedford, Massachusetts. Nat Guy, the longtime city champion—when city championships meant something and were played all across the country for bragging rights—faced Jules Cohen, a former number one at Yale and a player of no small reputation on the New England Lawn Tennis Association circuit. Guy was an area legend and both a hard working and formidable player that all the kids admired greatly.

Since it was a rarity in the late fifties and early sixties for any tennis to be televised—and with only a faint memory of tuning in to see "The Chief," Alex Olmedo, playing a U.S. Davis Cup tie on a grass court somewhere—I saw the game up close and personal for the first time. It was being played at a different level. Cohen was loose as a goose while Guy, for the first time ever, was noticeably tight, rigid, and robotic by comparison. I couldn't believe my eyes. In the end, the relentless weight and beautiful efficiency of Cohen's game, although matched throughout in hustle and resolve, was superior from start to finish, and my view of how the game could, and should, be played was dramatically changed.

Constantly monitoring muscle tension—particularly in your shoulders, arms, and hands—along with always aspiring to be a free flowing striker of the ball, will make you a better player almost immediately by allowing you to experience a level of consistency that you previously believed was well beyond your ability.

Most players can relate to the fact that on occasion, some of their absolute best shots occur when still playing out first serves—the serve is struck, you react, but at the very last moment, right as you're pulling the trigger, you realize that the ball is actually slightly out. Too late to hold back, you spontaneously let the racket go, but with an underlying awareness that it's not going to count, resulting in a completely relaxed and totally effortless stroke under no pressure. Wham-o, a monster return, a perfectly placed scorching would-be winner accomplished with no muscle at all . . . always indisputable proof in the pudding for being a loose goose instead of a dead duck.

The Other Swoosh

Sure, it's a long way from those less than substantial canvas "tennies" with the then-brand-new baby blue logo. You do remember them, don't you? They were first worn by a teenage John McEnroe, who surprised everyone by coming through qualies to reach the semis at Wimbledon in the early eighties. They carried the very same logo that today, twenty some years later, is in absolutely no need of accompanying text—the Nike swoosh.

For motivated tennis players always looking for answers, another swoosh exists, but this one is not seen, it can only be heard—by a very keen ear. Although not commonplace, if sufficiently isolated with enhanced courtside audio, a really expert network broadcast team is occasionally able to separate the "noise." This subtle but unmistakable sound of power and freedom—always an indicator of superior motor control and full commitment to the task—can actually be discernible from the usually audible sounds of footwork, breathing, and the ball being struck. A constant awareness of it will do a whole lot more for your game than any "look like a pro" embroidery plastered all over your shoes or apparel.

It especially stood out in the Sampras first serve motion, in the Tiger Wood's driver off the tee, or even in the mighty Barry "Asterisk" Bonds' whiff. Swoosh—the racket, club, and bat moving at exceptionally high speeds and audibly displacing air. It's also readily apparent in the nothing-but-net Shaq monster dunk, although it's technically more of a "swish" on that court.

The New York Times' Selena Roberts, while also taking certain sports cross-referencing liberties, captured it in her account of Monica Seles' resurgent but heartbreaking 6-7,6-4,6-4 loss to Martina Hingis in the 2000 Chase Championships final at Madison Square Garden. "It was the early 1990s again. And there was Seles, grunting and darting and swishing her racket with the pace of windshield wipers in a downpour."

Groundies, approaches, returns of serve, overheads, or even topspin lobs can collectively benefit from this particular swoosh as well. Only the preferred compactness of most volleys, the delicate nature of drop shots, and the softness of both half volleys and defensive lobs are executed without it.

Unfortunately, when asked to demonstrate a routine forehand, backhand, or serve *without* a ball, many players often produce a stroke that accelerates much too suddenly, and then decelerates just as abruptly. Some can even "arm" an imaginary ball—bring on the elbow braces, please. They are rigid, their muscles are tight and inflexible, they're hitting "at" instead of "through," their neuromuscular potential is adversely altered and undermined, the inherent ball propelling properties of the racket are severely compromised, and not a sound is heard . . . the silent swing.

Players stuck on the learning curve and failing to experience continued growth, but who have a sense that they should be striking the ball cleaner, commonly have a difficult time grasping the feeling of their racket literally cutting through the air. Typically, it is often those who grew up with little or no background in ball sports that struggle. However, once they have observed in close proximity a skilled player demonstrating a smoothly accelerating and decelerating stroke without a ball, and also experience actually *hearing* the racket displacing air in its swing path, they then get the idea and can capture the very same technique and feeling almost immediately.

In a matter of minutes, in live hitting, they are consistently doing less and getting more, happily to their amazement. Enough confidence is quickly developed to back off, relax, and allow the racket to go right through the ball without insecurely dragging along a tightly muscled anchor. No longer feeling the false sense of security that lies in guiding, steering, or pushing the racket, experienced by everyone at one time or another, their athletic computer is reconnected, reprogrammed, and they have successfully gotten out of their own way and stopped fighting themselves.

Strangely enough, although golfers at every level constantly rehearse their swing to retrain this parallel sensation, tennis players have never been interested in, or even aware of, practicing in the same way despite the obvious similarities and benefits.

At a bare minimum, take a few easy air displacing practice swings before you walk out on the court to begin your actual warm-up. At the very least, if you've missed the opportunity and find yourself already out there, do it immediately upon taking your racket out of your bag. Feel it. Hear it. Recapture this feeling every day since it can easily slip away, especially among serious players who at times fall victim to over-trying, and then, as a direct result, grossly under-utilize their racket as the hitting tool.

A player I have worked with on a number of occasions—already in possession of a very heavy two-handed backhand, but unable to pop a forehand with anything close to the same kind of authority—realized a dramatic improvement on her weaker side by regularly utilizing this exercise off court. Eventually, a much more efficient use of the racket became ingrained in her muscle memory.

Following the lead of baseball players and golfers, specifically their penchant for swing practice without a ball, is nothing short of a great way to build a better stroke.

DEFENDING THE COURT
AND FOOTWORK

Eye Foot, Eye Hand

The absolute necessity of eye-hand coordination in playing tennis, specifically in getting the sweet spot of the racket squarely on the ball at the ideal moment while conjuring up multiple kinds of shots, is immediately obvious to even the most casual observer of the game.

Strangely, far too many individuals playing the game on a regular basis do not realize that eye-foot coordination, clearly indispensable in a sport such as soccer, is also a huge part of the mix in consistently producing cleanly struck shots in tennis. British pro Steve Heron, an excellent mover in his own right, dryly put it to a gathering of his new American mates a few years ago over a couple of Bass Ales when he said, "No feet, no game, no future."

The majority of time spent in any point involves moving aggressively yet smoothly all around one's side of the court—all 1,053 square feet of it in singles, and the 1,404 square feet that's shared in doubles—to be repeatedly well-positioned to strike the ball both solidly and comfortably. In actuality, the shot-making moments represent only a very small portion of the time you have invested in the point—collective milliseconds. During a clinic once with Tom Gullikson, former U.S. Davis Cup Captain, Tom, after first pointing out and then skillfully demonstrating some of the finer points of movement on a tennis court, succinctly explained to a large gathering of attentive players that, "Footwork is the blue collar part of the game."

Similarly, in a 2000 interview in the USTA's High Performance Coaching Newsletter, Paul Annacone, best known as Pete Sampras' coach, but a top player himself, was asked what he thought the most important aspects of technique on groundstrokes were. Annacone replied, in part, "One thing that sticks out in my mind is the first time I hit with Jimmy Connors. I was amazed at his footwork and preparation on every ball. He would get his body in the right position to hit the ball every time. Very rarely would you see him reach over to hit a ball this way, or reach that way. He was always moving his feet, so he got it right where he wanted it."

Whether it's a groundie, volley, lob, approach, or even a return of serve, well-timed footwork is one of the important keys—a core fundamental—to making good shots. Specifically, you should be taking your final ball-striking step within the same time frame in which you are swinging the racket, not well before—triggering athletic versus technical tennis.

When positioning becomes particularly demanding you'll even find yourself landing your final ball-striking step noticeably *after* your shot has been struck, especially when hitting out of an open stance on the forehand—an increasingly popular approach. A bad bounce on clay, an exceptional amount of spin, the wind, or simply an especially good shot from your opponent that extends you out wide *or* jams you are the usual causes. Athletically striving to make adjustments while still in the act of hitting, when the ball *isn't* where you want it, is absolutely necessary and something for everyone to embrace.

To that point, let's once and for all eliminate a huge misconception that club players somehow consistently buy into: that accomplished players, particularly the tour players that these same folks are supposedly attempting to emulate, "get set," or planted, to make shots. Yes, they work to "set up" for their shots by timing their footwork to make them "on stride" in order to always be as well balanced and in as powerful a position as possible when striking the ball. Remember that tried-and-true phrase, albeit a bit dated: transfer your weight into the shot. This is precisely why the very best make it look "so easy," a comment that is often heard around the clubhouse. Just watch Roger Federer seemingly float about the court without even touching it while almost invisibly transferring himself into the ball and effortlessly firing laser-guided winners past the best of the best . . . the *Matrix* is indeed loaded in the form of the man from Switzerland.

Be wary of anyone who tells you that you didn't get set early enough as a reason for missing a shot. No doubt they are well-intentioned—these wannabe pros with their typically unsolicited advice—but it's both a misleading cue and an inaccurate one . . . double whammy.

While recently working on groundstrokes with a very athletic mover, a superb Jennifer Capriati-like "last moment adjuster," I was surprised to learn that she previously had been discouraged from utilizing her exceptional natural ability. Instead, she had been led to believe that it was incorrect to set up for shots as previously described, especially when last moment adjustments in position were also necessary, and had been encouraged to always be set, rooted in the court, waiting on every shot no matter what. On another occasion, on a particularly windy day while practicing returning serve, this same individual repeatedly expressed frustration with her ball-striking while simultaneously reeling off a number of totally successful and outrageously athletic returns—versus a good server—that required necessary and difficult last moment adjustments in position. Hopefully, in time, her classic misperception of movement, an unfortunate product of her previous conditioning, will be totally eliminated and set the considerable talent inside completely free.

You will not see accomplished players standing still while waiting for the ball to arrive. Complete lack of motion in a set position triggers a major loss of timing and rhythm, and literally disconnects you from the ball. Being stationary also most often leads to conscious left brain thought—"too much time to think"—dividing one's attention and making it very difficult to stay focused on the ball. It was amazing to watch a completely frustrated Marat Safin in a year-end match at the Masters Cup in Lisbon—not long after winning the 2000 U.S. Open over Pete Sampras with a dazzling display of energized shot-making—missing numerous routine, right up the middle of the court, backhands while standing completely flat footed. One can only assume that the cumulative grind of his year-end battle with Gustavo Kuerten for the number one ranking had completely drained his tank physically, mentally, and emotionally.

In many instances, much like the "easy" backhands that Safin was missing, the ball is hit directly to your existing position, leaving you with the feeling that there is no need to go anywhere, and that you're already in good position—which to a limited extent you are. But versus these kinds of balls, periodically directed right at you by cagey opponents, you must stay energized and *manufacture* sufficient movement and its accompanying rhythm by filling the time right up to the moment when you can pull the trigger. Jimmy Connors will always be *the* model for exceptional footwork, especially the way he always used those little trademark "stutter steps" whenever necessary in order to maintain his balance and rhythm leading up to the final ball-striking moment.

Pancho Segura, Connors' coach during his early years on tour, in reflecting on Kim Clijsters' rise to the top of the WTA tour in 2003 *without* being able to win a Grand Slam title said, "She's very good running a long distance, but she needs to work on quick footwork over a short distance so she can transition better and attack."

Unless you suffer from a serious hearing disability, you can't help but take notice of the Connors-inspired audible squeaking of shoes against the playing surface by the professional players of today in hard court events. It's a dead giveaway of the level of footwork, and the accompanying work ethic—such a key for a coach of Tom Gullikson's stature—that's employed at the very highest level of play.

In order to maximize your own shot-making ability, you're going to have to put forth a similar effort to support those skills with a level of movement that's not only energized, but always aimed at ending up being in all the right places right on time—the rapid fire synchronicity of first the eye, then the foot, and finally the hand.

Moving Well Equals Playing Well

The ability to cover the court through the efficiency of one's movement, along with being closely in tune with your physical self, are undeniably linked as crucial aspects of playing at the top of your game. Solid shot-making is not possible if you are continually out of position and out of balance.

The very best movers on tour, and among those on top at the club level, appear effortless when running down even challenging balls, whether wide or short. They also seem to recover for the ensuing shot with equal ease. They are especially fluid, even at full sprint, and are more than able to defend the court against all but the most heavily struck, perfectly placed shots. As a direct result, the cumulative next shot pressure they are able to exert on opponents becomes a considerable match play asset in singles or doubles.

Moving well always begins with a keen set of eyes. Yes, that's right— the eyes! The unique demands of tennis are such that they make participation especially difficult for those with impaired vision, and, unlike golf, completely impossible for the blind. The ability to habitually track each and every shot all the way to the opponent's strike point, and back to your own, is *the* connection to tennis-specific movement. The resulting recognition, or "reading" the other guy's shot at the earliest possible moment, is paramount in getting off the mark quickly with an explosive but, at the same time, relatively soft first step, creating plenty of time to get the job done.

When club players plant their feet firmly into the court and "dig in" for those previously noted "easy" shots "right to them," which includes so many returns of serve, not a muscle is stirring—never a good thing since bodies at rest stay at rest. Rhythm is severely compromised and the eyes predictably wander from the ball without your "motor" running. Would you turn the motor of your car off when encountering a red traffic light? Of course not, since once the light turned green you would be delayed and off to a slow start with horns blaring from behind. Other balls, ones that do require pursuit, can quickly go from reachable to unreachable in static moments lost locked in granite-like ready positions. You'll then find your reasonably speedy self somewhat puzzled over why you're so slow and having to say "nice shot" so often.

Instead, when already coiled up and in a good ball-striking position, keep your feet stimulated by rhythmically shifting your weight lightly from foot to foot, stalking the ball, cat-like, the entire time while momentarily stationary and "waiting" to make your shot. This practice will not only enable you to then better time your "split step" (more on this in the next few pages) when squared up on defense, but also get off the mark with exceptional quickness—bodies in motion stay in motion—to run balls down with comparative ease. The advantages of staying energized in this fashion go on. They especially include a far more relaxed first step—one that's relatively stress-free—which your knees, ankles, hips, and lower back will appreciate more than you would have ever experienced from any "glued to the court" approach.

When recovering from your own shot back into a defending position, move only as fast as necessary. It is a complete waste of effort, and worse yet rhythm breaking, to always strive to get back into position as quickly as possible—I know you've actually paid for that particular advice at one time or another—with absolutely no connection to the shot-exchanging tempo. Granted, at times you do have to put the pedal to the metal after being moved well off the court to close down a wide-open court, particularly when up against a sharp shooting opponent. However, much of the time, you can move back into a solid defending position far more efficiently by arriving back precisely at the moment of the opponent's point of impact—nothing more, nothing less.

Additionally, always make it a point to move as smoothly as possible, and avoid pounding around the court with those heavy clod-hopper foot plants you can painfully hear landing at any club in the world by those out of tune with their physical selves. The g-forces on your body will not only increase unnecessarily—asking for injury, particularly on hard courts—but you will also be *literally* slowing yourself down at the same time.

When coming to a stop in a "dead" point, always decelerate gradually by slowing to a halt versus suddenly slamming on the brakes. It could be after a full-out sprint for what turns out to be an unreachable ball, after a desperate but necessary attempt at a winner you know you will not be able to recover from, or in an unsuccessful serve and volley attempt. The point is already over. Forget that "no pain, no gain" baloney because completely eliminating unnecessary strain whenever possible will *always* result in lessening any potential pain.

Learning to move on *top* of the court is the bottom line on any surface. If you have ever experienced moving barefoot across red hot pavement—which always brings the beach parking lots of one's youth to mind—then you already know how to move both softly and quickly at the same time. And growing up in some landlocked, beachless place is never an excuse for routinely leaving your club's beautiful clay courts practically unplayable for those following you. Dragging your feet around like anvils for a couple of sets, and then making no effort to repair one's damage along the way, or minimally when finished, is an unacceptable no-class move. No self-respecting golfer would ever fail to replace a swing-produced divot in the grass or rake any sand trap unfortunately visited.

Additionally, if you choose to not bother yourself with making it a point to always wear high quality tennis-specific footwear, or are in the habit of hanging on far too long to even good shoes that have broken down internally, you might as well be playing barefoot. Soft court players are particularly vulnerable since their outsoles show little wear after weeks of play. If you're "frugal" and reluctant to periodically make the investment in good shoes, then at the very least replace the insoles often, or you might eventually find yourself playing the game a lot less, or worse yet, watching it from the sidelines.

Moving well is so essential to performing well, Loic Courteau, the coach of world number three Amelie Mauresmo, offered clear encouragement to his own player and the women's field in general going in to the 2004 Championships at Roland Garros by commenting on former number one Serena Williams' comeback from knee surgery. "Her ball-striking remains the same," he said, "but her movement seems to have suffered."

No better summary can be found than in the example of the incredible Muhammad Ali, who, in his prime in the sixties, was a master of both quickness and fluidity of movement in the ring—not so different from what's required to perform well on the tennis court—and who popularized a sports mantra as a testament to his genius. Coined by his flamboyant trainer Boudini Brown, it remains very apropos for tennis players seeking to not only maximize movement, but their shot-making as well—especially the non-Serenas of the world—and to even reduce injury for those in the habit of playing the game with cement shoes on. "Float like a butterfly, sting like a bee" . . . I believe that sums it all up pretty well.

Slide and Glide

It's not unusual at all for someone used to playing almost exclusively on a hard court to express their frustration with the footing, or their perception of the lack thereof, on even a perfectly maintained clay court. These players, conditioned to sure starting and stopping, especially stopping, can find themselves at odds with the comparative lack of shoe-to-court friction inherent in a granular playing surface.

Taken further, the tennis press has been guilty of both criticizing and simultaneously making excuses for the general lack of success on clay among American born and bred players for decades. The USTA, empowered with the long-standing rationale that we are always at a serious disadvantage versus the Europeans and South Americans who grew up on the "dirt," has overseen the evolution of the U.S. Open surface into the modern era, including the warm-up events that have always preceded it. Incredulously, first in the departure from the pre-Open era traditional grass courts at Forest Hills to a short-lived *clay* surface in the seventies while still held at the West Side Tennis Club. Ultimately, more rational heads prevailed and the championships returned to a fast surface in the Deco Turf II hard courts that are still favored twenty-plus years later at Flushing Meadow. Such is the perception of the difficulty involved for an American (North American that is) to succeed on clay.

At the ATP Atlanta event just prior to the 2001 French Open, Andre Agassi, a former winner in Paris despite his preference for a hard court style of movement on clay, was upset early on. In the post-match press conference, he explained that he "never got his footing" on what he perceived to be a slippery surface at the Atlanta Athletic Club, a clear indictment of the less than ideal comfort level shared by many with the footing on clay.

Clay courts can vary widely in their playing characteristics, always at the complete mercy of how the subsurface was constructed, how well they are maintained, and whether they are traditional European red or, as in Atlanta, what's become known as American "green clay." Commercially recognized as both Har-tru and Fast Dry, this USA brand recognition is steadily giving more of an identity to the still-maturing American Spring clay circuit that occurs just prior to the European red clay season, culminating with The French played out on—would you believe—crushed brick dust.

Professional players enjoy the luxury of choosing court-specific footwear in order to obtain the best possible traction, much in the same way that Formula 1 racing teams change tires to match a track's conditions. However, even shoes specifically designed for clay courts will be of little help, especially to club players—never mind an Andre Agassi—unwilling to adjust the way they move.

Thankfully, it doesn't involve that much in securing a relatively good feel for any clay court that's playing well—one with a firm sub base featuring a top dressing exhibiting a low friction coefficient that allows for both reasonably quick starts and controlled sliding. It's a combination of footwork that many find challenging.

Confidence can be gained fairly quickly during the warm-up by shuffling your feet around—much like skating—as much as possible, versus picking them up as you normally would on a hard court with an extremely high friction coefficient. You'll not only get an immediate sense of the differences in first step acceleration, but also in the timing necessary to put the brakes on and come to a stop exactly where you intend to.

On a hard packed clay court, particularly one that's somewhat dried out, this shakedown method is especially important in allowing you to get a solid take on just how much you can push off of your drive foot without slipping. Coming to a halt at the right place on a timely basis, and then reversing your field, is another matter entirely on this type of surface. Just ask Agassi.

The tennis press also loves to extol the ability of the tour's clay court specialists to use the inherent qualities of the clay to classically slide into any shots that they have to dig for out wide. By timing their movement to the ball in a way that will allow them to be relatively still just as they are making their shot, they are then able to recover back into the court without losing any precious time skidding out of control after the ball is struck.

Players without the ability to slide and glide find themselves feeling as if a layer of ball bearings is connected to the bottom of their shoes whenever they attempt to reverse directions—classic "banana peeling"—especially after having to really hustle to make a shot. Time lost starting and stopping in a start-stop sport like tennis will cost you dearly in match results, increase the possibility of injury in any sudden moments of lost balance or hyperextension, and occasionally result in you unceremoniously ending up on your backside. Diving for a shot is always respected, falling down without even being touched is downright embarrassing.

Some players take to sliding without any real trouble. I have repeatedly witnessed a player at a Lake Placid, New York club who is so completely at home with the technique he can even slide freely on a damp and somewhat soft early morning court. Others, even competent players, experience surprising difficulty. Typically, their problem lies in their overly high center of gravity, or lack of knee bend. More specifically, their last second apprehension—manifested in raising up on the ball of their lead foot as they initiate their slide—is what does them in. In working one time with a reasonably good athlete who was also an okay club player, I was astounded to see him repeatedly do just that. Despite my repeated demonstrations of staying down through the slide, he face-planted himself into the clay, in full push-up position, over and over again.

A good exercise in learning to be with the clay like the world's best dirtballer, Gustavo Kuerton—better make that *hopefully somewhat* like him—is to locate a dry court at midday when much of the moisture has evaporated out of the surface material. Then, with running starts, practice sliding back and forth across the baseline area where the court's firmness will be the most conducive. The key elements in getting the hang of it are: 1) first picking a spot where you intend to end your slide; 2) toting your racket just as you would in normal ball pursuit; 3) getting down into a very low center of gravity position when initiating the slide; 4) leading with either foot along with keeping the entire sole of your shoe in contact with the court's surface; 5) utilizing the back trailing leg for balance by inverting your shoe on to the toe cap with the laces down; and 6) making no overt effort to put the brakes on to stop the slide. In essence, you must learn to become comfortable with going with the flow, and avoid resisting it.

Eventually, you'll know instantly when you should slide, whether it's the condition of the playing surface or the nature of the shot you're chasing down, or both. Along the way, you'll become an adept slider, enabling you to steadily elevate your clay court play another full notch.

Split Stepping

The already mentioned "split step" represents one of the most underrated and single most important components in the game of tennis—another one of those core fundamentals. It is not only instrumental in defending the court as well as possible, but also a crucial element in creating the best opportunity to make your own shot as routine as possible.

Split stepping is the precise timing of simultaneously landing both feet, after a small jump, lightly on the court at the exact moment the opponent is striking the ball in order to make the transition into your next shot. It's a little hop step, occurring when either on the move or in a stationary position, that you've seen executed thousands of times when watching the pros on the tube. Yet the announcers, even Johnny Mac, curiously seldom make mention of it.

Some players, like Steffi Graf during her brilliant career, are very explosive and elevated in their execution. Others, such as Pete Sampras, are subtle and less obvious. Nonetheless, every accomplished player at any level religiously executes split stepping on every single shot, beginning with the return of serve.

Conversely, players who ready themselves for the opponent's reply without a well-timed split step experience a disconnected and out-of-sync-with-the-action feeling. This against-the-flow bad habit not only wastes energy, but is also a great way to jerk *yourself* around the court and actually contribute to whatever an opponent is attempting to do to cancel out your game.

Your overall goal is (also touched upon earlier) to time the speed of your recovery to coincide with your opponent's next shot point of impact. Ideally, in the fleeting moment after you have struck your own shot, you instantaneously calculate not only the pace and depth of your ball—along and the opponent's ability to run it down—but also their likely response, and how much court you'll have to gain back as well. Motoring back into position on time, capped off with the requisite split step, is very beneficial in creating a natural flow in the way in which you move about the court from shot to shot. I know that you have observed your favorite tour players so impressively covering the entire court with such ease, punctuated with split step after split step, and getting the movement job done in a very big way.

At times, when moved only slightly out of position, you'll be able to routinely recover by squaring off to the net out of your follow-through, and then laterally side stepping, easily and unhurriedly, back into position. When pulled considerably off the court, you'll sometimes have to get more aggressive and use a crossover-lateral step combination to catch back up to any ball that initially registers on the radar screen as trouble. When totally out of position, you'll have to turn the "jets" on and sprint full out back into the open court in order to recover as fast as you possibly can just to stay in the point.

Most importantly, at the very end of all three recovery methods, wherever you happen to find yourself at the very moment the opponent strikes their shot, it is 99.44 percent necessary to square off momentarily to the opponent and land a split step.

Hopefully, more often than not, you'll be able to achieve optimal position right on time. On other occasions, despite giving it your all, you will not be able to realize as good a defensive position as you would like. Nonetheless, you will still need to execute a split step to guard against an opponent hitting behind you. When hopelessly out of position, go ahead and run the court at full throttle to try and make one more save. One important qualification though, when the roles are reversed and you're in the driver's seat, never attempt to hit behind an old guy—club players galore—he's still there.

Split stepping on cue will enable you to change directions on a dime, and move to close down the open court explosively yet with a soft and relatively effortless first step. You'll also begin to reap the shot-making rewards that result from repeated precise, time saving movements, and will also defend the court with a greater physical presence that can draw errors from opponents feeling the pressure of having to thread a continually shrinking needle.

A final bonus, and a considerably underestimated one to be sure, will progressively take the form of much improved ball tracking—an invaluable byproduct. Consistently timing your split step precisely at shot impact will automatically focus your attention primarily on the flight of the ball—instead of on your opponent, the court, or, worse yet, nothing in particular at all—without thinking about it.

Decoding Games

Exactly why professional players, most notably in singles but in doubles as well, cover the court so well has already been addressed. Yes, they are indeed able to run the court effortlessly, almost as if they are not really running at all. Equally important, but not nearly as obvious, many also seem to possess a sixth sense with regard to knowing exactly where opponents are going to hit their shots.

Although some touring pros are more predisposed to naturally moving well—gazelles in tennis disguise—as a group, they are *not* always literally "guessing right," as we constantly hear from certain television commentators when these players not only reach seemingly unreachable balls, but then often do something special with them. In situations where they are at the mercy of an opponent, but somehow are able to wriggle their way out, it was at the very least a very educated "guess" that led to their success. Most can still picture Jimmy Connors, during his epic final run at the 1991 U.S. Open, doggedly and incredibly lobbing back umpteen Paul Haarhuis overhead smashes just to stay in the point before finally ripping a totally amazing passing shot—I remind you off of an overhead—perfectly down the line, right by the stunned Dutchman, for a winner. Connors demonstrated so much more than these lame guessing-right explanations: 1) a forcefield generating presence; 2) knowing an opponent's tendencies; and 3) getting them to hit it where you want it.

Some players have an absolutely uncanny knack for *never* appearing to be hurried or forced to scramble. On this subject, temporarily reignited at the time by the success and elegant smoothness exhibited by Karol Kucera in 1998 at Flushing Meadows, the buzz around the grounds, not surprisingly, also focused on another Czech, the legendary Miroslav Mecir, Kucera's coach, and one of the greatest movers and anticipators of all time. No one ever made it look easier than the "Big Cat," the human hovercraft, a large man who at his best never appeared to even touch the court. The guy had *soft feet*, a description of this kind of ability that has never become mainstream.

The key to great anticipation and court coverage is concentration—not exclusively raw foot speed, not pure first-step explosiveness, and certainly not long strides, although it's really advantageous if you already happen to possess those qualities. Fortunate genetics, and developed movement skills, can only help in a big way, but they will be greatly underutilized if you are unable to "read" an opponent's shot.

Legions of club players mistakenly believe that in order to read an opponent's shot you have to "watch their racket." I hear that all the time. But there is no way that you can actually see their racket speeding through the air. Certainly, as part of your read, you'll need to be aware of their racket coming to the ball since it relates directly to predicting their point of contact, but *only* through your periphery. You'll also get a sense of any applicable hip and shoulder tip-offs in the same way, especially as you become increasingly familiar with an opponent's game. But what you resolutely need to be paying attention to and is the flight of your shot, your own ball as it travels out and enters into the opponent's strike zone.

Since the ball can only go where the racket is facing at the exact moment of contact—lasting only a few thousandths of a second—estimating where the ball is going to be struck in relation to the opposing player's body position represents your best chance at decoding their game.

Simply, balls struck well in front of the body are going crosscourt. Balls struck slightly less in front will be directed right up the middle of the court. Balls struck the least in front are headed down the line. Granted, these are subtle differences, but the fact is that any place on the court can be reached by simply varying the point of impact by mere fractions in the strike zone. After all, isn't that mechanically how you go about directing your own shots?

The challenge is constantly being aware of these strike point differences in a variety of players with different stroking styles. This demands a big-time ability to stay focused on the ball for extended periods of time—over the course of an entire match or practice—once again, beginning with the outgoing flight of your own shots to provide you with a viable method of anticipating the direction of an opponent's response.

The one instance that will especially indicate if you are really hooked-up, and truly reading an opponent, is found in your reaction to a shot that is struck very late. Typically, it's your own penetrating shot that has "eaten them up" and made them late in "getting around." Your ball has traveled right through their optimal strike zone and the only place they can possibly go is down the line. Getting beat in this instance means that you're not paying attention—literally clueless—and, as a result, are very susceptible to spontaneous guessing. Taken further, it's incredibly deflating to nail your shot, fully penetrate your opponent, and then get passed down the line because you're still covering a cross-court possibility that's not possible. If you don't see this one coming from a mile away, you can be sure that you will not be able to antici-pate anything else either. You'll not only end up getting yanked around the court in singles, but won't be very adept at poaching, closing, or even defending in doubles.

In time, by making sure that you're truly focused on this particular task every time out, you'll find yourself covering more balls with con-siderably less scrambling. You'll be able to relax and economize, elimi-nate mindless random guessing, and become an accomplished reader of the ball and the ensuing shots being launched at you from the other side of the net.

Selling the Juke

When is the last time that you pulled off a miracle get, the one where the opposition had you dead to rights and you were that sitting duck? If you're being honest, and thinking about the time of the last leap year, you're probably not too far off. Nonetheless, every once in awhile you actually are able to randomly guess and keep yourself in the point. Miracles do happen.

But, all too often in these situations, players take off prematurely in a frantic attempt to close down a wide open part of the court that they have almost no hope of covering anyway. So, that being the case, what's the point?

Incredibly, even at the tour level—just watch the next televised event—players in the same predicament also routinely break too early, often half-heartedly to boot, in an exercise in futility. Factor in any professional player's ability to "hold" a shot until the very last moment, inviting overanxious opponents into overcommitting, and there appears to be no possible solution to staying in these points anyway. Or is there?

Since, in reality, there actually is, why concede the point like that? Unless you're in a predicament like young Andy Roddick at the 2001 Wimbledon Championships—where he was forced to completely guess on the return facing the event's ultimate winner, the rejuvenated and delightfully crazy Croat Goran Ivanisivic, who was serving huge ace after ace into the corners—don't do it. Otherwise, I'll never understand why the best players in tennis—never mind club players for the moment—unlike other world-class athletes in movement sports like football, basketball, and soccer for example, seldom ever even attempt to "juke" an opponent.

"Juking" has both offensive and defensive applications in sports, but in tennis it's especially useful when you're in big trouble. I've been using it in real play with reasonable success for years—probably as a result of playing a fair amount of sandlot football and basketball as a youngster— and teach it to all levels of players. If well executed (which always requires a good acting job), even very experienced opponents, including tour players—I know from personal experience in sparring sessions—will sometimes buy into it. You'll potentially be able to turn what appears to be the point ending moment into an opportunity to remain in the point for another shot. On occasion, you'll even be able to turn around a completely defensive posture into a winner of your own, outfoxing opponents initially in charge, and then catching them totally by surprise as a result.

The art of juking involves convincing your opponent that you are totally committed to defending the more vulnerable side of the court— the place you believe that they would logically choose to hit their would-be winner into—by breaking toward it with an exaggerated early start. You've got to sell them on your apparent abandonment of the less open side with an Oscar-winning performance of what appears to be an all-out sprint in the making. Then at the precise moment that they, now fully convinced, are about to strike their shot—now behind you—you turn and wheel completely back. Voila—the stealing away of a sure winner, and sometimes even more. I can't begin to tell you how often they'll take the hook, not go to the open court, and deliver the ball right back into the area of your original hopeless position—the only part of the court that you could have really covered anyway. Thank you very much.

This little move won't always work, especially if you're a bad actor and can't pull off the timing. But at the very least you're making a calculated effort to get opponents in charge to put the ball where you actually will have a realistic chance at it, instead of giving up so easily on a wild goose chase.

When you are able to pull this off, it's probably not a good idea to get smug about it; do not celebrate, do not even grin. Getting completely suckered and conned out of what appeared to be an easy put away is a bitter pill to swallow. . . . Well, at least don't let them see you grinning.

INNER TOUGHNESS

Not Getting It Done

The use of the term "mentally tough" to describe exceptional competitors has grown exponentially in the past fifteen to twenty years, not only in tennis, but also in other sports. Coined way back when by the now well-known performance psychologist and author Dr. Jim Loehr, it was the product of his on court research beginning in the 1970s at an indoor club in Denver and is now well entrenched in the lexicon of the day. His vision zeroed in on both identifying and defining the specific ingredients of the ever elusive, and previously almost entirely unaddressed, playing at your best from the neck up model.

I had the pleasure and advantage of working next to Dr. Loehr in the early to mid–1980s at the newly opened Jimmy Connors Tennis Center at Sanibel Harbour, Florida. I was already very familiar with his work in player development. Because, I suppose, of my own memories as a young, fairly talented, but undisciplined and poorly coached player frequently "shorting out," I was always motivated to learn more about the mental part of the game. My experience during that time would dramatically influence my approach to teaching, coaching, and playing the game from that point forward. It was clearly the whole player that, from head to toe, needed to be addressed . . . not just the strokes.

Loehr was on the cutting edge with this mental toughness training, which today is an essential component of any serious player's approach to the full development of their game. His successes resulted in him being the most sought after sports psychologist on both the men's and women's pro tours, as well as by other world-class athletes in individual, team, and various Olympic sports. Most have completely forgotten about his signature and pivotal role in Gabriella Sabatini's odds against Grand Slam triumph at the 1990 U.S. Open, or his behind the scenes work with the gold medal winning USA speed skater, the courageous Dan Jansen, at the Lillehammer Olympics in 1996, among others.

Although it continues to amaze me in 2004 when anyone "discovers" mental toughness (better late than never), Loehr's program has thankfully become standard fare for coaches in the know, and continues to be both recognized and embraced by the sports community worldwide. Psychologists specializing in this discipline are now a commonplace and integral part of today's sports landscape. More amazingly, Loehr's original model was so incredibly right on the money that it remains virtually unchanged among an entirely new breed of practitioners.

Along with his team at LGE Performance Systems in Orlando, Loehr continues to be heavily sought after by tennis players and other professional athletes in need. More recently, their high stress training techniques have caught the collective eye of corporate America, government agencies, security specialists, the medical community, and other professionals operating in competitive and potentially adverse circumstances seeking to utilize the sports model. Producing greater teamwork, productivity, creativity, success, and cool under fire in the new global marketplace and a geo-political world that is under relenting pressure—like the athletic arena—is at a huge premium. Curiously, it remains baffling how so many otherwise dedicated club tennis players are still completely unaware of, or if aware, sometimes boorishly poohpooh the mental and emotional side of tennis as if they've been impervious to never quitting on themselves, losing their temper, or choking a match away.

"Peak performance," another phrase brought into the mainstream by Loehr, whether in sport or everyday life, is of course not possible without a high level of mental toughness. Tennis, very much the "gentleman's game" on the surface, is in reality very primal in nature and repeatedly plays itself out in the form of "points" that are contested in a classic mano a mano setting. It is also unique in that well over half of the time spent in match play is spent not playing at all, but pausing in between points. As in all things, how well you deal with any adversity encountered—always lurking close by—along with how well you fill the time leading up to the moments of confrontation, is key to being a competitor to be consistently reckoned with.

Mental toughness comes easily when you are dominating a less skilled, less conditioned, or less experienced opponent. Everyone behaves, looks (sometimes even smiling), and especially feels like a champion when they are kicking butt and winning handily. True tests of real toughness and character occur when you are getting spanked by an individual or team perceived to be beatable, or involved in a very competitive match—a real battle—that could go either way.

Many things can go wrong and contribute to *not* being able to get it done. Dr. Loehr was the first to make all the possible contingencies exceedingly clear. Players lacking in resolve are the first to go away. They go in the "tank," as it is commonly known or, as player/commentator Luke Jensen likes to say, "They've put the flippers on." According to ESPN commentator and former tour player Cliff Drysdale, the great Australian champion Roy Emerson politely referred to it as "lacking interest." They stop trying, go through the motions, roll over, moan and groan, feel sorry for themselves, and ultimately play dead. These individuals like to tell us they easily could have played better—or even won—if they had felt like it, if their racket was gripped properly, if their strings were tighter, if it was less windy, if their partner didn't screw up so much, and so on. They are not only excuse makers but are also often unconsciously fearful of putting themselves totally on the line in full view, then having to take complete responsibility for an end result that could very well still spell failure.

Some players "lose it." They don't quit, but instead lose patience with themselves by commonly setting unrealistic shot goals. They then become frustrated, and ultimately lose their composure entirely in a very negative and ugly way. This outward display of anger, right there for everyone to see—whether audibly overt or clearly simmering inside—is born on a sub-conscious level. Often aimed at deflecting their embarrassment over their play, it's always an attempt to communicate, albeit insecurely, that they are normally a much better player, which often they are not.

More evolved players almost never give in to any unwelcome urge to tank, even for a second. They seldom ever lose their temper, and by and large handle themselves quite well in situations of normal pressure. Unfortunately, despite all their best intentions and commitment, they can choke when match play pressure is increased. It's obvious when they become overly careful and cautious, but much less so when *it* takes form in the urge to recklessly and desperately overhit. *Both* are classic examples of choking by those who never seem to be able to play to their potential when it really counts. Interestingly, long before Jim Loehr came along, these individuals were traditionally recognized as "head cases."

To be a peak performer, *at any skill level,* you must continually work on mastering the basic components of your inner game, and continually develop your mental toughness to consistently win the underlying, and always most important, contest with your self, regardless of the match at the time's outcome.

Jeff Greenwald, currently point man and founder of Mental Edge International in San Francisco—hardly a household name in his playing days—reached a career-best world ranking of 796 in 1990 before mercifully calling it a day. But with regrets still simmering over a decade later, he embarked on a mission to "play at a higher level by training his mind," the state of which he recognized was not always a positive force when he was trying to survive on the incredibly deep-with-talent ATP tour. At the end of 2001, he proved his point by becoming both the ITF's and USTA's world number one in the 35s, and in the process validated his long-held sense of the difference a well-conditioned mind can make in sport.

More recently, Vince Spadea resurrected himself by (incredibly) reaching number 23 on the ATP entry rankings, and number 11 on the 2004 champion's race, after completely reversing his fortunes by winning in Scottsdale—his first ever title—and then reaching the semis at Key Biscayne. At the end of 2000, he inexplicably had plummeted from being a top twenty player to being ranked number 229. Although his shotmaking ability didn't suddenly disappear, from the neck up he somehow began underachieving and fell from grace into a near career-ending funk. Spadea now reflects, "I lost a couple of matches, my confidence, my passion, my interest. I was playing seventy-five percent into it."

On Court Philippe Chatrier at the 2004 French Open, a somewhat difficult second-round victory by Jennifer Capriati over the lowly-ranked but capable, Kveta Peschke, led to the Czech Republic dirtballer's post-match, new twist analysis of Capriati's game: "I think she has the fitness in the head. She's very strong."

Two recognizable household names, legends of the game Jimmy Connors and Chris Evert, are among the very best models of having the fitness in the head, i.e., being mentally tough. Although they exhibited very different on-court demeanors, they both played with passion and confidence, never gave matches away by tanking, never exhibited anger toward themselves, and were consistently able to limit fear and any choking episodes to very few and far between. They almost always were resilient enough to dominate the contest with themselves, and in the end usually succeeded in *getting it done* consistently in impressive fashion.

Hanging Tough Instead

Delivering a solid competitive performance every time that you step out on the court is not always easy, and can certainly *never* be taken for granted. A consistently high level of resolve and commitment is necessary day in and day out, month in and month out, and year in and year out in order to realize one's true potential.

Fighting for every point, controlling your anger, managing your mind, and keeping your body revved-up are a few of the non-ball-striking skills that come into play.

In my mind, the absolute most important component of always being close to or at the top of your game is *always* visualizing successful shots. When positively motivated, we generally get, by and large, exactly what we expect. But this corollary can also work in reverse. If you are prone to seeing failure in your mind's eye, especially in its most deadly completely unconscious form, your chances of then realizing those exact same negative expectations can also, in the end, become predictably self-fulfilling. Future baseball Hall-of-Famer, Tony Gwynn, was recognized by most as the best pure hitter in the major leagues for many years. Now retired, and sharing his vast knowledge as head baseball coach at San Diego State University, he explains the mindset that he always took into the batter's box to face the pitcher: "Let's see who's better. You've got to go to the plate believing you are. Otherwise, you're toast."

If you always believe that you can, that it's at least possible, that you'll grow in the process regardless of the outcome, and you're willing to give it your all out of respect for yourself, then tanking a match will never be an option. Charles Schwab Sr. once said, "Man can succeed at almost anything that he has enthusiasm for."

Performance coach (as they are referred to today) Jim Fannin, a journeyman touring pro long ago, currently an in demand—among professional athletes—exponent of his Score Performance System, offers an intriguing view of the learned make-up of the more success-ful players in any sport. "Superstars don't think like everyone else," Fannin said. "The average person has 2,000 to 3,000 thoughts per day, and sixty percent of the average person's thoughts are in chaos. The superstar has 1,100 to 1,300 thoughts a day. They eliminate worry, envy, jealousy, embarrassment and anger. The superstar thinks a lot less and holds a thought longer." In commenting to reporters in a feeding fren-zy on long-time client Alex Rodriguez's—the other A-Rod to tennis fans—dismal start to the 2004 major league baseball season as its most valuable and highest paid player, Fannin said, "It's on everybody else's mind. It's not on his mind."

Anger control is, at the very least, linked in part to successfully being able to dial in a comfortable level of shot margins and pace that is both realistic and doable. Maintaining a high level of patience with your existing "player self" is equally important. If you're in the habit of attempting more than you can deliver on a consistent basis—an emo-tional explosion in the making—you are setting yourself up to fail, and that's going to be more often than you like because of stubbornly push-ing the envelope one step too far. If that strikes a chord, perhaps you should reevaluate and consider re-strategizing your game's goals. Additionally, if you tend to be *impatient* about allowing reasonable time to find a ball-striking groove early on, or typically not disciplined enough to stay within yourself when achieved, then you'll never get "there"—the true level of play *within* your capabilities—anyway.

Breathing, the value of which is woefully underestimated by mil-lions of tennis players, represents the single most important anti-chok-ing technique. Not only will it raise the level of your shotmaking, but the physicality of exhaling at least somewhat demonstratively during and through impact also reduces the emotional stress of the moment, relaxes potentially tight muscles, and contributes mightily to remaining relatively unconscious while warding off any technical over-considera-tions or general over-thinking. Apprehension is neutralized as much as possible, courage is bolstered, and you are then following the teachings of St. Nike—the patron saint of tennis—by literally (more than a marketing slogan) "just doing it."

Optimal pacing between points is another technique that can also enhance one's belief in self and overall mental toughness. Develop a clear sense of the amount of time you generally need to feel comfortable, positive, and secure. Especially avoid rushing to start the next point during times of difficulty, almost always because you're in a big hurry to erase your previous error or poor play. It's vital to take a little extra time to regroup positively. And *never ever* stand absolutely still between points—it's a guaranteed kiss of competitive death. Your mind will wander and your body will either go to sleep or seize up completely. It's imperative to keep moving, pacing like a lion in a cage right up until the next point is about to begin. Even world *chess champion* Garry Kasparov, who successfully met the challenge of the IBM computer Deep Blue, prefers to leave the table after making a move in order to pace back and forth a few feet away and maintain his focus versus sitting motionless while waiting. It's universal.

Back on court, keeping your feet engaged and busy triggers the stimulation of the thousands of nerve endings in your feet (You've had them tickled, haven't you?) so that your existing muscle memory remains keen and connected when not actually playing.

Positive body language, along with always maintaining an appropriate "game face," can also lead to a higher level of play. Carrying yourself like a winner, no matter the score, can pay big dividends. *Tennis Week* contributor Douglas Robson, in commenting on the new-and-improved Roger Federer's emergence as the world's supreme player after his breathtaking play in the finals at the 2004 Australian Open, cleverly put it this way, "Federer's body language remained, as it had all tournament, Swiss neutral."

Similarly, the expression on your face and the look in your eye during the actual shot-making moment—one of can-do determination versus one of fear and indecision—also breeds greater overall confidence on a deep primal level.

Completely eliminating negative self talk—you know, that berating and/or whining to yourself crap, especially in the third person—is also a must. It's such a complete waste of what should be an in between point self-coaching opportunity. As the well-known corporate consultant, Tom Peters, used to reflexively say on this subject, "Shut up and compete."

Rituals represent the final primary piece in the elusive mental toughness puzzle. They are present in all of sport. In golf, better players go through an intricate routine of body loosening movements, twitches, and ticks before hitting every single shot. They refer to it as their "pre-shot routine." I believe that Sergio Garcia, Martina Hingis' former love interest, at one point was recognized as the number one exponent of rituals on the PGA tour.

Tennis players need similar rituals on serve and return of serve. These two shots begin every point from a static start, exactly like golfers on every shot. Always creating a feel-good rhythm prior to launching a serve by bouncing the ball a few times and then rocking back and forth a bit with your entire body, in your own idiosyncratic way, is absolutely essential in creating a positive mental and emotional climate. Not long ago a New York City-area club player, Marilyn H., frustrated with her form, uniquely and accurately expressed to me her reacquired serving success, triggered *solely* by helping her develop a distinct ritual, as "getting the kinks out."

Returning serve also requires a certain level of energizing that's typically created through a slight upper body rotation, including the racket in a fixed position, along with a simultaneous rhythmic foot-to-foot weight transfer while waiting and poised in the ready position. Try visualizing, right at that very moment, any of your tour favorites getting ready to serve or return. Make some version of their habits yours.

However, all the training in the world isn't going to amount to much if you lose faith. Never losing faith should be a given. It's a prerequisite for all of the above techniques, but is often far more difficult in reality. Twenty-six year old non-superstar Thomas Johansson hung tough in the 2002 Australian Open final to ultimately prevail over the heavily favored Russian sensation, Marat Safin, despite every possible obstacle at the outset.

Beginning with the immensely talented Safin's cocksure entrance into the stadium—flashing a "V" for victory sign to his entourage—compared to Johansson's pensive at best arrival, the Swede ended up being very much against it in the early going. After breaking serve in the opening game, a relaxed and supremely confident Safin paused to re-tie his apparently too loose shoes—quite the message sent—to then, one could surmise, really apply himself.

Despite eventually going on to lose the first set, the initially tightly wound Johansson *did not* lose faith. He hung on to the knowledge that he had nonetheless created six break point chances against the Safin serve, despite having failed to convert a single one. To compound things he was also terribly inconsistent on his own serve, normally a strength. *New York Times* sports writer, Christopher Clarey, succinctly captured—in the end—the winning essence of the no nonsense stay-the-course attitude, and belief in self, exhibited by Johansson at the start of the pivotal second set with, "There were strong hints that this [losing] was not a given." Hanging tough at its finest.

In time, these kinds of practices will go a long way toward galvanizing you as a never say die, consistently focused, under control peak performer—win, lose, or draw.

Getting Into the Point

Whether it's singles or doubles, serving and receiving always represent the most important, most difficult, and most opportunistic shots in the game. Moreover, these point starting "stationaries" are not the beneficiaries of the movement-generated rhythm that players are able to tap into once the point is ongoing. It's actually quite the opposite. Delving further, the server is free to choose the most advantageous place to serve from, while the receiver responds by choosing a position to best defend the service box from—advantage server. The server has two totally free shots if necessary, and after all, among relative equals, good serving should prevail over good returning.

To make the task of negating the serve less daunting, first consider, for example, that you dress yourself every morning in the exact same article of clothing order, and that you also always brush your teeth precisely the same way every day. You don't think about it; you just do it reflexively. Muscle memory on autopilot in its purest and most efficient form.

In sport, these types of routines, as noted earlier, are ritualistic in nature and are both kinesthetically and consciously developed simultaneously in order to make difficult athletic tasks—specifically those initiated from still positions—not only physically less demanding but also considerably more mentally and emotionally secure.

Tour players, and the very best club players, all go through a specific pre-return routine prior to the server striking the ball. The routine is always the same: first the pacing in place forward and back while waiting for the server, then the settling into a committed position of engagement, and finally initiating a side to side hip and shoulder rotation repeated in a relaxed rhythm while waiting in place. With the feet intermittently shifting weight from one to the other in concert with the upper body dance, ultimately leading up to a split step that's landed precisely as the serve is being struck, timing the serve can be viewed as a welcomed opportunity.

Experienced players, recognizing times of particular pressure and importance—or, conversely, when feeling a little sluggish—will precede their normal routine with a moment or two of light, energized lateral skipping in place to rev the engine. When facing smart bombs coming in at high rates of speed from a mere seventy-eight feet away, there is no time to spare and one's motor must already be purring, versus waiting motionless and rigid in a totally defensive mode as so many do.

These routines are universal in sport, and they are by no means trivial. Professional golfers always come to mind "addressing the ball" ad infinitum (Sergio Garcia), always in a very patterned manner with all that so-called "wiggling and waggling" before each and every shot. Since we're on the subject, it's baseball players who, when preparing to hit, are by far the all-time most ritualistic athletes (Nomar Garciaparra of the Red Sox, for example). Once they enter the batter's box they settle themselves in for *their* moment of truth with an assortment of gyrations and ticks involving their uniform, spikes, cap, hitting gloves, bat, and even body parts that shall go unmentioned here. And who can blame them with the pitcher, only sixty feet, six inches away, looking down at them from an elevated mound and firing potentially lethal hard balls that do amazing things at varying speeds often exceeding over ninety miles per hour. The batter, insufficiently armed with a round wooden stick and its miniscule sweet spot, is at a distinct disadvantage that's solvable only one-third of the time on a good day. Hence, the old and still relevant baseball wisdom—very much applicable with sports' considerable crossover relevance—good pitching beats good hitting.

No two tennis professionals are quite the same in their ritual practices. There exists an easily observed total individualization with each player's signature clearly on it. Some appear more energized and animated than others, or is it the other way around? Whatever, it's all about dialing in a good feeling for being able to react quickly, make the shot, and eliminate any conscious thoughts of how to accomplish it technically by always pre-visualizing your return.

At the moment the ball is struck, the returner's goal is to have already created a physical, mental, emotional, and tactical climate of readiness featuring a high level of self-belief. We're talking about thousandths of a second to react positively off either side to ideally produce a perfectly timed swing of the racket that dominates the collision with the ball and redirects it back over the net with near or matching authority.

As an important side bar, never allow an opponent to quick serve you before you have readied yourself. At the club level, it's typically done without intent, but you should never attempt the return if you were not allowed sufficient time to perform your routine in order to be truly ready. Simply hold up your hand, announce that you were not ready, retrieve the ball, and restart the point. In any event, it's always prudent to approach your actual return position from a location well behind it before settling in. This practice will allow you enough time to gather yourself properly and wave off the server if necessary.

As you develop an affinity for your own particular return of serve ritual, you will, without a doubt, begin to more fully appreciate that there are many degrees of readiness. Returning rituals that are very deliberately and consistently executed will provide you with a real opportunity—the *only* opportunity—to make full use of your existing skill and get you into the point in good shape more often than not.

The Mind Body Connection

To this day, I can clearly remember playing a practice set against an experienced older player when I was still just a kid. At the time, I had been told that I had some raw skills, and was beginning to believe in myself a little bit, but I wasn't totally sure I could hang with this guy, never mind beat him. To up the ante, he seemed especially keen to give me a lesson since, in part at least, I had been assigned to regularly work out with his very talented, nationally-ranked twelve-year-old son, green as I was as a teacher/coach. During the course of easily besting him, as it unexpectedly turned out, he, embarrassed by his plight, blurted out to our one spectator in disbelief, "He's unconscious," and he was absolutely right. I had absolutely no conscious idea of what I was doing, or exactly how I was doing it, but I was doing everything right and could do no wrong. I was "playing out of my mind," to quote another popular phrase of the day, although in reality I was actually very much in my mind—the right hemisphere of it, that is.

Seventeen year-old Maria Sharapova's stunning upset of Serena Williams in the 2004 Wimbledon final mirrored my own humble experience. "To tell you the truth, I don't know what happened in the match," the thirteenth-seeded Russian Chernobyl escapee said. "I don't know what the tactics were. I was just out there. I was just playing. I could really care less what was going on outside me. I was in my own little world. I don't know what that world was really." That particular world is familiarly referred to as "the zone," where paralysis through over-analysis never occurs.

A few years after my experience with the older player, I was matched against a player preceded by a considerable reputation at a USLTA (as it was then called, the "L" stood for "Lawn" for those of you too young to remember) New England summer circuit tournament on Cape Cod in Massachusetts. This guy was all over me from the start, full of confidence and bravado, serving and volleying even on second serves despite the slow clay, and chipping and charging otherwise at every possible opportunity. As usual, I was spraying any groundies that I had to hit all over the place with no rhyme or reason.

I couldn't help but notice that 2004 U.S. Olympic pole vault hopeful, diamond in the rough Jeremy Scott, articulated my exact approach off the ground at the time in a self-analysis of his pursuit of a more enlightened vaulting technique when he said, "I was [previously] relying on running fast and hanging on."

Back to the match—both my return game and passing shots were, as usual, respectable, and at times better. I used the same strokes and same mechanics, but with totally different results. When he was coming in, and especially when already in, I somehow instinctively visualized precisely where I needed to place my shots to pass him cleanly if any kind of opening was there, or at least make him play a difficult low volley if it wasn't. It took years for me to recognize and fully comprehend what had taken place. I had absolutely no conscious knowledge of mental imagery at the time, but in my mind's eye I managed to picture both his position and the top of the net itself as points of reference for the exact place, or window, that I intended to hit my shots through. When he did stay back and took my "target" away, thankfully not very often, my focus switched to consciously hoping not to make errors, triggering classic left brain contemplation resulting in errant shots struck without conviction or purpose. These were shots described best, in retrospect, as vaguely launched in the direction of "somewhere over there." If I only knew then what I didn't learn until years later when my playing window had already passed me by.

Mental skills are such an incredibly important component of a game that initially appears to be, on the surface, nothing more than a strictly physical one. Yet, picturing shots in advance every single time without fail—a direct function of the creative "walk and chew gum" right hemisphere of one's brain—is a vital part of the mix. The conscious analytical left side, ideally shut down during in point activity, should only be accessed for between-point problem solving on an as needed basis. Since you've been in the game for a while, and have worked hard to develop respectable mechanical and physical skills, this thinking-non-thinking man's tennis can represent the gateway to consistently playing to your potential right in your own signature zone.

Yannick Noah, after upsetting Jimmy Connors at the 1999 Nuveen Masters in Naples, Florida, in an early round robin match said, "The big points don't have to do with technique or physical condition, it's a mental condition. For me it comes down to controlling my breathing, my thoughts and my emotions." It follows that it's extremely difficult to be under control if your shot goals are routinely vague at best.

The mind-body connection has everything to do with taking full advantage of an incredibly able neuromuscular network. Although much has been learned about the brain's role in tennis and athletics in general, particularly its uncanny role in orchestrating both gross *and* finite motor control simultaneously, its study remains a never-ending pursuit. As a motivated player, you should at least have a basic sense of how you're wired for the game, and what makes you tick, along with exactly what's taking place when it all clicks.

Developing solid and reliable ball-striking skills in all areas of your game makes effective muscle memory response literally a no-brainer. Obviously—although sometimes not so obviously to some—no practice, no repetition, no proven mechanics to draw upon, and then no confidence lead to an overriding apprehension with sporadic and limited results. However, the great news is that success is well within reach since both rank beginners and novices—even those without a great deal of athletic ability—can, upon request, grasp visualizing fairly quickly and then crudely direct their shots more to the right, more to the left, higher, or lower with either very little or no knowledge of mechanics. Such is the awesome power of the mind and the body working in concert.

Unfortunately, even experienced club players with high NTRP ratings, after particularly bad shots, tend to fog over when asked exactly where they were trying to direct the ball. Replies like, "Well, I'm not really sure. I guess I just wanted to get it back over," or, "You know, I really didn't know," are not unusual at all. Some, in denial, actually try to lie about not visualizing by attempting to give me the "right" answer. Believe me, I hear it all every single day. It's exceedingly difficult to recall what wasn't ever *there* in the first place. If you're not precisely sure, crystal clear, about where you had at least intended for your shot to go, then where is it going to go? The answer is—just as I experienced as a frustrated young player from the back of the court—somewhere over there. The bad news is that the court isn't big enough, nor is the net low enough, for that approach to be very successful, especially under pressure.

At the tour level, we see even the best of the best occasionally and inexplicably miss an easy put away by a huge margin. Despite all their ball-striking wizardry, they can also be distracted from clear visualizing by the conscious mind contemplating, for even a mere millisecond, the consequences of blowing an important winning opportunity that had been hard earned through a considerable physical effort. In the spirit of don't drink and drive—don't think and hit.

Californian Tom Chivington, in commenting on the evolution of his former player, Brad Gilbert, into a master tour coach and Andre Agassi's Svengali, gave us an insider's view of them both when he said, "When Agassi confessed he didn't think about where he was aiming his serve until he threw his toss up, Gilbert was aghast. 'Are you nuts?' he asked Agassi. 'I think about where I'm serving two weeks before I walk on the court.'"

The shot-making chain of events is, thankfully, unwaveringly sequential. Upon recognizing an opponent's shot—right at or even before impact with an educated read—you lean into your shoulder turn, start coiling up while beginning to prepare the racket, and instantaneously compute the right place and time to meet the approaching ball. A fleeting moment later, you're visualizing your response: the direction, margins, trajectory, spin, and pace of your shot all rolled instantly into one in your mind's eye. Then, with what feels like is plenty of time—compared to not visualizing—you pull the trigger at the moment of truth, unhurried and secure, and begin tracking your shot back to the other side of the court.

I always recall a general characterization of the game by LGE partner Dr. Jack Groppel as "one of constantly occurring emergencies." Fair enough, but it doesn't have to be, and it certainly shouldn't be. The better you understand the inner workings of your mental, physical, and emotional capabilities, the better you can calm yourself and manage the difficult moments more methodically, deliberately, uneventfully, and ultimately more successfully.

In *Derivative Sport in Tornado Alley*, an essay on his youthful adventures in Central Illinois junior tennis, avant-garde writer, David Foster Wallace, perfectly distills the essence of the game in one sentence, "It is chess on the run."

Aspire to never think about mechanics, and certainly not winning and losing, in the midst of any point. Just feel the real deal kinesthetically and enjoy the ride. Embrace having no conscious idea of how you're doing what you're doing, when you're doing it. Focus your total attention on the flight of the ball. Picture your desired result well before you strike your shot, and have the courage to let the chips fall where they may. It's far too late to be inventing or reinventing one's technique in the middle of the point. Jean Butler, the spectacular lead Irish dancer in the original stage production of *Riverdance*, succinctly explained her very best performances this way, "On a good night, nothing goes through my mind."

After clinching the United States Davis Cup team's 2004 quarter-final win over an outstanding Swedish team, world number two Andy Roddick, in commenting on his dispatching of the more than capable Jonas Bjorkman in straight sets, particularly his play in a stunning 6-0 display of nearly perfect all-court tennis in the third that he capped off with a world record 152 m.p.h. serve, said, "I felt great out there in the third set. I wasn't even thinking. It was just kind of like my instincts took over. That's as clean as I've ever felt on the tennis court in a long time and maybe ever."

Since pressure exists on each and every shot to one degree or another, the challenge is to have total faith and confidence in focusing on the opportunity for success, and reject and block out any and all negative intrusions of self-doubt. Trusting every shot to your existing muscle memory—by thinking clearly in pictures—will not only make you a better competitor, but also much more the player that you aspire to be, seen previously only here and there in brief flashes.

Lance Armstrong, Tour de France cyclist superman, is obsessively committed to "pre-stage" visualization—according to his coach Chris Carmichael in *The Ultimate Ride*—by picturing every contingency from road hazards, the best lines through the corners, the crowd presence at the edge of the pavement, and the frenetic sprints, all culminating in a success.

Personally, when I feel that I have put forth a determined effort, and have performed reasonably well, but still get beaten by the better player that day, it's not such a bad thing. Then it's simply getting back to the drawing board to improve exactly what kept me from playing my best and possibly getting the win. But, if I lose to *anyone* because of umpteen unforced errors resulting in large part from generally poor self-management—creating a heavily weighted negative differential between winners and errors—then I'm left with considerable disappointment in myself for such an undisciplined, unfocused, lackadaisical, out of control effort.

After all, as usual, at the end of the day, on or off the court, you get pretty much what you expected all along.

By the way, if the net were a brick wall instead of the see-through netting that it is, I am absolutely positive there would be far fewer errors in the net, and visualizing would come much more naturally to all players early on in their development.

You Gotta Fight Right

Being a tough competitor is essential in riding out the many momentum shifts that can take place in tennis, as well as any mechanical or emotional glitches that also can occur in match play at any level.

Committed players instinctively try harder when the going gets tough. It's the nature of the animal. If not properly managed, the thousands of years of man's evolved "fight or flight" adrenaline-flowing response—to defeat, escape from, or, if all went wrong, be killed by tribal enemies and predators in ancient times—typically leads to an undermining increase in hitting arm muscle tension, rapid and shallow breathing, and a runaway pulse. Although seemingly appropriate, this condition is not exactly ideal when attempting to meet a challenge and raise one's level in an arena where exceptional finite motor control and cool under fire is essential.

Never, in regard to *making shots*, try harder. Not only is this approach to trouble extremely inefficient, it flat out doesn't work. Instead, find the courage to try to be softer, smoother, easier, and even slower. Consciously lower your muscle tension. Relax both physically and emotionally. Quiet your mind and get back into the flow of the points, one at a time. Be on the inside *with* "it," versus on the outside *against* "it," trying to force square pegs into round holes. Good things will happen. Following his five-set loss to Arnaud Clement in the semifinals of the 2001 Australian Open, after being up two sets to none, Sebastien Grosjean said, "I think I started well, but Arnaud kept fighting. He started to play better. It was good fighting. But he came back and he played better at the end."

Quite another view of the Clement turnaround, that of the insightful *New York Times* tennis writer Selena Roberts, zeroed in on Grosjean's loss of composure and control, "Suddenly, the 22-year-old Grosjean was visibly tight. Beneath his backward cap, he looked panic-stricken."

The incredible Austrian skier, Stephan Eberharter, holder of *forty-three* World Cup medals over a long and distinguished career, finally won the gold at the Salt Lake City Olympics after, for him, below par performances in first winning a bronze and a silver medal. When asked about the pressure he faced in his final event triumph, he said, "I was disappointed about the last two races. But trying extra hard doesn't usually get you anywhere. You do what you know how to."

Somewhat closer to our world (not really), Dmitry Tursunov, the 205th ranked tennis player on planet Earth, upon reaching the final of the 2003 Bronx Tennis Classic and qualifying for the U.S. Open said, "I think if you look at it physically, there are not too many exceptions at the highest level. Not many players can serve like Andy Roddick or have the quickness returning of Andre Agassi, but generally the skills are the same. The toughest part of the game at this level is learning how to deal with pressure. This is what I'm still trying to grasp."

Brad Gilbert takes it further when he says, "Andre and Andy have so many more weapons than I ever did that they don't have to play a garbage game like me—now we are getting closer. They have way more offense. But they've still got to learn how to grub their way through. That's competition—two guys, toe-to-toe."

This is not to suggest that you shouldn't dig deeper regarding your overall hustle, and more specifically your level of footwork, to both defend the court with abandon and be in better shot-making positions as well. In any event, always keep in mind that tennis is a differential relaxation sport—the lower body is going hard and fast so that the upper body can comparatively go soft and slow.

Your attitude toward the ball—yes, the *ball*—can also play an uncanny role in playing your way out of trouble and avoiding any loss of form. Players in distress unconsciously are apt to begin viewing the approaching ball as the enemy, as if it has somehow conspired with the opponent against them, and tend to rid themselves of it as quickly as possible. Turn that perception around and team up with the ball. Spend some time with it. Chill, the ball can be very user-friendly if you allow it. As usual, it's all what you make of it. Welcome its arrival to your side of the court: 1) you expect it to come back, 2) you don't mind, and 3) just perform to the best of your ability. After all, you came to play, not to avoid playing.

When you're losing the battle with yourself, and self-destructing through unforced errors, the solution is not pressuring yourself to raise your game by hitting winners. Cool it and get back to basics by engaging the opponent in longer rallies in order to first settle down, and then get back into a good rhythm. When "stalemating," you're positioning yourself to win, *not* lose. In his five-set win over Patrick Rafter in the other Aussie Open 2001 semis—after being down two sets to one—Andre Agassi explained his strategy against the relentless net rushing Australian, "At the end of the day, you just want to make him earn it if he wins. That's all I was trying to do, just play a great match. It turned out to be a great match that happened to go my way."

The philosopher Kierkegaard must have been a very solid tennis player in his day since he once offered, "Be with what is, so that what is to be, may become." Now there's another guy secure enough to let the chips fall where they may.

After all, in the end, it's only a game. Hockey legend Wayne Gretzky had a great take on preparing for the big games, "I'm looking forward to enjoying the pressure." And why not relish it as an opportunity, much like Serena Williams in the Wimbledon finals showdown with Maria Sharapova, albeit unsuccessful? "She's a very tough girl, and she's a fighter, and we share those similarities. So I'm looking forward to a very tough match," said Williams. There's that "looking forward to" phrase again.

You can put it in perspective by considering the challenge faced by the licensed to kill Samurai warriors—to remain relaxed and calm, in the face of possibly getting their heads lopped off, in order to perform their best and get the "win." Now that's *really* having to fight right!

As a final reminder, you absolutely have to drop the histrionics and negative self-talk when things are not going your way. You are just distancing yourself further from righting your game. Be like a mature, happy Martina Hingis, who evolved far beyond her bratty French Open temper tantrum meltdown of a few years ago—after being taken to school by a past-her-prime Steffi Graf—and have a little fun out there. Or, be like Pete Sampras—don't act as if it's the end of the world when things are not going all that well—best exemplified by the nightmarish loss the six-time Wimbledon champion, the king of lawn tennis, suffered after winning the first two sets against clay court specialist Alex Corretja on home grass versus Spain in a 2002 Davis Cup tie. And how about Gaston Gaudio's post-match revelation after coming back from a petrified two sets down start—in which he won only three of the first fifteen games—to win the 2004 French Open title from the prematurely anointed fellow Argentine Guillermo Coria, 8-6 in the fifth? "After that I start to relax a bit more, trying to enjoy the moment I was living, being in the final," said Gaudio, in response to the fifteen thousand-plus fans performing an extended wave, ignoring the chair umpire's repeated pleas for silence, in an attempt to urge him on at the crucial juncture in the pivotal third set. Once a smiling Gaudio dropped his racket and applauded the crowd, the ice was broken.

These were important lessons to be learned from three of the very best, two of whom reigned as world number ones in multiple years and cared more about winning and doing their best than we can probably ever imagine.

Taming the Beast Within

In the heat of battle, when you're well over any pre-match jitters, but with the outcome still very much in question, if getting the win is important, one's mind can be flooded with unwelcome thoughts, emotions, and images that are overridingly distracting from the task at hand. They run the gamut from suddenly experiencing negative thoughts about your returning ability on a big point, to thinking that you're going to double-fault, or even to avoiding the challenge by "going away" and focusing instead on who is talking so loud in the courtside bleachers.

Actually visualizing losing the match because of a bad patch, early on, in a contest still headed down to the wire, with plenty of time left, is another version. Leaving the present and worrying about not being able to close out a match that heretofore was going well, and there for the taking, is still another. Building a comfortable, but not insurmountable, lead over an opponent that you've never won even a set from previously, and then falling victim to a debilitating apprehension, is another classic.

Remaining in a consistently attentive and positive can-do mode, even a defiant one, takes every single ounce of concentration and resolve you can muster in the face of such undermining and overwhelming possibilities—taming the beast. On a relatively equal ball-striking playing field, self-doubt, confusion, panic, or all of the above are far more of an enemy than the player across the net. Daily disciplining of your on *and* off court thought process and mindset—cumulative positive experience, external *and* internal, absolutely can build confidence—will eventually reward you with the avoidance of, or at the very least an insurance policy against, an especially embarrassing or maddening day.

Never let your mind wander because it's only the Wednesday afternoon social mixed-doubles scramble. Avoid practicing imperfectly, since you will always be a product of exactly how you do practice. Expecting to somehow be able to flip on an "all is well" switch when in serious match play, after you have played rather carelessly previously, is totally unrealistic.

In recounting his career changing straight set victory over Pete Sampras at the 2001 Ericsson Open in Key Biscayne, Andy Roddick wrote in a journal he kept for *Tennis Magazine,* "The only shaky moment I had was when I got up a break in the second. I couldn't help but think, 'Like, I actually might beat Pete Sampras.' But I fought hard to shut it out." Roddick also caught himself initially losing focus in the warm-up when he peeked across the net and thought, "Ooooohhh-kaaaayyyy, I'm playing Pete Sampras, in front of 15,000 people, and it's on national television." A potentially disastrous mindset was averted, nipped in the bud, and he was able to start the match on solid mental ground. Not bad for an eighteen-year-old banger who, at the time, already understood perfectly well that it takes more than just bashing forehands and firing aces to succeed.

Personally, two recent playing experiences in the very competitive Naples, Florida, club pros league can serve to illustrate both the consequences of losing focus and the rewards of continuing on no matter what. While serving at 0-6 in a match-deciding super-breaker (first to 10 by 2) I was interrupted three times right as I began my ritual by a public address system operator gone wild—would you believe Gene Autry singing, "Back in the Saddle Again." Still focused and undeterred, and with nothing more than a slim thread of hope, I finally got the fourth attempt launched and into play. Fourteen points later, my partner and I somehow managed to come through and win the breaker 11-9. Nice reward. Conversely, in another breaker the very next week, once again for all the marbles, leading 8-5 and serving after battling back from being down 5-2, I couldn't help but think that we had done it again—it just happened. Unfortunately, I allowed my concentration to be broken and divided in a brief moment of weakness, and with the tennis gods overseeing the transgression—*they always are*—we proceeded to go down 10-8 in what seemed like the blink of an eye. Fitting punishment.

The beast within can emerge completely unrecognized. It can be triggered on the spot by simply looking at your watch for a brief moment in anticipation of where you have to be after the match. You're gone, also referred to by ESPN's Fred Stolle as, "leaving the office a little early."

In 1990, John McEnroe arrived in Melbourne primed to win the Australian Slam. In winning his first three matches, he had lost a grand total of just fifteen games and was on a roll, playing his best tennis in years. However, in the fourth round against a resurgent Mikael Pernfors, all went wrong. A combative Mac—what a surprise—let his emotions get the best of him in arguing profusely over an abuse of racket point penalty that followed a previous warning over intimidating an official. Thinking in the back of his mind that he still had two infractions to play with before getting the heave ho—forgetting that the point penalty system rules had just been changed from a four-step process to just three to start the new year—he pressed on. An audible obscenity, possibly his worst ever, directed at the officials, but also heard by *everyone* else nearby, followed. What resulted was historic, the very first default of a player in a major tennis event, ever. When all was said and done, McEnroe himself admitted that it was first allowing his mind to wander *prior to the match* that opened the floodgates for his loss of control in the tumultuous second set. "I knew how well I was hitting the ball. I wasn't serving as well as I can, but I was hitting the ball as well as I ever have. But instead of thinking about winning the Australian, I started thinking about my schedule (the likelihood of having to be on the road for nearly *two* months). That should have been the last thing in the world I was thinking about, especially in the middle of a Grand Slam tournament."

This monster within can also, over even a couple of days, methodically gain a foothold while just lying in wait, egged on by a distinct disdain for an upcoming opponent for stupid personal reasons difficult to rationalize. Or, it can suddenly arrive along with an opponent's constant chatter in between almost every point at the same time that you're trying to keep your already inconsistent game from unraveling completely. The list goes on ad infinitum. Once the beast gets in, it's often too late to stem the tide, and you've already morphed into a wreck in the making.

There are indeed countless examples in sports, especially individual sports, when players falter under pressure and the worst in them prevails. Well documented, and ever dissected by the media and the sport shrinks, they are painful to watch, particularly at the highest levels of the game where the fall from grace is the steepest. Even the best of the best are not immune. If I were a betting man, I would have made book on all the action that I could find with Jana Novotna leading Steffi Graf 4-1 in the third, and serving at 40-30 in the 1993 Wimbledon final. And I would have also bet the farm on Greg Norman prevailing over Nick Faldo at the 1996 Masters golf showdown while enjoying a huge lead on the final day with a mere ten holes to go. I would have lost my shirt in both instances, since both Novotna and Norman, highly ranked seasoned world-class performers and proven winners, completely collapsed in a heap with the finish line in sight.

At the 2000 Olympic trials for track and field, Clint Wells, the top-rated Native American distance runner today, was seemingly well positioned in third place—the top three finishers would qualify for Sydney—in the 3,000 meter steeplechase finals with three-quarters of a lap remaining, only to finish fifth. He later told mentor and 1964 gold medal-winning (10,000 meters) Billy Mills, an Oglala Sioux: "Billy, for the first time I could taste the Olympics. Then I thought, 'Are they going to catch me?' and I started thinking backward instead of forward."

Record-setting long distance swimming phenom Lynne Cox, at fifteen, swam the English Channel faster than anyone before her. She then went on to conquer the Strait of Magellan, the Cook Strait in New Zealand, the Cape of Good Hope, the Bering Sea from Alaska to the Soviet Union, and the Antarctic Ocean in thirty-two degree-plus water. In her book *Swimming To Antarctica*, she revealed her constant inner battles with fear, self-doubt, and impatience. And, boys and girls, we're talking extremely high-risk and potentially life-and-death stuff here, not just bouncing fuzzy rubber balls in a secure cage. Perspective is always a good thing.

During Pete Sampras' retirement "party" at the 2003 U.S. Open, he recognized the taming of his own inner beast by crediting his 1992 U.S. Open final *loss* to Stefan Edberg as setting the stage for the rest of his career. "I felt like I gave in that match; I felt it was good enough getting into the final. After that, the fact that I gave in bothered me a lot," he admitted.

There exists no panacea for falling victim to your own thoughts and demons, although the old adage of "practice, practice, practice"— Sampras' exact solution: "I did more work . . ."—does come to mind since a strong sense of security is the product of repetition. Everyone has experienced these kinds of nightmares—in actuality, *daymares.* Thankfully, everyone lives to tell us about theirs, when and if they're willing to actually admit them. After all, losing because of a physical problem is acceptable, but losing because of a mental one is perceived as inexcusable and a sign of serious weakness.

Thankfully, there are antidotes that, if monitored and worked on every time you step out on the court, can make a difference, especially long term, in keeping your hair from catching fire and your psyche from melting down when it's show time.

Habitually warming up as quickly as possible shows absolutely no respect for the game, or the continued development of your own skills. It is an absolutely great way to set yourself up to be overwhelmed *from within* in a close match. I call it "zone avoidance," and it's frustrating that so many continue to practice it on a daily basis. I recently made it the subject of a clinic I presented to a group of club players as part of a French Open celebration. The very next day a foursome of the very same players in attendance warmed up for no more than five minutes on the court right next to me, took zero practice serves, and announced, "f.b.i" ("First ball in," for those of you, thankfully, unfamiliar with the term). Hello? Methodically reinventing every phase of your game during every single warm-up is unequivocally essential.

Other tactics that can be very beneficial in keeping you on the straight and narrow are establishing very methodical serving and receiving rituals, and settling into an in-between point tempo and rhythm that feels just right to you—not too fast or hurried and not too slow or de-energizing either.

Sitting down on the changeovers in tournament or league play, naturally when you're fatigued, but also to always gather your thoughts— although never to wallow in any failures—and touch base with either yourself or your partner, even if only briefly, tired or not, is another relevant self-management technique.

Still another is avoiding being overly friendly with any opponent—

cordial is good enough—since you could very easily lose your edge. Avoid being overly unfriendly as well, since you could not only become too intense overall, but it could also become personal, possibly making operating coolly and collectively more difficult.

Naturally, always make tough, but fair line calls—when in doubt, "It is absolutely *not* out!" is what should be bandied about, versus the in jest exact opposite, on this subject—especially on the big points where some players want "it" so bad their dark side emerges. Any reluctance to do so will gain you an unfavorable reputation and is asking for a festering headache that could, if you have a conscience, gnaw away at your focusing powers the rest of the day.

Not keeping your eyes and ears fixated on your own court, typically manifested in looking all over the place between points—actually watching points on an adjoining court or listening in on a disputed line call three courts down—will also, sooner or later, conjure up the demons lurking inside. You should know by now that they wait just below the surface of even a game seemingly firing on all cylinders for the opportune moment to enter the equation and nudge open the door to misfortune.

Finally, never start the next point without knowing the score. Keeping close track of the score is necessary to decide not only what your strategy is on each and every point, but also exactly how you're tactically going to go about getting it done. Always play to the score.

Tournament play, league play, or any kind of match play can potentially create a completely useless cacophony of noise in one's head. Taming the beast involves *never* underestimating the importance of monitoring and orchestrating one's mind. Creating the right climate by thinking the right thoughts when it's time to think, and then calmly pulling off the ultimate trick of being able to think no thoughts at all when it's time to just physically do what you've practiced hundreds of times, is a developed skill.

Internationally recognized concert pianist Artur Schnabel, who understood the challenge all too well, said regarding his performances, "The notes I handle no better than many pianists. But the pauses between the notes—ah, that is where the art resides!"

Breathing

Have you ever noticed that after witnessing professional players compete, especially if you're fortunate enough to be up close and personal at a live venue, the level of your play when you return home always immediately improves. You spontaneously begin emulating, with a renewed enthusiasm for the game, the best of what you have seen. Your strokes are longer, smoother, and cleaner. Your footwork and court coverage are more energized. Even your demeanor, both in and out of the point, shows greater confidence and composure under pressure. The experience has taken complete advantage of your innate visual learning ability.

A much more subtle method of improvement involves auditory learning—learning from what you hear. Unfortunately, club players seldom return from attending world-class tennis events benefiting in a similar fashion from what they actually *heard* from the best players in the world.

To that point, the vast majority of these folks tend to be big-time breath-holders. Unlike one hundred percent of professional players today, they—until a more sophisticated level of play is reached—hold their breath every time they strike a ball. This practice guarantees excessive muscle tension, increased emotional stress, and the onset of oxygen debt. Not only does ball-striking become inefficient by seriously negating the role of the racket, but, least desirable of all, stamina is also undermined and the brain eventually shorts out from oxygen deprivation. For anyone with a few miles on their odometer, especially if you're a few pounds heavier than you'd like to be, holding your breath on every shot is also extremely unhealthy and potentially dangerous to your overall well-being.

I especially like Naples pro Joe Obidegwa's "questionnaire" on the topic. He first asks how long one can go without eating; then, how long one can last without drinking; and finally, how long one can survive without breathing. Everybody gets that!

Top players exhale at the moment of impact on every shot. Again, that's *every* shot. Simply put, they breathe all the time. Sounds like a good idea! They inhale just prior to making their shot and then exhale through the shot. Long, sustained exhalations for groundies, serves, et cetera, short abbreviated exhalations on volleys. The serve in particular can be the greatest beneficiary of breathing by inhaling during the toss, and then exhaling as the ball is being struck.

Television commentators like to refer to this technique as "grunting," which is absolutely true in the usual examples being noted, set regularly for our impressionable younger players by Monica Seles for years, and now Serena Williams, who regularly breaks the sound barrier. Yet the former top players typically doing the analysis consistently fail to offer some brief tutorial on what's normally necessary to get the breathing job done—*without* screaming. Many in the tennis industry have come to regard these exaggerations as a disservice to the viewing audience, the game itself, and sometimes the opponent, i.e., the hindrance rule.

At times, jacked-up courtside microphones amplify the player's breathing to the point that it hypes the grunt card and becomes misleading to those listening at home. Although the practice is indeed more guttural and louder in certain players, some of the very best, past and present, were and are barely audible. Tennis *is not*, after all, power lifting hundreds of pounds over your head.

Some professional players even alter their "sound" based upon the type of shot, the emotional stress of the moment—such as a particularly big point or when the match is slipping away—or their level of physical exertion. In Venus Williams' third round upset loss to Lisa Raymond at the 2004 Australian Open, sports reporter Christopher Clarey noted, "Williams seldom raises her volume unless she needs to raise her game, and she was in serious need as the baseline rallies stretched on and the unforced errors piled up. But although Williams could change the soundtrack, she could not change the flow of the surprising match . . ."

A recent Animal Planet channel program of note featured a deep-in-the-wild black bear field study conducted by a groundbreaking researcher who, based upon his astonishing up close and personal experiences with numerous subjects, said, "Just the way they breathe tells me what they're thinking."

In the modern game, others, raising the breathing bar still further, consistently make use of two-syllable exhalations. The first exhalation is just prior to hitting their shot, and the second is right though impact. This practice, first utilized by Mr. Connors and later popularized by Seles, also appears to be on the rise in popularity among certain tour players.

In any event, well executed exhaling at each shot's moment of truth physically relaxes your muscles—including eliminating any counterproductive jaw clenching. It also reduces emotional stress dramatically, assists in keeping you literally in your right mind, and ensures the continual supply of oxygen to the body as a whole, and, more specifically, to the brain. Tired players in oxygen debt not only lose motor control, but also make very poor decisions—not a good combination.

Learn to not be self-conscious about performing like the pros—as so many are—especially in this incredibly important component of the game. Once again, you do not have to be loud, or grunt. Being overly demonstrative can easily backfire. It not only can waste energy, but also trigger excessive emotion and a loss of calmness if a certain line is crossed. Always keep in mind that once you've made the commitment to breathe—and you are not screaming—any negative comment about it, from either a partner or an opponent, is coming from someone who clearly *does not know the game* despite any outward appearances of credibility.

Ever wonder where the athletic expression "choke" came from? Could it be a reference to not being able to breathe, and then, as a direct result, not being able to perform as usual? In the form of another irony, what about those instances in daily life when someone describes to you a situation in which they were so apprehensive that they were "holding their breath" *hoping* that everything would turn out alright—not a sound approach to getting results on the tennis court.

When you do succeed at making breathing an integral part of your game, whatever else you're capable of will be quickly solidified in a big way. And, although not exactly measurable, you will only then not be leaving anything out in your otherwise positive efforts to learn from the pro example.

The Man Who Breathed for Two

In the mid–1980s, the Paine Webber Classic Super Series tour event was alive and well at the Sanibel Harbour Resort. Jimmy Connors, the properties' touring pro (whose name was on the stadium court), would meet Ivan Lendl, ranked number one in the world, in the finals at week's end to the delight of all Jimmy's new Southwest Florida fans.

It was a heady time for the area to be hosting such a big time world-class tournament, complete with national television coverage, and a thirty-two player field so strong that a previously injured Pat Cash, a recent Wimbledon champion, had to come through qualifying. But something else noteworthy took place during an early round match that NBC completely missed, and I suspect that most either never noticed in the first place, or, if they did, have long since forgotten about. Jay Lapidus, a former number one at Princeton, and a solid journeyman pro, would breathe for two.

With Jim Loehr in residence, and his on-site work with visiting tour players looking for an edge gaining notoriety, his Mentally Tough program was in full swing. Today the term "mental toughness" is in the vocabulary of even the most Neanderthal of coaches in just about any sport, not to mention its now commonplace usage by television commentators and print journalists as well. New England Patriot quarterback Tom Brady, after coming from behind late in an early 2003 season game to then win in overtime versus the Dolphins in the uninviting hot and humid Miami weather, said, "If there's one thing our coach [Bill Belichick, hardly a Neanderthal type] preaches, it's mental toughness." And the fact that the Army (U.S. Military Academy) football team

(0-13 for 2003), leaders and future officers all, includes a "mental coach" puts the discipline well into the mainstream.

Breathing with a purpose represented one of his most essential components in harnessing and managing one's full ability, both physiologically and psychologically, and was being recognized by serious tennis players in large numbers at every level of the game. So what better place or time than at Jimmy Connors' new home—after all, Jimmy was *the* original model for demonstrative breathing—for Lapidus to go where no man had ever gone before on a tennis court.

Upon entering the stadium for an early round match, I immediately saw—no, make that heard—that something very strange and unusual was taking place. Lapidus was not only audibly exhaling on his own shots, but incredibly, was also exhaling when his opponent struck the ball as well! I was always amazed when top players would come in to work with Dr. Jim, despite their previous successes, and turn out to be either marginal or full-blown breath holders, but this was something else all together. It was at first glance/listen an apparent aberration of considerable magnitude. Yet, after the initial novelty wore off, and with jaw back in place, regulating one's breathing pattern one hundred percent to the rhythm and dynamic of the give-and-take action at hand, at *both* ends of the court, made some sense.

This was breath control on the tennis court, shot-making inhaling and exhaling on cue, in its most precise form. What a great tool for focusing, relaxing, reducing stress, maintaining an uninterrupted supply of oxygen to the body, and giving in to being unconscious at all the right times. Lapidus was so committed to this controlled breathing pattern that it was easy to see that any potential distraction would be hard pressed to penetrate his single-minded effort. It then boiled down to, I suspect he thought, mechanics, pure and simple, and getting the very most out of his ball-striking talents.

Inhaling just prior to the shot, exhaling during the shot. Then inhaling just prior to the opponent's shot, and exhaling during the opponent's shot. In and out, over and over again, much in the same way an Olympic swimmer coordinates their considerably more challenging breathing task to their stroke count out of the necessity of being submerged in water a good portion of the time during their event.

He was impressive, going into a little trance while huffing and puffing his way around the court with tremendous focus and an unflappable presence. This guy was way down deep in the points. Hell, he was the point.

Now, fifteen-plus years later, none of this ever became mainstream, not even, curiously, as an exercise in breathing at the junior camps and tennis schools around the country. Today, Jay Lapidus is in charge of a solid men's program at Duke University. I don't know if he ever utilizes "breathing for two" in team practices, but I do believe that there was no madness to his method, particularly in light of its clear potential as a viable training device.

In our daily programs at the resort, we would ask beginning breathers, sometimes even highly skilled players, to say "yes" in the place of a pure exhalation as a way to introduce breath control. In this same vein, especially for tightly wound breath holders, breathing for two can create an immediate and very acute awareness of one's breathing patterns. It can also provide a lesson in how efficient breathing can either enhance performance, or adversely affect it if not practiced methodically, or especially if not at all. And please, don't try to tell me that you can't handle breathing and watching the ball at the same time.

If you are still working on your breathing—aren't we all—it's definitely not a bad idea to give either method a try at least once, preferably when just hitting with a friend. Don't tell them what you're up to. They probably won't notice anyway since it is *not necessary* to be overly audible to be effective, and being relatively quiet is, in most instances, physically more economical.

If you are discovered breathing for two, just call it the Lapidus Maneuver. It won't have quite the same impact as Heimlich's technique, but it will definitely add something to your understanding and appreciation of breathing, and its positive effect on the continued growth and release of your inner game.

How Could I Miss That Shot?

You have most likely heard a number of opponents and partners say just that. And I'll wager that you've expressed the very same thing over making one of those dreaded "easy" errors that suddenly ends a point, which you thought was absolutely yours to win. Typically, these points have been well constructed: methodically, calmly, and with controlled aggression, right up to the very moment the finishing opportunity presents itself. The opponent has been maneuvered well out of position and what should be the winning shot is right in front of you, right there for the taking, and you blow it.

These mistakes, in particular, are perhaps the most frustrating in the game. But wide open court chances can trigger last second disruptions of focus, affecting both rhythm and timing, that result in seemingly inexplicable errors at the most opportune moments, at any level, but especially among over-eager players. A non-stat on the pro tours, tracking open court conversions would be very revealing in club tennis.

In order to remain in control in these "more difficult than one might think" situations, and avoid self-destruction, it is important to develop the "nothing more than just another placement" mindset, versus emotionally salivating over the prospect of a spectacular winner. Expectations of shots that absolutely must end the point, especially ones that an opponent also won't even be able to get their racket on, cause huge increases in last second pressure, making execution a very dicey proposition at best.

Self-control is crucial at munch and crunch time. In order to prevent rushing one's shots—actively encouraged by hustling opponents

closing down what initially was a completely open court—and to, ultimately, completely eliminate those kinds of unnecessary errors that can
turn the tide, you must remain calm. It's demoralizing to invest so much
and then suddenly lose it all when it's right within your grasp. If you
blow enough of these chances, according to one of my regular students,
Woody W., "You'll end up on a slippery slope, into the spiral of death,
and well on your way to the zone of no return." And we've *all* been
there.

Unnecessarily increasing your pace of shot, right along with
decreasing your margins to the lines, puts you on thin ice. Factor in the
not-uncommon tendency to commit prematurely to a position to
launch the shot from, leading to invariably looking up at the inviting
open court just prior to striking the ball, and it gets worse because, in
failure, you know you shouldn't have possibly missed.

Learn to stay cool and collected when you've got a balloon right
there for the bursting. Keeping your feet working right up until it's the
appropriate time to make the shot is an absolute must. You've got to fill
the time. Never allow an opponent, or a doubles team that covers the
court well, to influence the timing of your shot. In the face of a shrinking opening that you have no real control over, remain completely
focused on the ball and stay in the very same point-building rhythm
and tempo that got you "there" in the first place.

Learn to treat these opportunistic situations as just another ball, just
another placement. What's the problem? What's the big rush? After all,
that's all they really are.

Numero Uno

"I just didn't concentrate today" is another example of what tennis players say after a particularly bad outing. How often have you found yourself thinking the very same thing after putting forth a determined, solid physical effort, but end up still well short of playing up to your expectations? Exactly what does "*not* concentrating" really mean anyway, and precisely what was it that was not being concentrated on?

The great news is that the answer is simple: the ball. But the task of focusing one's attention solely on a small yellow sphere traveling through the air at a varying and dizzying array of speeds, spins, and trajectories, while simultaneously blocking out distractions and then intercepting it at the best possible place and time, is no easy feat.

After a lifetime of teaching and coaching the game, it continues to surprise me just how many players, even experienced ones who have benefited from years of lessons, do not fully appreciate that watching the ball is the single most difficult and important skill in tennis. Often duped into believing that they actually were focused on the ball, sometimes even after a particularly bad unforced error, club players will often defend their misperception with both confidence and passion. They will earnestly inform you that they can specifically recall "seeing it" when asked at the point's conclusion. But, when their game is breaking down and they're making too many mistakes, they often fail to recognize that, yes, they "saw" the ball alright, but only in a glancing fashion. At best, it was only through their periphery, which will not be nearly good enough to get the job done. When these players are also asked, "Are you good enough to play without watching the ball?" they always respond with an equally emphatic, "No." Upon pointing out to them that they are indeed good enough to play without watching the ball—after all, they just did—but that it will be very poor play, a deeply impacted chord is usually struck among thoughtful players. The bottom line is that there is watching, and there is *watching*.

I was once the recipient of a flattering ball watching compliment in a losing effort against the tough Texan, Benny Simms—currently Chandra Rubin's coach—in the finals of a small New England event. After the match, Simms graciously consoled me with, "If I ever have a son I'll bring him to you to learn to watch the ball." Although it actually never ended up taking place, that experience struck the same chord for me, thankfully a life-long reinforcing one, but, nonetheless, still a work in progress.

Realizing the distinct difference between absolute focus and peripheral sighting is the first step in becoming an exceptional watcher of the ball. Then, as you increasingly become able to nip any tracking problems in the bud, you will develop the ability to right your game quickly. You'll also spare yourself wasted energy on disconnected and completely irrelevant over-analysis of technique—a classic habit annoyingly exhibited by far too many club players typically intent on demonstrating their "knowledge" of the game to anyone who will listen.

Hopefully, you are not one of them since, in reality, it's actually sloppy ball watching that is often the number one cause of the majority of errors if you're a fairly accomplished player. Symptoms of ball watching failure can both manifest *and* mask themselves in many mechanical forms, which are typically not the root cause of poor play among players with normally good all-around ball-striking skills and prudent shot selection.

Effective in point concentration demands following the flight of the ball from the moment the opponent makes contact completely to your own strike point. Then, and this represents a core fundamental that always separates the bigger dogs from the pack, continuing to watch the ball, to the best of your visual ability, from your own moment of impact totally back to the opponent's, back and forth, over and over, again and again.

For those of you who feel compelled to cite the inadequacies of the human eye, it's true that when the ball is exploding off the racket face, and at times off the court itself, you are momentarily unable to actually see such an exceptionally fast-moving object. (Although some claim that they can actually see a yellow strobe at these critical moments, much like Ted Williams, the greatest pure hitter in baseball history, who claimed he could see the stitches on the baseball as it left the pitcher's hand.) The best you can do is auto-project, from experience, exactly where it's both coming and then going to. Thankfully, the eye-brain connection is incredibly adept at "locking on."

So when do you look at the court? How about never! It's not going anywhere and they're all exactly the same size. The court is a constant; the ball is the variable.

Continuing, when do you focus directly on an opponent? Never in singles, and only in certain instances in doubles, mostly when required to momentarily occupy a service line position to defend against a possible poach. Other than that, and a few other tricky doubles situations—it's a totally different game than singles and far more difficult in many ways—opposing players should be visible only through one's periphery.

While we're on the subject, when should you watch an opponent's racket? You're right of course, you don't—you can't really see it anyway because of, once again, the limitations of the eye. However, it's in the mix strictly through your periphery, only you are not focusing directly on it.

This level of concentration will allow you to develop an exceptional visual fix on the ball, eliminate disrupting split second voids in tracking, dramatically improve timing and anticipation, and also result in a startling perception of having more time. The only thing worse than actually being rushed—brought to bear by big-hitting opponents—is the disarming feeling of being rushed that occurs unnecessarily against any opponent when the ball is "lost," even for a fraction of a second.

That stated, without maintaining a relatively still head position during the course of following the ball, particularly when striking your shots with moving body parts and all the running around, all the best intentions will be completely and totally undermined. Not only will you alter your stroking path—when the head moves the body follows—you will also lose the ball at the very moment you are about to strike it, producing mis-hit, errant shots. What kind of photograph would you get back from the lab if you accidentally jerked the camera slightly while taking the shot? An out of focus image without a doubt—it's very much the same principle.

This aspect of the game always reminds me of a very determined club player that I worked with on many occasions. Paul always exhibited a wonderfully dry sense of humor. One day, upon experiencing a new level of ball watching understanding, but still very much challenged by the task, he asked with a sly grin, "How do you expect me to watch the ball when I can be thinking of so many other things?" He finally understood that it was impossible to stay focused on the ball if you're busy concerning yourself with technique, or anything else, in the midst of a shot.

Thinking will literally distract you from watching the ball, and put you square in your left brain, resulting in a wide field of vision with no particular focus at all. Never think about mechanics in the middle of the action. Monitor your strokes instead by *feeling* mechanics on a kinesthetic or sensory level only. And do not stray from always visualizing—in your right brain mind's eye—precisely where you intend to place every single shot, using the net itself as a reference point, from the very first ball in the warm-up. With your undivided attention now squarely on the ball, you will be doing the absolute *most* that you're capable of during the point.

In between points—when you observe tour players staring into their strings (and actually straightening them when necessary) or looking down at the court—is *the* time to concern yourself with any needed adjustments in ball-striking and tactics, to encourage yourself to keep fighting, or to, better yet, reinforce success.

I once attended a coaches clinic in Tucson conducted by the great Aussie Roy Emerson, who, many years after his retirement, was finally surpassed by Pete Sampras' win at the 2000 Wimbledon Championships as the holder of the most Grand Slam singles titles in tennis history. He described in great detail how he, the legendary Rod Laver, and all the other "boys" used to train for Davis Cup ties under Harry Hopman when they dominated the sport. But there was nothing particularly innovative about their exceptionally hard working two-a-day's approach. Despite being well past his prime, Emmo convincingly demonstrated that the years had not severely impacted the developed skills of such a dedicated early regimen when he took on a few of the young lions in a reflex volley drill. Although the effects of a few pints here and there over the years were evident around the waistline, he was more than impressive to say the least, another reminder of the many, many levels of the game. Yet, we still hadn't heard the pearl that I'm sure everyone came for. But one could sense it was forthcoming and we waited patiently and respectfully. Finally, right at the very end of his presentation, he didn't disappoint with, "And after a couple of weeks of that we could see the ball pretty well. Any questions?"

The moment of silence, and the accompanying reverence, led me to believe that everyone got the message—that seeing the ball well must be continually developed, re-invented daily, and never taken for granted in order to fully realize your game and its ultimate potential.

The Toughest Ball Watched

There are many players who look good hitting their groundies, playing the net, returning serve, and even when in transition. Unfortunately, a large number of these same individuals, and an overwhelming majority of lesser players, do not look nearly as capable when they are serving—nor are they.

The serve, typically the last shot to be fully developed (if ever developed by aspiring clubbers) and the first to break down under pressure, is both mechanically and emotionally the most challenging in tennis. It also represents, surprisingly, perhaps the most difficult ball watching task in the game.

Those who have grown up in throwing sports usually enjoy a distinct muscle memory advantage in that serving is very much the same motion. At the same time, these individuals can be at risk because of the exact same conditioning. In all previous throwing sport experience, they became, unknowingly but quite naturally, conditioned to look at the target being thrown to when releasing a ball.

Amazingly, even those with limited throwing sport experience as youngsters are also subject to some degree of the same look-at-the-target muscle memory as a result of even only occasionally throwing any object at all outside of sports, i.e. snowballs, rocks, et cetera.

If you can imagine seeing a baseball pitcher looking upward when throwing a pitch, you can just sense how totally unnatural that would be. If you cannot readily visualize that, then go ahead and try it, right now, with a crumpled up piece of paper. You will immediately be able to relate to the completely alien feeling. Yet, when serving a tennis ball,

that's exactly what you're required to do, which is very much in conflict with the normal mechanics of throwing. Now you can begin to
fully appreciate why serving can be so difficult and tenuous for so many,
and why, at least in part, we hold excellent servers at the club level in
such high esteem. Yet curiously, at the professional level, far too many
choose to jump on the current bandwagon and denigrate tour players
with exceptional first serve weaponry that can produce numerous aces
and unreturnables, calling it "boring" tennis.

Although impossible to quantify, but with nearly forty years of
teaching and coaching experience to draw upon, I can tell you that
median age club level men—the same ones who typically grew up
throwing all kinds of balls around—often do not watch the ball quite
as well as their female counterparts when serving. On the other hand,
the service motion mechanics of many of these same ladies, the same
ones who grew up generally not throwing, are typically not as fluid or
developed as those of the guys.

Optimal ball watching normally demands tracking the ball in both
directions of flight, incoming and outgoing, on all shots, to the best of
one's visual ability. But watching the ball when serving, or when hitting
mechanically similar overheads, requires a slightly different and somewhat unnatural technique of keeping one's head up while the ball is
being struck. Then, *after* the serve is well on its way, reacquiring it as it
lands in the service box—or the court, in the instance of overheads—a
fraction of a second later.

Along with previous throwing conditioning, there are other factors
that contribute to the struggle with the serve. One is severe trunk flex-
ing. Inadequate leg drive, caused by a lack of hip and shoulder rotation
as the ball is tossed, makes it nearly impossible to stay up with the ball
through impact. Conversely, sufficient rotation triggers natural knee
bend and a powerful and upward uncoiling of the entire body. As an
added bonus, keeping one's head up, eyes locked onto the ball, becomes
much more easily accomplished.

Another is poor or non-existent pre-serve visualization habits that
lead to an apprehensive and out of focus "I hope I get it in" mindset.
This random serving approach also contributes mightily to premature
peeking across the net, or "coming off the ball," well before it is even
struck. Reminder—the head moves, the body follows.

I did, however, witness the unbelievably talented Miroslav Mecir actually pulling this off, by design, at the '89 U.S. Open on an outer field court in the face of a particularly blinding afternoon sun, one that was directly in his normal tossing path and strike zone. An amazing feat—"wild and wacky stuff" as Johnny Carson used to put it—he was starting the points by putting his serve into play without even looking at the ball, an approach probably best left to the game's magicians, past and present.

Besides leg drive, hip and shoulder rotation, and visualization, there are other techniques that can also be instrumental in supporting effective ball watching on serve. A full range of motion ball-tossing movement—already difficult enough since it's with your non-dominant hand—featuring the greatest possible extension, highest possible release point, and no spin, is vitally important. Consistently putting the ball exactly where you want it, and expect it to be, obviously reduces ball-tracking difficulty.

A centered point of physical strength and stability is another. Bolstered by inhaling during the toss, and located in the upper chest, it will allow you to remain tall and strong through impact and create an enhanced opportunity for the arm/wrist/racket "whip" to come freely through the ball.

Finally, a particular focus on striking the ball at your perceived ideal moment, give or take a little for tossing individuality (tour players typically toss the ball slightly higher, about six inches, than they can reach), as opposed to trying hard to "watch it"—watch what?—is a much more easily managed task for many.

Two axioms come to mind in putting this task into perspective. The first is credited to the funniest, best coach ever, Vic Braden: "There's only one ball, you've got it, what's the hurry?" The second, which could very well be another "Bradenism," is: "If the court moves, I'll let you know."

Hopefully, with this added insight, you'll gain a much greater respect for what it takes to be continually working toward mastering the toughest ball watched, and improve both the quality and consistency of your serve simultaneously.

Hearing the Game

The visual aspect of tennis is obviously the number one learning component in the game. However, tapping into the auditory input you also receive every time out can also make a significant contribution to producing your best level of play. The sound of your own shot at impact, the opponent's shot, even an awareness of one's own footwork and breathing, can collectively make a considerable difference if consistently monitored.

Auditory stimulation is so important to tour players that David Dinkins, the former mayor of New York City and an avid tennis player, took it upon himself to divert the nearby airport traffic away from Flushing Meadows during the U.S. Open. Previously, it was not unusual for bewildered players to be completely unable to hear these vital sounds whenever the jets flew overhead at low altitudes, resulting in a significant rise in player tentativeness and an immediate drop in the level of play. They were playing deaf, prompting the big serving South African, Kevin Curren, a Wimbledon finalist in 1982, to offer the now-classic quote: "They should drop a bomb on this place."

The collision of the racket and ball is especially revealing since you can actually hear the distinct differences between shots hit flat, or with varying amounts of spin, power, touch, and all the rest in between. The instantaneous feedback can heighten your anticipation of pace, trajectory, weight of shot, and improve your overall ability to not only read an opponent's shots, but also to respond more effectively with your own shot-making.

Personally, I have always found it first irritating, then extremely challenging, when the grounds crew invariably decides to cut the grass immediately next to the court that I'm playing on in prime time. Focusing becomes strained and even more critical without the usual sounds of the game that are normally taken totally for granted.

On the other hand, some courts, most notably those indoors—especially bubbles—enjoy incredibly heightened acoustics compared to all but the most ideally protected outdoor settings. Under these conditions, players typically sense a greater connection to the game and often perform at a level higher than their norm. It's somewhat analogous to listening to your favorite music at a higher volume since every sound is brought out and you experience the piece more fully.

I would be remiss at this juncture if I failed to address the function of the various shock absorbers that club players, and even some professional players, attach to their strings. First of all, it's well documented that they absorb precious little shock—a very small percentage from only the strings themselves, not the frame—and have absolutely no actual effect regarding the overall feel of the racket. Yet players will actually like or dislike a racket depending upon whether it has one or not. What they do accomplish is an alteration of the sound the racket and the strings produce upon impact. Players who reject them prefer the traditional high-pitched "ping" sound. Those who opt for placing long, worm-like absorbers across most of the main strings at the throat experience a sound best described as a "thud." Other individuals insert nickel-sized ones between the two center strings, which creates a sound somewhere between the ping and the thud. Whatever one's tonal preference, it can have a very positive influence on your play if the shots are sounding "good" to you.

A number of years ago I experienced a true coaching revelation while working with an accomplished individual—off the court—who was also a very motivated club player. She always aspired higher, but had seemingly plateaued on the court. After trying every trick in the book, I was still unable to find a reliable trigger to get her to relax and work *with* the ball instead of fighting it every inch of the way. In grasping at a final straw, after a particularly well-struck forehand, I impulsively asked her if she liked the way the shot sounded. Since she did, I suggested that she make every shot, for the remainder of the session, produce the same sound. The startling result was an immediate new level of play that completely surprised us both, and it marked the beginning of a newfound self-confidence on the tennis court—yes, she could do it. This individual, as it turned out, was far more auditory wired than was average—more than I ever dreamed possible at the time—and went on to become an acute listener of her own game, and a better player as well.

I have continued to periodically suggest to students, particularly those not responding as quickly as I believe they could, visually and kinesthetically, that they make their primary focus producing shots that sound particularly good, once again, using a previously nailed ball with the "right" sound as the frame of reference.

If you need a little more convincing, keep in mind that those who regain consciousness after being in a coma reacquire their sense of hearing before any of the other senses return. If that's not enough, one's ability to hear is also the last to remain functional just prior to going comatose.

When next watching tennis on television, go ahead and really juice the volume during the points when the announcers, hopefully, have stopped talking. You will clearly hear the subtle, and not so subtle, differences in ball-striking, the sounds of high-energy footwork against the surface of the court, and even the uniquely individual sounds of exhaling during the shots as well. Regarding the latter, in the context of maintaining a healthy respect for the original spirit of the game, there are those that need to learn to refrain from making so much unnecessary noise. Not only is it at a volume that's quasi theatrical, but it's also distracting to players on adjoining courts and annoying to anyone else within earshot.

In time, with an improved awareness, these sounds will be immediately recognized and exposed. In hearing the game, you'll be able to take another step along the never-ending path toward being both a better and more complete player.

Modeling

Wouldn't it be nice to be able to play even a little bit like your favorite tour player: the way they strike the ball, the signature shot, their demeanor, the way they move around the court, or just the way they in which they go about playing the game?

Modeling, touched upon earlier while we explored breathing, is patterning oneself after another. It is utilized in all walks of life by motivated achievers seeking to improve performance. We do it all the time, often unconsciously, by emulating the habits and routines of those that we are impressed by. In tennis, as in life, modeling oneself after someone who gets results represents a potentially fast track to improvement and success.

Typically, it's a player that you are especially drawn to, one that can be readily visualized on demand, someone you have seen on numerous occasions on television, or, if you've been fortunate, right up close at a tour event. At the same time, unless you have seen a fair amount of reasonably well-produced video of yourself in actual match play, it is next to impossible to accurately picture your own game as both an improvement and trouble-shooting tool.

Without having access to a stadium court, where an unmanned camera can be positioned high enough at the north or south end of the court to catch you in action from the same perspective that professional tennis is viewed on television, you're out of luck. Nonetheless, although far from ideal, any video shot courtside from various angles— a side view of the baseline from both sides, from directly behind the player just inside the fence with the widest lens setting, from the net posts—is considerably better than not seeing yourself in play at all.

The natural merging of your own approach to the game and that of your chosen model is a positive step. Even the best in the world, past and present, have patterned themselves (at least to a certain extent) after other great players. Pete Sampras, for example, has always held the great Australian champions of an earlier era in high esteem, and both his game and style clearly show it in so many ways. And, although I've never read or heard anything to confirm it, you have to believe that Jimmy Connors was a significant influence for the young Monica Seles.

A few years ago, frustrated with my own form, I was motivated by the performance of the Slovak, Karol Kucera, which included an upset over Andre Agassi at the U.S. Open. His was an approach to playing the game that I naturally gravitated to—better yet, aspired to—and, following his lead, I enjoyed an especially good stretch of play. On another occasion, this time many years ago, when Ivan Lendl was the best player on the planet and competing and practicing for a full week at my home club, I recall that I was able to raise my own level considerably after absorbing and emulating such an incredible model. I can still remember a regular practice partner, whom I began completely dominating once Ivan's example and inspiration had taken hold, sarcastically offering, "Boy, you were a lot of fun tonight." Apparently I had embraced the Lendl demeanor as well.

Young children are among the very best at modeling. They are complete naturals. They practice continually as developing beings. At an inner city kids clinic held in conjunction with the then-Lipton sponsored tour event at Key Biscayne in the early 1990s, I was assigned to introduce the serve to a number of six- and seven-year-old children. Any over-teaching, especially any hint of techno babble, would be lost on these little ones. Instead, we played "copycat tennis," which they took to immediately. We bounced the ball twice, we did the Boris Becker look-alike "rocking horse" three times, we delicately tossed an "egg" up in the air that we were careful not to break, and then we smooshed it with great glee when it took a "nap" in midair. In no time at all, these kids mimicked me with a full service motion—no one at any age needs that idiotic "scratch your back" stuff that can screw your service motion up for life. They not only made contact much of the time, but also managed to get a few in to their delight (much cheering), and mine (more cheering). All the while, Arthur Ashe was monitoring the process on our court just a few feet away. This was modeling at its best, in its purest form.

Learning can be accelerated, and performance enhanced, if you're willing at times to let go and not be so caught up with your own, most likely less than perfect, exact technique. It can also get you off that occasionally overly self-conscious hook. To this day, I can still see old friend Tom Monahan, now a stockbroker living in the San Diego area and an active player on the USTA national 45s circuit, being a master court impressionist of the top players of the day in the late 1970s. It was always interesting that he appeared to play even better, especially much looser, when he was acting out someone else's game. Yet, when playing his own perfectly good game—one good enough to be a New England small college champion—he sometimes appeared to be comparatively less comfortable in his own skin.

Don't you always play better after witnessing the pro game live? You were modeling! Go ahead and start incorporating more of the same into your game on a regular basis. Get the television schedule and tune in, even if just for a few minutes at a time. Cherry pick—choose those elements of various players' games that you're attracted to, that you would ultimately like to add to your own game, and that intuitively, in the gut, seem right for you.

Remember, however, to be realistic in your goals with regard to your current skill level, athleticism, overall fitness, and experience. Choosing the Venus Williams free-swinging topspin forehand volley hit from mid-court, for example, would be an unrealistic choice if you're not yet routinely producing topspin on your forehand ground stroke. Or, emulating the Marcelo Rios one-legged-hop two-handed backhand might prove to be too idiosyncratic. Then again, perhaps not. You never know for sure until you give anything new a fair try.

A Cheat Sheet

On occasion, Arthur Ashe was known to refer to notes that he had brought to the court during changeovers. More recently, during her ascent to number one in the world, Serena Williams has been seen utilizing the very same practice. And, actually, nothing could be further from cheating.

Increasingly, some tour coaches have been lobbying the game, thankfully unsuccessfully to date, to allow on court coaching during matches, as is currently allowed only in Davis Cup, Fed Cup, and in high school and collegiate tennis. Players *not* taught to be self-sufficient, and lacking in problem solving skills, often look with predictable anguish to their coaches on tour, their parents in the stands at junior events, or to their teammates in USTA team tennis for answers when things aren't going well as a result. Club players especially, always without the luxury of traveling coaches to sneak them a little hand signal when in trouble—which is cheating and very much against the rules—might consider keeping a troubleshooting checklist in their racket bag in the event that all is going wrong. In a sport as all-inclusive as tennis, it inevitably happens to everyone.

Here's a good place to start:

1. Focus primarily on the ball, not the opponent.
2. Prepare early.
3. Step as you strike; do not get set or planted.
4. Be aggressive, but within safe margins.

5. Do only what's necessary to get the job done.

6. Swing only as fast as you can control.

7. Play within yourself.

8. Work with the ball, not against it.

9. The ball ideally leaves the racket when it's good and ready.

10. Let the racket do the hitting.

11. Stalemating is on the way to winning, not losing.

12. The last ball in the court wins the point . . . every single time.

13. The first and last points of each game are the most important.

14. Play in the present.

15. Leave your judgmental side at home.

16. Shut up and compete.

17. Enjoy the pressure.

18. If all goes wrong try softer/smoother/better, not harder.

19. Do not think *in* the point; play dumb.

20. Visualize to realize.

21. See success; you get what you expect.

22. Breathe your way through choking.

23. Always give them the runaround.

24. Never hit behind an old guy; he's still there.

25. No feet, no game, no future.

26. Patience and perseverance.

27. Tame the beast.

28. The answers come from within.

PLAY BOOK

Warming Up the Player Inside

Over the years, I've listened to dozens and dozens of players express their frustration over the detrimental warm-up habits of their peers, whom, after playing the game for years, you would think would know better. Yet, the "let's hurry up and play" mentality unfortunately prevails all too often.

In other sports, even rookies seem to have a greater appreciation for preparing to perform. Tennis players, however, classically step out on the court and go with comments like, "I don't want to tire myself out in the warm-up," or, "Let's start, it isn't going to get any better." Hello, is anyone home?

Runners certainly get it in their sport. Golfers especially get it—and they're not even going to have to run—in that they are very diligent about arriving to the course early enough to spend some quality time at both the practice area and the putting green. In fact, weekend warriors of all sorts, such as those involved in pick-up soccer, organized softball, or even bikers out for a long trek, have at least some respect for the importance of warming up their body, and their skills, or both as applicable. Still, at any club or public park in the country at any given time, there are thousands of tennis players, who are required to move suddenly while simultaneously performing difficult finite motor tasks, who do not warm up. Unfortunately, as a direct result of their generally poor warm-up habits, along with an apparently zero appreciation of what's really necessary, this group shortchanges themselves every single time out. Go figure.

If you expect your game to keep steadily improving and evolving in a climate in which the bar is continually being raised around you, the skill and discipline with which you warm up, in a "run and gun" sport like tennis, is an absolutely necessary ingredient in realizing the skill within. Players who routinely take the warm-up for granted, who pay little attention to its management—actually carrying on conversations with their partners and opponents at the same time—will *never* be fully able to consistently tap into whatever it is that they are truly capable of. Whether it's starting a match positively or sustaining a solid level of play throughout, they will be negatively affected over the long haul . . . guaranteed.

Hopefully, you've been fortunate enough to attend the U.S. Open, or any professional event for that matter. But, if you have not hung out at the practice courts for any length of time, there is no way you can fully appreciate how the best players on the planet go about warming up *their* games.

Sure, tour players always have the advantage of warming up well before their actual match time—it's their job. It could be with their coach, a regular sparring partner, or even a potential future opponent who is also a friend. The typical length of this warm-up is about forty-five minutes to an hour, and sometimes longer if they feel the need for extra practice time and a court is available. Far more important than the length of their hit is the way in which they trade shots with their counterpart in such a cooperative way. They work *with* each other, not *against* each other, and they are in no way competing, at least not overtly.

Starting up totally relaxed with soft grips from a position a few steps *behind* the service line is always a good idea for club level players in friendly situations. Never begin inside the service box, as so many misinformed club players attempt to, since there is simply too little room for a full swinging path leading to an immediate reinforcement of slapping at the ball instead of hitting through it. Getting started prudently involves trading very easy forehand and backhand groundstrokes—*not* volleys—with minimal muscle tension, and, once again, a relaxed grip minus any sudden unnecessary movement. Professionals and smart club players, ever mindful of the routine, allow balls to bounce twice early on rather than moving quickly, or, if just a little out of reach, don't run at all and let it go. *Their* warm-up is about rhythm, timing, and getting a good *feel* for the ball. I repeat: getting a good feel for the ball. It is not initially about hustle or exhibiting foot speed, and there is no urge to attempt one's highest level of play in the early stages—an immediate sign of insecurity in clubbers. Additionally, a given at the highest levels of the game but definitely worth addressing for the vast majority at the local level, the warm-up is also *the* time to get your attention focused, particularly on—what else—the ball!

Placing the ball right back to the other player, it is not uncommon for the very best to engage in an extended yet unspoken forehand to forehand exchange in order to find a groove. Whatever the pattern, or lack thereof in some instances, there exists a high level of patience and respect for what it takes to gain that feel for not only the ball, but the court, the general conditions of the day, and the opponent. Ideally, as the warm-up proceeds, the pace and intensity of the exchanges is gradually and incrementally elevated to a level that the respective players typically perceive as one that they will be able to successfully operate at in the actual match to follow a couple of hours later. After all, what does the winning player typically say in the post-match courtside interview? "I saw the ball pretty well today, and I moved well out there. And, you know, I had a really good feel for the ball."

Neither player is hitting winners during the warm-up—club pros, *please* inform your players. The goal is to hit as many balls as possible at a comfortable tempo. The more methodically one progresses, the greater the potential to play well. Completely avoid the well-intentioned but doomed "slam, bang, boom" approach exhibited by so many players beginning with the very first ball. If you don't, I absolutely guarantee that you will be victimized by a lack of consistency, and run the risk of possible injury—not to mention depriving your opponent of a fair (i.e., sportsmanship) warm-up opportunity.

Since you're not on tour, there is most often no earlier practice court available at busy clubs—and you're not about to locate some obscure but perfectly okay public court to really prepare—you typically have ten to fifteen minutes, at best, before everyone is eager to start the match. No matter. Follow the model of the pros as much as possible and I guarantee that you will end up playing at a higher level even if—worst scenario—the first set is part of the process. You'll enjoy your tennis more, precisely because you will have evolved beyond being one of those individuals who is always complaining that it takes them at least a set to warm up. It's an obvious choice.

If you're not involved in an inter-club team match, or an official tournament—where the time spent is being monitored—go ahead and extend your warm-up. Two well-played sets is a whole lot more satisfying than the completely absurd mindset of warming up as quickly as possible in order to have extra time to play three lousy sets. Keep in mind those self-fulfilling players we all know, always in a hurry, who hit for a minute or two and announce that they're ready because they're "not going to get any better"—yup, exactly right, they're not.

Similarly, all players must take their practice serves prior to the start of the first game. Those are the rules. There are no more practice shots after the match begins—nothing like starting the match and then restarting it three more times in doubles. C'mon! Do golfers go back to the driving range after the third hole? And do not even think about f.b.i. Does the receiver, already at a disadvantage, get the same opportunity? That would be f.r.i.—of course not! So, whatever your level of play, let's get with the program and take all practice serves before you begin the match, friendly or otherwise.

Let us also not forget about the widely ignored universal protocol of the pre-match warm-up that's strictly adhered to and respected by veteran players. Groundstrokes are exchanged first from the back of the court—the key word being "exchanged." Remember, visualization is one hundred percent transferable from right at them to effectively away from them once the match begins for those of you who continue to selfishly hang onto and whine, "But I don't want to practice hitting at them." The luxury of the behind the service line three-quarter court start-up is *not* applicable to official match play unless mutually agreed upon by the participating players—typically old enough to have taken up the game when it was played exclusively with wood. Then get to the net to take your volleys, but begin a little farther away than usual for the first few to create a bit more space and time while the volley is still cold. Once you've moved forward and the net game is on the mark, ask for "a few up," or signal by pointing skyward, to practice the overhead. Again, allow them to return it. When completely finished—do not allow a pushy opponent to take the net prematurely because you had to momentarily retrieve a ball in the back of the court—return to the baseline in order to allow your opponent their turn. Note: always try to be the first to the net since you'll end up with two practice opportunities from the baseline if proper protocol is followed.

When everyone is finally ready—make sure that in doubles you always consult with your partner first should they need "a few more"—move on to the serve. Should the other player begin returning your practice serves immediately, ask them, "Aren't you going to take any?" You might need to remind less knowledgeable players that you're under time constraints and that they're using up their serving time. Also, consider warming up with two new cans of balls or a four-ball can if available. It's affordable if you've purchased this book, and the tennis industry will get to report greater participation—"growing the game" by any means possible validates the "blue blazer" salaries and perks—through increased ball sales. Nonetheless, nothing is more inefficient and frustrating than warming up for a doubles match with just three balls. (Could it be that well accepted tennis mores possibly "shrink" the game?) Even the world's best are not so unrealistic to think that four players can have a good warm-up with just three balls—another reason why club players, in frustration, resign themselves to the non-warm-up. The four-ball can has been popular in Europe for some time, but not here because of—would you believe—the ball manufacturer's price point, sales paranoia.

Finally, if your warm-up partner/opponent persists in attempting winners, even after you've politely requested that you rally back and forth *to* each other so that *both* players benefit the most, then demand that you start the match immediately. They are indeed practicing something, but at the same time denying you the same opportunity of a level playing field. In doubles, you can actually request to warm up with your own partner should your opponents be uncooperative for whatever reason. Hopefully, it never becomes so ugly and lacking in sportsmanship that it comes to that.

Eventually, with repeated practice, warming up much more efficiently will help you tap into the better you that already resides inside. Ironically, you'll not only dial in your game more quickly, but also cumulatively pave the way for a steadily increasing level of play.

Winning the Warm-Up

An inordinate interest in the pre-match warm-up, with all of its ramifications, began in earnest for me about thirty years ago. Living less than an hour's drive from the Newport Casino in Rhode Island—now home to the International Tennis Hall of Fame—I was afforded an annual opportunity to check out the game's very best players at one of its most classy, intimate, and tradition-filled venues.

The intrigue for me involved closely observing tour players during the warm-up, from the very first ball hit, in order to try and forecast the winner of the match, especially one viewed as a toss up. I evaluated the players not so much by any comparisons in strengths or even possible chinks in armor regarding ball-striking or court coverage, but instead through demeanor and game face, energy and intensity, focus and determination.

I remember being increasingly surprised that, as a young coach and aspiring teacher of the game, I was often correct in predicting the winners of those matches that on paper did appear to be an even bet, and particularly between players whose games I was not very familiar with. Occasionally, I could even recognize the scent of an upset in what was supposed to be a non-contest, long before it was "in the making," precisely by taking in every nuance of the warm-up. Such were the differences of the mostly free-spirited players of that era, almost exclusively left to their own devices without the advantage of a full-time coach at their side to always keep them on the straight and narrow. Either they made positive use of the warm-up on that day or instead went through the motions, cavalierly taking it for granted, and running the risk of getting off badly and possibly not being able to regroup before it was too late.

Today's mostly "always all business" professional players, with their support teams and entourages catering to their every need, can be far more difficult to read. But at the club level, the beat goes steadily on, and these not so readily visible intangibles very much remain a determining factor in pulling together a one hundred percent totally committed effort. Among ninety-nine percent of those playing the game worldwide—a group totally lacking in both world class ball-striking capability and personal coaches in tow—an ability to deftly control the dynamic of the warm-up can be a huge factor in gaining an edge at the start of a match. And, it can be done without violating the parameters of sportsmanship.

By taking charge of the warm-up, you can maximize the gearing up of your own game while simultaneously, but subtly, countering an opponent's ability to do the same. While still affording them a fair opportunity to hit their fair share of balls, you begin the contest with the very first swing of your racket.

As you begin to trade forehands and backhands, first evaluate an opponent's stronger side, then isolate their weakness by concentrating mostly on their strength. You'll not only get a better sense of handling and neutralizing their big gun, but also, at the same time, reduce their opportunity to groove their less able suspect stroke, often the backhand.

As previously noted, waste no time in being the first to the net to take volleys. Initially, take the first few just inside the "T" before assuming a closer, more offensive position. This will provide a better opportunity to get a read on their ball speed and ensure against possibly being robbed of enough time and space to comfortably dial in your net game—especially if they're immediately, and blatantly, coming right at you with heat to both test and intimidate you. Simultaneously, try and direct most of your warm-up volleys deep and right at your opponent, including freely running the risk of sending a few beyond the baseline in the process. You'll soon find the range and a good comfort level, all while legitimately inhibiting their effort just enough to prevent them from getting an equally good feel for the passing game that they're going to need once the gun sounds.

Upon asking for "a few up" *before* retreating back to the baseline—warm-up protocol again—position yourself back around the "T," or beyond if necessary, to better deal with any potentially overzealous, out of control, or excessively deep lobbing. By just stroking back the first few offered, at far less than match pace, you'll be effectively displaying the three "Cs" of dialing in your overhead from your advantaged position: consistency, coverage, and confidence. Anyone skilled enough to tee them up for you just the way you like shouldn't pose any problem at all, as long as you repeatedly give them that chance by refraining from hitting warm-up wasting winners.

Once *they're* at the net, immediately elevate the pace of your previous groundies to match level and go primarily right at *their* belt buckle to tie them up. Since this is your second go around from the baseline after being the first to the net, they will not get another chance at their backcourt game if protocol is followed. If their responses are well off the mark, do not go out of your way to chase them down to accommodate them—after all, the warm-up clock is now ticking right along in your favor.

Respond to their request for lobs with higher and deeper-than-average offerings on the first few, a potentially difficult ball with which to begin warming up the overhead. You'll get a good look at their true confidence level, after which you can follow with short, low lobs that a twelve-and-under would lick their chops over. If done well, the first lob you put up in the match, a hopefully deep but absolutely sky-high number, will immediately push their self-doubt button if any cracks in their overhead exist.

Once serving, do not be intent on any overt display of firepower, especially if you've got an opponent stubbornly practicing their return of serve while neglecting their own serve, despite protocol. Ease off the throttle and actually assist them in honing in on a serve that's actually not even the equal of your typical second. Once the match starts, you should be able to dial up the pace fairly easily to your norm with a two-to-make-one strategy and undermine *their* questionable effort of timing your serve. These folks always cross the line to have it both ways. Unfortunately for them, you've got answers.

No one is keeping score in the warm-up, except you! Albeit a different kind of scoring, you'll be setting the match stage by proactively directing and manipulating the pace, tempo, and the dynamic of the exchanges between the two of you while putting them in a mostly reactive mode. After all, isn't that going to be your exact intention once the match does begin—to rule the other player?

Ideally, when the figurative man in the chair says, "Play," you've *already* been playing for fifteen minutes or so and have control of the reigns right at the match's beginning, which hopefully you'll then be able to consolidate and build upon early on to a successful conclusion.

Prior to new world number one Roger Federer's straight set victory over the on-a-roll Marat Safin for the 2004 Australian Open title, the dazzling Swiss superstar succinctly put it in perspective with, "The beginning of the match will certainly be important."

Singles 101

Singles, in stark contrast to the complexities of doubles play, is a comparatively simple game. But it does require a particular mindset and a clear understanding of how to maneuver opponents out of position, and then do damage in the open court while simultaneously zealously defending it against the same.

Reliable shot-making is at a premium since you will only be as good as your weakest shot versus a skilled and experienced opponent. You cannot hide, for example, a weak backhand the way you can in doubles. There's no room for mechanical breakdowns, which consistently have a remarkable knack of occurring when you can least afford them.

Assuming that both players are relatively equal in ball-striking, court coverage, fitness level, and in their command of offensive and defensive tactics, the outcome, in great part, will ultimately be decided by possessing the greatest resolve and exuding the same, right to the end, every single time.

Solid players begin this show of strength and confidence right off by beginning the match with the first ball struck in the warm-up, without fail. They are bent on establishing a high level of error-free consistency that sends the ultimate message to opponents: I do not miss, I am not going anywhere, and you will have to hit winners to beat me.

Once the actual match has begun, especially in clubland, fearlessly stalemating your opponent shot for shot, point after point, is *the* number one tactic in imposing your will in no uncertain terms. The reality that you're willing to hit as many balls as it takes to get the job done will come through loud and clear. Learn to welcome and enjoy the longer rallies necessary in singles versus the "ticking time bomb" mindset exhibited by some players who suddenly become unsure of themselves when the point extends into the fourth, fifth, sixth shot, and beyond. Take your time. The slower you go, the faster you will get to where you want to be, and the less fuel you will burn along the way.

Never feel pressure, or the need to hit, on call, winners. It's a generally foolhardy adventure for all but the very best players. Instead, visualize nothing more than relatively safe placement after placement, *not* glorious point-ending spectacular shots. Placements that are still aggressive, with pace, but at the same time realistic in terms of margins to the lines *and* the net, equate to playing within yourself, right at the limit of your skills, which is everything. The best news of all is that if a placement is good enough, you'll experience, much to your surprise, more than your fair share of winners without even trying for them!

With a total commitment to this kind of core strategy and game plan, you cannot lose. You will not self-destruct, as so many players routinely do, and beat yourself with repeated unforced errors that are always a result of attempting to play, as a long-standing phrase puts it so well, "over your head." Accept the player that you are and hang tough— really tough. Be true to the existing skill and fitness level that you have brought to the match on any given day—no more, no less—and get the absolute most out of it. Do not be like a 10k runner I remember from my road racing days who, lacking sufficient early resolve, failed to keep pace with the leaders. He then fell too far behind, resulting in an all-out sprint at the race's end to no avail, to which he exclaimed, with misperceived pride, to all within earshot, "Oh, I still had plenty left."

The better the opponent, the *more* consistent you have to be. Again: *the better the opponent, the more consistent you have to be.* Avoid the temptation to go for bigger shots than you normally would because you are facing someone allegedly better, or minimally your equal—it's not the answer—and then have the courage to be secure enough to let the chips fall where they may.

You can now only be *beaten* by a player who can consistently make penetrating shots that you cannot handle, or who can make placements that you are not able to run down, or both. Either they have forced an error, or have thumped it completely past you. In these instances, you have not lost the point, they have won it. There is a huge difference.

Make them play. Make them prove their reputation or on-paper supe-riority, and at the very least make them earn it, every bit of it. You'll inch ever closer in any ensuing encounters as a direct result.

In 1959, the world's top amateur, Lew Hoad, signed on with the fledgling Jack Kramer Pro Tour and would, for the first time, get paid over the table instead of under it. He arrived in New York fresh from his second triumph at Wimbledon to play in a ten thousand dollar Round Robin—a paltry amount by today's standards, but big sports money for a week's work at the time—at Forest Hills. After a promis-ing 2-1 start, Hoad then lost two straight matches leading up to his first meeting with Pancho Gonzales, regarded as the best player in the world at that time. After suffering still another loss, Hoad came away from the experience with not only a heightened respect for Gonzales, but also a new perspective of what it would take to play with these renegade true professionals. On the power-playing Gonzales' mystique, determination, and skill, Hoad said, "All this comes from an intense, searing belief in the pre-eminence of his own game. I would have to defeat him; he would not defeat himself. He was the most consistent player I have ever met, a man with vast physical toughness and unwavering mental strength who had reduced his percentage of errors lower than any man has ever done."

Tactically, while always factoring in the court surface, there are nonetheless a few singles rules of thumb to follow. When playing at the baseline—either on clay or a slow- to medium-speed hardcourt—posi-tioned anywhere in the middle three-fifths of the court when striking your shot, you can safely probe any part of the court since you'll be able to easily recover back into a good defending position. When, however, you are forced onto the outside of the court on either side, or "out on the wing," you must be able to routinely direct that shot back crosscourt versus a well-positioned opponent. But, if you're playing on grass, or more realistically on a fast hardcourt, you'll have an opportunity for far more viable down-the-line possibilities minus the defending liability. Generally, when recovering back toward the center of the court after going crosscourt, remain slightly off center, or more, since the center of the court you're defending—as if it's on a constantly angling turntable—changes in relationship to the opponent's hitting position. Always remember that every angle, of course, creates an opportunity for an equal or even greater one.

Unfortunately, club players tend to be notoriously down-the-line happy and become wide-eyed at just the thought. If you do consistently choose to go down the line instead when forced off the court, you'll become easy prey to crosscourt counters that are angling increasingly away while you futilely attempt to recover and run them down. Of course, if you're somehow more often than not able to absolutely nail the low percentage winner—in your dreams—be my guest. This is exactly why you witness so much crosscourt dueling at the tour level, at least until one player outmaneuvers the other, typically moving them so far off the court that they cannot recover sufficiently in time and *then* become vulnerable down the line. The point then begins to unfold and almost always ends favorably for the player who managed the angle duel best.

This lesson can be quickly learned firsthand in a controlled drill session with players of relatively equal skill. With the "runaround" not allowed, one player is required to hit all of their shots crosscourt, while the other is committed to placing all of their shots down the line. The player assigned the crosscourt task will completely dominate the down-the-liner. Even a slightly lesser player can more than hold their own in this match simulation if given the crosscourt advantage. It's that big of a difference.

If, despite your best efforts in managing the crosscourt, you find yourself getting consistently outmaneuvered in down-the-line contests, then it becomes time to frequently take the angle opportunities away from an opponent with a dominating hot hand. In the U.S. victory over Spain in the 2000 Fed Cup, Coach Billie Jean King gave Lindsay Davenport, whose court coverage was hampered by a strained calf muscle, an adjustment in her game plan against a threatening Conchita Martinez. Davenport explained in the post-match celebration, "She said, 'Let's just go back to hitting hard and up the middle, and don't give her a lot of angles.' I think that helped. I knew it was going to be a tough match." It doesn't get any simpler, but, once again, simplicity rules.

Of course, all bets are off if you get a short ball to take complete advantage of and then come into the net behind. Your bread and butter tactic in this instance will be to direct these approaches primarily down the line, or, if positioned right in the middle of the court, direct it into the opponent's weaker passing side. A well-struck penetrating down-the-liner will make the crosscourt passing shot very difficult to pull off, and you'll be able to sit on the line and knock off some routine volleys for crosscourt winners. Once an opponent begins to overplay your approaches, reverse your pattern and nail a few crosscourt to keep them honest and off balance.

When facing a steady baseliner who can run everything down— usually from a position well behind the baseline—you'll have to go to the drop shot early and often in order to bring them in closer to the line, giving your groundies a bit more bite and penetration.

Some additional intangible rules of thumb include—no matter what—always hitting the ball only as hard as you can consistently control at any given time, which can vary widely at different stages of the match. Riding the wave of a hot hand with an increased confidence level is one thing, but also recognizing a loss of timing and feel, or an increase in pressure, and backing off the pace of your shots a little until you right yourself is quite another. And, only placing your shots as close to the lines as you can consistently manage, to give yourself a little margin for error, is *always* prudent advice.

Positively take advantage of every single weak second serve, and, whenever possible, follow up by taking the net to finish the job. Lobbing when really in trouble, when you have absolutely no shot and need to buy time to recover, is playing smart. Putting up offensive lobs when an opponent has his nose over the net—to cut your passing lanes down—will positively pose a future threat and get them off the top of the net.

There's more. You've got to be willing to play "frustro-ball" as a last resort—repeatedly sending back really high, looping balls, preferably with topspin—when you're *completely* outgunned and out of options, unless you insist on going down in flames with your spurs on. This will at least keep you in a contest with no timeclock a little longer, and you never know, they might "gag," have trouble finishing, and something good might happen.

Your drop shot will come in handy once again when faced with an extremely low approach shot opportunity that you're barely going to reach versus a deeply positioned opponent expecting more.

Returning first serves deep and right up the gut, slightly crosscourt, at least until you've got the timing dialed in and sense that you can do a little more, represents solid percentage tennis that takes *their* angle completely away.

You should also serve and volley on occasion to ideally apply some added pressure. This is effective versus opponents who consistently float your first serves back, and particularly when the burden is exclusively on them to come up with a good return to either get back into the game or save a game point with a big shot.

And, rule of rules, always get a high percentage of first serves in to avoid allowing capable opponents too many looks at your second serve—especially if it's not the greatest. That will always set the tone for a more positive outing overall.

Finally, always set realistic goals—ones of a solid performance first and foremost versus any inhibiting preoccupation solely with winning and losing—not only to enjoy the c-o-n-t-e-s-t with your opponents, but especially the one with yourself.

World and Olympic champion swimmer, Ian Thorpe, when queried about his expectations for the 2004 Athens Games, said, "I don't swim for medals; I swim for performances. The difference between trying to swim for medals and trying to swim your best performance, you have control over your performance. You don't have control over where you finish in a race. I think that's the right way, the best way to approach it."

Taking Down the Pusherman

In boxing—a contest similar to tennis in many ways—if one of the fighters is unwilling to engage the other in a test of skill to see who is the best, they are first warned by the referee and then ultimately disqualified. Continually holding and clinching, or avoiding confrontation completely by running away, is not tolerated. Unfortunately, tennis ain't boxing, and moonballing, dropshotting, lob-happy players face no such punishment. The last player to hit the ball in the court rules, period. It's really ugly stuff, but in violation of no rule.

In singles, these "pushers" typically move very well and cover the court like a blanket, hence the other common reference to them as "rabbits." In doubles, it's most often just the opposite in that mobility is a problem, and fast-paced exchanges are avoided by the slow-footed and slow-handed (see the Team Tennis section). Nonetheless, the bottom line is that none of these folks want to shoot it out. By sharing one of my playing experiences from a couple of years ago, I'll hopefully be able to enlighten you as to how you might fare better versus these types of players.

Upon entering a USTA senior singles event on a whim, to my absolute amazement and initial frustration, I drew the exact same individual that I had played in my very last singles foray fifteen years before. He was the crème de la crème of pushers, and this match-up was not what I had envisioned when I decided to enter a "real" tournament. I had in mind a nice, clean match versus a player who *did* want to get it on. I was seeking confrontation, not the Death Valley Ultra Marathon with a little backyard badminton thrown in.

After an encouraging warm-up—he was actually hitting the ball crisply, which, curiously, he was indeed always capable of—I got out to a further reinforcing early lead. Naturally, I was pleased that he was going shot for shot with me, and it was a respectable level of tennis. But, apparently seeing the light, he switched gears and went into full push-er mode. Now, when I drove him out wide, he began putting up these ridiculously deep sixty-foot-plus smart lobs, daring me to knock win-ners off out of the air, a challenge that, of course, I was not about to back away from. With an adept drop shot also in his repertoire, he'd mix it up and catch me off guard on occasion with good disguise whenev-er I showed any reluctance to come in. And, in our now yin-and-yang backcourt exchanges, he also started moonballing me, especially deep and high to my backhand.

At about the 1:15 mark, I had lost the first set in a tiebreaker after working my fanny off on the excruciatingly slow clay but, nonetheless, squandered countless chances with far too many wild unforced errors in the process. It was over ninety degrees, the sun was penetrating, and the Florida humidity was at its worst. During the changeover, I actual-ly visualized that I was back in my air-conditioned home sipping a nice cold Heineken instead of dealing with this annoying, afraid-to-play-me, scourge of tennis. This was not what I came out of "retirement" for; I wanted to rumble. I believe you can relate.

But I had beaten him in a final that last time we met, so I was damn sure not going to lose to him now in the first round, in less than great shape or not. I eliminated any negative thoughts from my mind, and instinctively removed my watch. I had always played with my watch on—a habit born from giving thousands of lessons over the years—but I now recognized that if I was going to prevail I would have to be in it for the long haul, even if I was facing playing another round that day if I could somehow get through. Although nothing more than symbolic, being watchless actually helped me gather myself, embrace a more patient mindset, and start *completely* over in the now-blazing heat of high noon. I was going to have to hit a ton of balls, and then I was going to have to hit some more.

I began making inroads in the second set. I was aware that he could see I wasn't going away, and my footwork was getting better and bet-ter—always at a premium versus any slow baller on clay. I even felt bet-

ter physically after resigning myself to the ordeal, always an underestimated intangible.

The cumulative effect of relentlessly running him side to side started to not only slow him down, but also affect the previous uncanny
precision of his defensive lobbing. At the same time, my overhead started to click because I wasn't as desperate, or motivated, to scorch him
with ego-driven bombs because I perceived myself as "the man" on that
court. Instead, I relied on disciplined placements with safer margins to
the lines and less overwhelming pace. If he got it back, I'd keep moving my feet and just hit another, and another, and as many as it took
until I finally got a meatball that I could easily drive through the court.

With the absolute all-important anti-pusher component of my
game solidified, I started reading his drop shots much earlier, and, now
able to run them down more easily, I dropped him back at every opportunity—a little taste of his own medicine! I was even sneaking in here
and there—delaying my approach from all the way back at the baseline
until the very last moment when I saw the moonball coming—successfully volleying a number of those "ducks" into the open court for
spontaneous winners, while still just making placements.

Slowly but surely, I was taking the rabbit's legs away. He knew he
couldn't outbang me, and now he also knew he couldn't outlast me by
waiting for me to self-destruct. Although still aggressive, I continued to
be extremely patient and in no hurry at all. There was no way that I was
going to beat myself—I'd die in the process from exhaustion before I
would let *that* happen. Then, his demeanor started to change, and the
look in his eye betrayed his waning resolve. The pusher was nearly dead;
long live the "players" everywhere.

The final score was 6-7, 6-3, 6-2, and the final two sets, although I
was going "slower," took about as long as the first set when I was in a
bit of a hurry. It was satisfying since he had not taken fifteen years off
from tournament play, and especially because I had come within a
whisker of allowing myself to cave in mentally, emotionally, and physically to a less skilled player at the first set's end. Although a complete
gentleman in calling the lines, he had to inform me that it was too bad
that he had tweaked his hamstring in the second set. What he failed to
recognize, while licking his ego-centered wound, was that *I* was the one
doing the tweaking.

Prior to an earlier meeting, when we were both considerably

younger, he had defeated me both in practice and in a tournament match as well, for the same reasons that I dropped the first set in the encounter described above. A supportive crowd had gathered at my home club, made up almost entirely of the "choir" that I had been preaching to for a couple of years. The pressure was *really* on.

Back then, I wasn't confident that I could flat out beat him, i.e., take it to him and knock him right off the court. I knew that I was neither sharp enough, nor fit enough to get that very physically demanding job done. Yet, I couldn't lose to a lowly pusher in front of my students, even if he was a legitimate national caliber player. After all, you can dress him up, but he's still a damn pusher, afraid of putting it on the line and at least attempting to play "real" ball. But, under the circumstances, I had only one option if I was going to get the "W"—to go "ugly."

I decided that it would be paramount to warm up very methodically, and I was fully focused from the very first ball. Although I'd been good enough to reach the finals, an additional message needed to be sent. I struck the ball well below my normal pace of shot throughout the entire warm-up—groundies, volleys, overheads, serves. It was already well beyond ugly in my mind, and I can still clearly recall being unsure if I would be able to remain committed to such an anemic "strategy." It just wasn't my nature. Hell, in college my teammates used to refer to me as "C.P." (Crowd Pleaser) for my athletic storm and swarm tactics.

But about three-quarters of the way through the warm-up, two things occurred to me: first, I hadn't missed one single ball—not one; second, as a direct result, he was the one making the mistakes. I wondered—could my lack of pace be bothering the no-pace counter puncher, and could my totally uncharacteristic, ultraconservative error-free approach be getting into his pusher head? After the brief match, as it turned out, one of my fellow pros informed me that he thought I had broken him down right there in the warm-up with, as he described it, my "came to play attitude."

At 4-1 in the first set, the writing was on the wall. He was the one still making the errors, especially versus the balls that I purposely fed him right up the middle of the court with no pace, daring *him* to initiate something, a role he was clearly not comfortable in. It was also obvious to me that we were involved in one of the all-time poorest displays of how the game is supposed to be played, but sometimes you do what you have to do. When he announced to the umpire that he couldn't continue because he had hurt his knee (the "injury" that time), I was very happy to get out of there alive.

If it's doable, because it's a relatively equal playing field, all you have to do is make up your mind that you can do it. Without that, you've got nothing—no matter how good you are—and you might as well go home. Once committed, you've got to take your time, be patient in your shot selection, and be willing to expire out there. Since pushers (unlike boxers) are never going to be DQ'd for their "style" of play, you've got to learn to deal with, although against the normal grain for most, such a completely frustrating opponent, especially on clay where these "backboards" thrive.

Because you're mostly used to playing against balls struck with at least some pace, but suddenly find yourself faced with incoming balls that do not even remotely resemble that norm, it's incredibly difficult—unless you're just off the tour—to operate at the same tempo and pace of shot that you're accustomed to. Just as a poor dancer makes a perfectly good partner look bad, a pusher lowers the bar dramatically on the tennis court. If, on a scale of one to ten, you are a level seven club player, it will be extremely difficult to maintain that standard versus an adept level four pusher. They make it extremely difficult to get into your normal groove. In fact, their goal *is* to take you out of your comfort zone, disrupt your rhythm, and put you out of synch—not to mention scramble your brain. So, unless you can just go out there and blow them away—not an easy task—you, just as I had to, are going to have to adjust your game accordingly, and probably remove *your* watch as well.

Shifting Gears

It's never uninteresting when the always brutally honest John McEnroe—the only one on television who can succinctly explain what's actually taking place on the court—is at a loss for words. I can recall one instance when an out of character momentary brain lock occurred over why a particularly hard-hitting player, whom he had previously alluded to as a hardheaded one as well, was making countless, unforced, stupid errors, game after game, and wouldn't "back off." You could just see him in the booth, off camera, cocking his head into that "you cannot be serious" tilt.

This necessary playing-within-yourself business is a serious challenge for motivated players at any level. Club players in particular are notorious for falling victim to the "two seconds of stardom" trap: you have just hit a blistering forehand down the line, inches from the corner for an outright winner . . . the trap is set. Then, as the delusions of grandeur set in, you begin overhitting everything in sight in the unrealistic belief that you can and ought to be able to make those kind of shots all of the time because that's the real you. Wrong—that's *not* the real you, and it just doesn't work that way.

The necessity of having total control over all your shots on a consistent basis is always an extremely delicate balance of a number of factors. How fast you're able to swing the stick, and how much pace you are generating as a direct result, is huge. Racket head speed must always be closely monitored and should vary depending on one's success at the time, level of accompanying confidence, sense of rhythm, degree of spin, court position, and, of course, the score.

Going with what feels good at the time must also be factored in. Some days the flatter forehand is right there, on others it's the looping topspin that's zeroed in. Then there are those times when the second serve is unsteady, dictating that you take some pace off your first in order to get a higher percentage in and reduce the number of second serves necessary. Or your opponent is eating up your topspin backhand, yet appears to be bothered by the slice.

Andre Agassi, in the throes of a number of consecutive first-round losses a few years ago on his quest back from number 141 in the world, explained courtside, after finally winning one, the dilemma of playing well consistently: "Confidence leads to winning, but you have to win to build confidence." All players have to constantly be in touch with whether they are doing too much, not enough, or are happily centered right in between when it counts.

Even a complete unknown, like five-foot-four-inch, one-hundred pound Venezuelan Milagros Sequera, in explaining her progress—not only her gold medal performance at the 2003 Pan American Games, but also her surprising dominance over the bigger, stronger top young Americans—said, "Confidence. That's the main thing."

At the same time, the quality of an opponent's shot, and all the intangibles that come with that recognition, are an integral part of the mix. Shot selection is a product of your split-second "read" of the approaching ball, which involves instantaneously calculating the placement, pace, and spin of that shot all rolled into one.

Players in control operate at a safe distance from their level of incompetence, producing shots at varying levels of pace—three in general—to take advantage whenever possible, and to stay out of trouble when necessary. Recognizing your very best results, ideally hit by design on those occasions when you're able to raise your game on call, but otherwise often spontaneous through exceptionally good timing, as "overdrive," creates a clear reference for the remaining two—"low gear" and "cruise control."

Low gear is used to ride out the very best shots that—assuming you can reach them—an opponent has to offer. Quicker preparation, softer hands, and an immediate stroke start collectively allow for a slower swing speed aimed at absorbing the blow and staying in the point. A clear and impacting message is then sent that their best stuff doesn't make a dent in your game, and that it's going to take much more than "that"—winners, to be precise—to be successful against *you*. Pouring a little water on the "fire" represents a much more prudent strategy than going ego-emotional and trying to do them one better. Since, unfortunately for some, tennis is not a contact sport, there is no opportunity to strike back with a good stiff forearm in the facemask. But, take heart, opponents do become frustrated in the face of such resiliency and often respond by attempting even better stuff, impatiently going for winners that they cannot consistently produce. Using their pace and laughing in their face—not a bad credo—and showing them that they've got nothing, can not only be maddening to them and push their buttons, but also be extremely gratifying for you. And it's no different at the tour level, exemplified by veteran Wayne Ferreira's comments about one of the most beautiful sights in tennis—seeing an opponent lose his cool when under steady pressure, just as heavily favored Juan Carlos Ferrero did in his upset loss to Ferreira in the quarter-finals of the 2003 Australian Open.

Cruise control represents the middle ground that is the meat and potatoes of your shot-making. This is a level of play that you can confidently control once you've dialed it in. You can still be aggressive—always—but you know what you can and cannot consistently produce. You are well within your self. You are relaxed, yet still intense. Your pace is very solid, but you are not attempting to press large square pegs into small round holes. You are committed to the game that you arrived with and more than willing to mix it up with the opposition without fear or panic in an extended rally. This is you at your consistent and realistic best, win or lose.

Recently, after recognizing a USTA league player's ease of timing in striking such an exceptionally heavy ball, I was able, over time, to convince her that, precisely because of this outstanding natural ability, playing comfortably in medium gear was all that she needed to play the tennis she aspired to. Her previous well-intentioned attempts to succeed by hitting harder and harder early on, followed by becoming overly careful as the match wore on and the errors accumulated, brought frustrating results. Not only in terms of wins and losses, but, more importantly, she would be left, even worse, very out of sync with her true game by the end of each outing.

Striving to become a very good "cruiser" is where it's at if you're ever going to go further—short-, mid-, and especially long-term. Pick your spots realistically to occasionally shift into overdrive—a very small bump up in racket speed is all that's necessary—when the opportunity is just right or when you're on a roll. Equally important, be willing to downshift into low gear in order to survive any challenging moments when in a bit of trouble or when dealing with a red-hot opponent. Watching an opponent's game self-destruct—exactly like Ferreira did—instead of your own for a change, is much more rewarding than you ever imagined, not to mention that you will ultimately also automatically expand your offensive capabilities—surprise, surprise—during the process. Minimally, it represents a great game plan, singles or doubles, to at least start your day on the court and then adjust as necessary from there.

There are countless matches that can be won at the club level, and at the highest levels of the game as well—just watch the French Open—with nothing more.

Diffusing the Breaker

The natural state of things in match play usually results in tiebreakers being perceived by most players as the pressure cooker of tennis. I'm betting that rings true to you, too. Even tour players with considerable reputations have fallen victim at times with spotty won–loss breaker records. After all, whether it's the tour or your regular doubles game at the club, no one relishes the idea of having played dead even through twelve games only to blow the set in the end with a poor tiebreaker performance.

Better tiebreaker results begin with more focused regular play, or playing every single point as if it's match point. Closely contested matches are always won by whoever got the best of the big points. Winning these "swing points," those opportune moments in a scoring system that should be embraced as always working *for* you, makes all the difference. The ones that, for example, bring you back to 30–all from 15–30, versus falling to 15–40; or those that result in holding serve on the very first game point; or those that convert first chance break points when returning; or playing solidly on all the ad points to either close a game out or level the score. And, last but not least, capturing as many first points as possible to start each new game is also key.

On occasion, there are some instances that do allow for a little breathing room and more daring play. There are other moments, however, when a seemingly secure lead can cause a momentary, and sometimes irreversible, letdown. There is never much room for loose play in any kind of match, most especially a tight one. Players who separate themselves from the pack always play to the score and have conditioned themselves, mentally and physically, to never allow themselves to play carelessly, or precariously close to a losing line (a.k.a. "the edge of doom"). They are consistently relentless. I'm sure that the names Connors and Evert then, and more recently Seles (even after the stabbing, with diminished skills) and Rafter, and now Hewitt and the Williams sisters, especially Serena, ring a bell.

The best, at any level, always know the score, its ramifications, and the resulting task at hand—whether it's to close the gap, level, hold a lead, or open up a lead. Every point is "big" in its own particular way among players who make winning a habit.

In playing breakers, it's obvious to everyone that each point does indeed count for more, and that the pressure is undoubtedly on in a big way—especially if you really want the win. With the finish line in sight, it's hardly the time to glaze over in fear or play indecisively. Some unintentionally crawl into a shell, some panic and go for reckless get-rich-quick shots, and some can't even recall the points in any kind of detail after it's all said and done.

But no worries if you're already with me and have decided that the biggest step in diffusing heightened tiebreaker tension is to play every point to the fullest, *all of the time*, in normal play. Hardened to the challenge, day in and day out, your perception of breakers, and actual performance within, will grow very nicely in time.

Armed with a new level of confidence and stress-reducing decisiveness, always have a plan. First identify, and then stick with, whatever worked for you in the set. At the same time, make every possible effort to deny your opponent(s) the opportunity to play to *their* obvious strengths. Stay aggressive—even look aggressive—because every little bit helps whether it's on the outside or the inside, but always continue to hit your shots at the same pace that got you there. Reduce any unnecessary risk by giving yourself slightly safer margins to both the lines and the net. Increase your first serve percentage by adding more spin, and use your return of serve to primarily get safely into the point. Making a concerted effort to win the first point for a potentially big psychological boost either way—whether it's the initial mini-hold or mini-break—and then running every single ball down the rest of the way, like there's no tomorrow because often there isn't, is about all you can do.

In short, make them play! Put the "breaker baker" on and get *them* to buy into pressing, overhitting, and going for winners as their only chance to succeed, versus your rock solid play and their perception of the same. Create a climate of desperation on *their* side of the net. Your belief in self, bolstered by an unwavering will and resolve, is always instrumental in succeeding. Stick to your plan, don't get flustered, and stay positive. As Fred Stolle used to like to say on ESPN tennis, "Keep your nerve and settle to the task." And, as I will *always* say, visualize to realize.

Breathing in breakers has added importance in that the necessity for efficient breathing is in direct proportion to the increased pressure inherent in such a crapshoot. Breath-holding in tense moments is a normal human reaction that can and will do you in. You've got to rid yourself of self-consciousness about being a little more audible than usual when exhaling in order to help combat any occurring moments of apprehension at a tiebreaker's crucial junctures. Once again, do you not model yourself after the pros in every other phase of your game?

Upon first realizing that the possibility of a breaker is looming, the work that you've hopefully put in on a daily basis will result in a more positive attitude, and you'll eventually come to enjoy and relish the short track challenge that so perfectly puts you to the test.

Special thanks to Jimmy Van Allen, the originator of VASSS, the Van Allen Simplified Scoring System—the precursor to the exciting tiebreakers of today first utilized at the Newport Casino Invitational grass court circuit events in the late 1960s. I know from firsthand experience since I once had the pleasure of being pummeled by the world number twelve at the time, 31-12, 31-10, although I continue to claim to have held my own in the warm-up . . . my fifteen minutes of playing fame.

Out on the Jazz

Okay, you did manage to paint the line with that crosscourt buggy whip forehand pass, the one that you defied the laws of physics with on the dead run? Very impressive, I must admit. But let us not forget that you haven't made that shot, not that you don't keep trying it on a daily basis, since Rod Laver won his first Grand Slam. So how about first considering counting your lucky stars, and then coming back down to reality land where heady players do not get delusional, i.e., "out on the jazz," after pulling an occasional rabbit out of the hat.

I'll never forget a young pro that I met and played a couple of sets with years ago. As we warmed up, he looked like a million bucks—very stylish too. On the very first point, he absolutely nailed a pretty good serve out wide for a return winner down the line. It immediately occurred to me that any previous concerns I had of being late for my next lesson appointment could be erased very quickly.

But from that point forward, with much bravado, he proceeded to go big, and bigger throughout both sets on his way to imploding 6-1, 6-1. Unfortunately for him, he'd fallen victim to his own myth on that outrageous very first service return—always a dangerous possibility for anyone starting a match out with an immediate blaze of glory—and then spent the rest of the day foolishly attempting to live up to it. At the time, I wasn't sure exactly who he was hell bent on showing—me or himself—that his start-up winner was an accurate representation of his normal game. Yeah, right, uh-huh. I don't think so.

This guy was so far out on the jazz that only John Coltrane himself could have possibly related to where he was going. But this was tennis, and he was charting a course that his game couldn't possibly follow. Nonetheless, the delirious attempts continued with conversions that were very few and far between . . . classic shot-making denial at its best.

As the match was clearly slipping away, he expressed growing frustration with each and every error in a way that suggested he was, without a doubt, used to making all of these inane attempts. In the end, he apologized for not giving me a better match with, "I was off my game today," a way for him to protect the misconception of being a better player than he obviously was, or, more importantly, ever worked hard enough to be.

By chance, one of the best of the new breed of young tennis directors in the country, Denny Rager, played doubles with this same player at a Gulf Coast Florida pro event not long ago. He gave me the sad update—same old deal a decade and a half later. The guy is still hammering balls all over the place, still looking pretty in the process, and still acting baffled by all the errors. The really bad news is that there actually are individuals like this involved in the underachieving USTA Player Development Program, as coaches! What's that? Perhaps he's a product of what I periodically hear certain teaching pros offering in jest for their lack of game, "It's more important to look good than to actually be good." Unfortunately, for these pros and aspiring club players alike, this mindset often serves as camouflage for not caring enough to stay relatively fit, or to maintain one's skills to a credible degree, or for never having been a reasonably solid and accomplished player in the first place.

Naturally, there are exceptions to everything, but to be one in an extremely difficult game like tennis you had better be oozing with talent. Old friend and former LSU number one, Jimmy Carl Winslow, who was in residence when a young Andres Gomez was also training at the legendary Harry Hopman Academy in Florida, reported that, at the time, Gomez—despite the big forehand—was by no means the best player in camp. Although much to the chagrin of those who were holding their own with Gomez in practice matches, the old master singled out the South American for greater tournament exposure at a higher level, and continued to urge him on with the now-classic Hopman directives—to "hit more balls" and "go for the lines." I believe you know the rest.

Yet, as the very talented Gomez fully developed into a tour force, and an eventual Grand Slam champion just as Hopman thought he could, he did much more than just blast balls at the lines to win. Like all great players, including those players who stand out at the club level, he learned to pick his spots intelligently, build points methodically, and avoid trying to outdo himself, or the other guy, especially immediately after a particularly well-struck shot.

Playing your best tennis is a considerable balancing act, to say the least. You have to be prepared to go out and reinvent the wheel every single day—where to hit, how hard or soft to hit, how much spin to use or not use, how to pace the match, whether or not to stay back or come in. And you have to continually monitor and tweak it in order to bring out the best you have to offer, while simultaneously calculating how to negate an opponent's effort to do the same. 2003 U.S. Open champion Andy Roddick came ever so close to not realizing his dream by trying to blow out the accomplished Argentine, David Nalbandian—a former Wimbledon finalist—in the semis. Had Nalbandian not tired from a much tougher draw, I believe he would have converted his two-sets-to-none lead to a place in the finals. You could see Roddick's new coach and savior, Brad Gilbert, pulling his hair out in the stands. You could also see a much more disciplined and selective Roddick actually dominate Juan Carlos Ferrero the very next day in the final after, no doubt, a wake-up call from the master strategist and handler Gilbert.

I once had the distinct pleasure of listening to Arthur Ashe tell a story with a great message about playing Davis Cup in his prime under then-U.S. team captain, the indomitable Pancho Gonzales—a great player himself, a legend, and ultimately much more than just the extremely tough hombre persona that he always displayed.

The Tie was on grass—a surface on which Ashe had few peers at the time—versus a Caribbean Zone team led by a far-more-than-just-capable grasscourter, Richard Russell of Jamaica. Upon being asked by Gonzales how he intended to play, Ashe related that he said, "Well, I'll just play my game." Then, with full effect, Arthur demonstrated on himself the full aggressiveness of the finger that "Gorgo" repeatedly stuck in his chest, after which Gonzales said emphatically, "No, you'll play whatever game it takes to win."

Clint Eastwood, after doing in a reckless bad guy in one of his

Dirty Harry movies without any frills, gave tennis players at all levels the perfect line to avoid getting out on the jazz with: "A man's got to know his limitations."

Be real. Know and respect your own.

Giving Them the Runaround

Many players believe there are but two groundstrokes: the forehand and backhand. But in fact, thankfully, there is an optional and often underutilized third one that could, and should, become a big part of both your play in the back court and in your approach game as well—the "runaround."

Adept players, whenever there is sufficient time and an advantageous court position, step around as many balls as possible on their backhand side in order to hit their forehand instead. Referred to as "inside out" or "off crosscourt" when typically delivered from the ad court in singles, it can also be useful in the deuce court on the service return, and generally from either side in doubles play.

The very best players in the world, and the best players at any club—surely you've noticed—jump on this shot at every possible opportunity with great effectiveness. At the tour level, just about everyone hits a little bigger off the forehand wing, and opt to whenever possible even though they have no problem—unlike so many club level players—hitting backhands. You can too by quickly moving yourself a bit off the center of the court in singles versus balls either right up the middle or those headed in tight on your backhand side. In doubles, without nearly as much court to cover, you can especially create ad court runaround opportunities that, along with inviting angles of attack, can be much more penetrating than your routine backhand. Daringly positioning yourself well out into the area of the alley results in your backhand becoming nearly inaccessible.

Early recognition of an opportunity for this third groundie is a necessity. A quick jump on the ball allows you to "load" the racket as quickly as possible by rotating your hips and shoulders in reverse of a normal forehand turn. With the hitting shoulder moving away from the court toward the back fence, you'll be able to backpedal into position without missing a beat, and more often than not get the ball right where you want it in your forehand strike zone.

Disguise can make this shot even more effective since the hip and shoulder turn must be exaggerated from the ad court in the direction of the open court when setting up. Opponents must then defend the court by "cheating" to their ad side vulnerability. Skilled players work this inside out angle repeatedly until an opponent begins to both over-anticipate and overplay that side. Then, by suddenly striking the ball slightly more in front from the very same shoulder turn, you can spank the shot right down the line on the right occasions, with no warning, against a surprised and defenseless opponent. The same result can be achieved in doubles—again especially from the ad court—when an opposing net man fails to protect the line, has become complacent in the face of your repeated crosscourt untouchables, or is overeager and "on the early bus" in attempting to poach.

The runaround is also paramount in avoiding being jammed on the backhand, especially in returning serve when the server is attempting to direct the ball tight into your body. Instead of pushing back a weak return from a handcuffed position, you can still have a free swing at the ball by quickly pivoting, once again, away from the line of the serve. You will almost never see it the other way around since it is athletically much more difficult for any player to run around what could have been a forehand to play a backhand. While on the subject, never purposely avoid hitting a forehand in order to "practice" your backhand since it's a tactic that you would never want to incorporate into match play.

Steffi Graf, a great study on this shot, had one of the most exaggerated *and* lethal runarounds on tour. She was so quick off the mark with that signature explosive split step, and extremely fast as well once on the move, that it was not unusual for her to get around even wide backhands that resulted in her being positioned well over into the ad side (and beyond in doubles) in order to really pop that patented last second, but still big forehand. Keep in mind that even Graf then had to hustle back to defend against a possible down-the-line counter in singles, or recover somewhat in doubles, too.

In the less athletic and more rigid days of tennis, running around your backhand was considered very bad form. It just wasn't "proper." Would you believe that I continue to hear that occasionally during my summers in the still potentially stodgy Northeast, a place where somewhat dated approaches to the game have been passed on for generations? I swear it's true. But times do change, and all sports have evolved due to technological advances in equipment. The rackets of today allow for some outrageous shot-making power, even when off balance and late, and alter the way the game is now played, not to mention the fact that tennis athletes have become more mainstream by working off the court to become bigger, faster, and stronger.

At the 2002 Salt Lake City Olympics, the latest advances in ski design allowed *all* the skiers to be more aggressive in the way that they made their turns. Picabo Street's previous forte, exceptional strength and gliding ability, were somewhat negated as a result, prompting her to say, "All the new stuff we're using now has taken a lot of the joy of the sport out of it for me. I liked it better the way it was." Street's up-and-coming U.S. teammate Caroline Lalive expressed a different take on the transformation of the skis: "Sports equipment evolves. You either change or get off the mountain." Once and for all, there is absolutely nothing wrong with running around your backhand, that is, unless they insist on still wearing the old "whites" at your club—long pants and skirts below the knee—and you're still using a Jack Kramer autograph or a Maxply Fort.

It's never too late to start developing and enjoying a new weapon, especially in doubles where you can "cheat" like crazy in the ad court and nail forehands all day long from the so-called "backhand side." And while you're hammering away, don't worry—any attempts to beat you up the middle can be easily picked off by a good partner at the net. If not, anything getting through becomes not only a running forehand that brings you back *into* the court in good position, but also a made-to-order off crosscourt opportunity with no downside since it can still be struck successfully even when a bit late.

Taking It to Them

There just might not be anything else in the game that's more exhilarating than successfully taking it to an opponent by going right at them. To experience this rush you're going to have to be willing and eager to: 1) take full advantage of all short balls or weak replies; 2) serve and volley in all the right spots; and 3) attack from all the way back at the baseline behind groundies that you know right at impact are going to be big and difficult to handle. Regarding the latter, according to Kim Clijsters, "You feel things when they come off the racquet. I've been playing for twelve years. Now, as soon as I hit the ball, I probably know if it's going in or out." Regarding all three points of aggressive play, opponents periodically faced with then having to make perfect passes or lobs, with you in their face, will be under a great deal of pressure—double jeopardy.

During his last hurrah as an overachieving thirty-nine year old deep into the '91 U.S. Open, Jimmy Connors screamed into the CBS court-side microphone, "He's going to have to pass me sixty times," while climbing all over the net at every possible opportunity versus Aaron Krickstein in their quarterfinal spectacle. As you may recall, Krickstein, a very successful top ten counter puncher and viewed by many as the stronger player at that stage of the tournament versus the old veteran running on borrowed time, nonetheless ultimately succumbed to the weight of the relentless and fearless Connors onslaught.

Patrick Rafter, perhaps the most skilled closer in recent years, whether on serve and volley or approaching off the ground, put it this way, "My attitude is guys don't like you coming to net, so I'll chip and charge their serve. I'll try to hustle them, rush them, give them no rhythm."

At the club level, the easiest pickings of all are the second serve "tap-ins," the ultimate meatballs, especially in doubles where the option exists for whaling away on even a skilled net man, a.k.a. the "naval destroyer." You've got to move in considerably to receive these puny serves. And also freely cheat on position, and I mean *freely*, since there's nothing that an inept server can do about it. That means leaving plenty of room on the typically stronger forehand side, about 80/20, and also using the runaround if necessary to get a really good whack at it. By always making it a point to strike these balls at their highest point off the bounce, you'll enjoy a favorable downward angle of attack, one that will allow your shots to pass safely over the net, land comfortably in the court, and hopefully feature some serious juice. Closing in behind this kind of penetrating service return can and should result in relatively easy volley and overhead opportunities, and also force a bunch of errors without having to hit another shot.

Groundies landing short during play offer an invitation similar to weak second serves, the difference being that the attacking player is moving in all the way from the baseline versus a position initiated from approximately no-man's land on the return. Again, this opportune ball should be struck at its apex, contrary to the bad habit of many club players of allowing this ball to drop down low, knee- to thigh-high, into their preferred strike zone, resulting in the net becoming a much greater obstacle to negotiate.

In either instance, the approach can be hit either with topspin or underspin, or even somewhat flat due to this ball's comparatively high strike position relative to the net at impact. But really big hitters, especially those still stubbornly clinging to their old school flat grips, will need to move over a tad more to get the racket face adequately closed for additional topspin that will create a truly risk-free swing on the "up" ball.

Rafter's reference to "chip and charge" is mostly regarding his one-handed slice backhand approach, although he did occasionally make use of the same technique on the forehand side as well. Either one can get the job done very nicely with a skidding bounce that both goes through the court and stays low, making it very difficult for any opponent to pass off of. Even at the tour level, many players elect to not go for heavy topspin on the high one-handed backhand approach, and instead, true to the Rafter example, most often slide the ball through the court with underspin. Topspin, in this instance, can be an especially difficult proposition for the average one-handed club player. But not so for most two-handers who, with the top hand more readily dominant and driving through the ball, are often more able to generate topspin without nearly as much difficulty.

Serve and volley represents the most direct and brash in-your-face challenge. Obviously, you must possess a highly developed serve, one that has weight *and* ample trajectory—to give those less fleet of foot than they once were time to get in—along with sure placement, especially on second serve, if you're going to pull this one off. However, always keep in mind that if an opponent demonstrates that their return easily handles your better serves on average, stay away from this tactic, except as an occasional surprise to keep them honest, especially when they're under pressure on a big point. Otherwise, wait for the higher percentage short ball chance to come in on. This goes for doubles too. Aspiring higher is always the way to go, but club players whose ambitions and misperceptions are considerably bigger than their serves are asking for trouble against a solid returner happily taking target practice.

When all is said and done, never forget that your effectiveness attacking will be directly linked to the quality of the shots that you came in behind. Be patient and selective, but never shy away from an obvious opportunity. Take the shot and make the move, you absolutely have to take the initiative whenever an invitation is extended.

Dirtball

The second Grand Slam of the year, the French Open, takes place every May/June—Le Printemps a Paris—and is recognized as the most grueling test of the year's four elite events. The slow European red clay surface featured at Roland Garros is capable of bringing some of the best players on the planet to their knees, and often does. All it takes is a quick reflection of Pete Sampras' incredible career; he was a legend on every other surface, but relatively unsuccessful at The French. Instantaneous shot-making rewards are very hard to come by. Focusing on getting one more ball in play, and stubbornly working the point in a battle of attrition, is most often the rule of the day among today's quick-footed professionals who can run down just about everything thrown at them on the "dirt."

Since you've most likely been playing long enough to know the difference, you're well aware of the physical benefits of playing on clay. The reduced stress on the feet, ankles, knees, hips, back, and, best of all, the considerable "give" in the court when putting the brakes on or, better yet, when actually sliding into your shot, make a huge difference versus playing on a hardcourt. Yet, at the same time that your body is enjoying less pounding, you're faced with the yin and yang of clay in that you're going to have to hit a lot more balls—at least a kinder and gentler pounding. As a result, a particular style of play, and a bulletproof mindset, is necessary to succeed at any level because of the considerably slower than normal playing conditions, and higher bounce potential, that any type of clay court, including "American green clay"—har-tru or Fast Dry—presents.

The rewards of sharp shooting with authority are immediate on the slick grass at the All-England Lawn and Croquet Club, evident on the Rebound Ace rubberized surface at the Australian (particularly when the roof is closed), and always on the by-design-faster U.S. Open Deco Turf II hardcourts. But when on clay, club players especially need *not* visualize the kind of tennis that's played at the above noted fast zones. Instead, you'll have to be far more patient, prepared to do lots of extra running, hit with more topspin and/or underspin for greater consistency, pace yourself for a longer contest, and exhibit an overall toughness—inner and outer—that clearly communicates that you're there for the duration.

Since an average point lasts longer on clay, in both singles and doubles, you must be at first content to accept that clay court play means, more than anything else, drawing as many unforced errors as possible. Naturally, you'll play aggressively and take any winning placements when you can get them, but primarily you're really going to have to be willing to work the point to death. And, at all times, keep in mind, once again, that the last player or team to hit the ball in the court *always* wins the point. There have never been, and never will be, any additional points awarded solely for initiative, style, or difficulty of shot. Thankfully, tennis will never be judged like figure skating.

Endurance enters into the mix specifically because of the additional court coverage inherent in the longer rallies of soft court tennis. Your fitness level, in combination with your breathing skills, will determine whether or not you can both keep your feet moving—an absolute necessity on clay more than any other surface—and stay strong over a couple of hours plus if necessary. Conditioning can be a great equalizer, particularly versus a better shot maker who may ultimately *not* be able to, or have the stomach for, hanging with you physically. If you have the resolve to play every point, and do not get discouraged in the early going when this type of opponent is still fresh and might be out hitting you, you can eventually get it done. Be patient and look for any signs of fatigue, such as increasingly heavy breathing, stalling in between points, impatience during the point, and the gradual onset of an overly ambitious shot selection.

Muhammad Ali, in his stunning upset over a heavily favored George Foreman, utilized this strategy to perfection, and in his own inimitable way referred to it as, "Rope a dope." Sometimes, especially in the heat, the telltale signs can begin as early as midway through the first set in singles, or a little beyond the start of the second set in a hard fought doubles match. If you're diligent, you will also occasionally experience even solid veteran opponents who, when all appeared well, will suddenly fold like a deck chair—physically, mentally, or both—when the red light goes on and the tank goes on empty.

At the same time, you will still always play as aggressively as possible in order to jerk your opponent(s) all over the court. When on the attacking track, you'll need to utilize safe margins to keep your own unforced errors to a bare minimum, much like the Michael Chang/Arantxa Sanchez-Vicario model of the nineties. They were able to consistently move opponents without giving away many cheap points.

Most errors, simply, are long or short, either beyond the baseline or into the net. Any errors that occur outside the singles sideline, or the alley in doubles, will be far fewer in number. The use of additional topspin off both sides, particularly on the forehand—especially including the runaround if coming over the ball on the backhand is not in your repertoire—will create some clear cut advantages. A resulting rainbow shot trajectory will ensure greater safety in clearing the net, better rhythm retention versus those troubling opponents with little or no pace, and provide the ability to sharply bend balls down at the feet of attacking players whenever needed.

In time, your determination and commitment to making the adjustment to the special demands of playing on the dirt will have a huge impact on your performance, win or lose. If you are patient with yourself, give everything that you have physically, and allow yourself realistic margins all around, then you will have performed well and you'll definitely pick up a few more W's as a direct result.

Pam Shriver, former top player, Hall-of-Famer, and current television analyst, made an off-the-cuff general observation about the mettle of successful players, on any surface, while working the booth at the 1999 Key Biscayne tour event: "Tennis players by nature are a very stubborn bunch." It's definitely something to always aspire to, especially whenever you find yourself playing dirtball.

Smoke and Mirrors

Players who are able to selectively up the pace of their shots at opportune moments, and also couple it with deft disguise, make it exceedingly difficult for opponents to both defend the court and maintain a comfortable shot-making rhythm of their own at the same time.

At the 1996 U.S. Open final, Pete Sampras was so penetrating *and* stealthy off the ground—yes, *off the ground*, not the first image of Sampras that comes to mind—that he was able to completely negate groundstroke specialist Michael Chang's signature foot speed, and the game's best court coverage, to the point that it appeared as if Chang wasn't trying. Of course, he was giving it his all as always, but Sampras' fluidity, effortlessness, and undetectable changes in racket speed and point of impact left Chang visibly mystified and completely out of sync until he was far too deep into the match to mount a significant comeback. I loved Harvey Araton's take on that match in his *New York Times* column celebrating the Sampras genius the day after his retirement ceremony at the National Tennis Center: "Boring? Sampras once dismantled Michael Chang, then in his prime as the game's premier plugger, in three startling sets of night-time shot-making that left the men's locker room abuzz well into the next afternoon."

Witnessing the subtlety of the Sampras magic from a vantage point just a few rows up from the baseline made me fully appreciate, for the first time, that Pistol Pete's game wasn't just about outright serve and volley raw power. If you saw his all-court game performance a few years later at the 1999 Wimbledon final against an on-a-roll French Open champion Andre Agassi, you certainly did, as expected, see him serving like a god. But even gods do not win on grass without a return game. Inspired by that same groundstroking prowess that, although never touted, always looked the same—almost generic—Sampras was also able to break serve on the lightening fast grass when he needed to with an eclectic mix of placements featuring both pace and spin.

Tampa-based Gewan Maharaj, arguably one of the best over-fifty players in the country, was waiting for me after I prevailed in my "comeback" encounter with the pusherman (referred to earlier in the book). I thought that I remembered his game fairly well from our last, albeit distant, meeting, a close but straight set loss in the finals of a small USPTA event in Boston. But, in the end, I realized that I had completely forgotten about his exceptional ability to hold back as much as possible while still remaining solidly competitive, and then suddenly elevate his game—without looking like he had—at all the crucial junctures. Game, set, and match Maharaj. Stealth and its accompanying surprise will always be crucial elements in any attack among relative equals.

Pedro Martinez, the ace of the Boston Red Sox staff, regarded by most as the best pitcher in baseball despite a comparatively smallish stature, continually fools the hitters in that game, much like Sampras in his prime and the Maharajas of the club pro circuit, with an uncannily deceptive effortlessness. His former manager, Jimy Williams, once said, "He just sort of slings the ball, like a rubber band." That's loose! Now-retired New York Yankee third baseman, Scott Brosius, probably understood how Chang must have felt after the Yankees faced Martinez on one of *his* special days. "His arm and motion is just so free and easy," he said. "He has that real easy cheese, that easy fast ball. He's not an intimidating guy as far as size. Pedro is nice and loose and—wap!—he's on you. You know he throws hard, but he's sneaky." That would be smoke and mirrors described to a T.

Sampras was, and Martinez still is, on a different planet when it comes to getting so much out of what appears to be, on the surface, so very little. It takes superior ability above and below the neck, coupled with years of never-ending practice and constant tweaking to both maintain and streamline the signature mechanics and accompanying nuances—along with the absolutely necessary help from *their* coaches—in order for that talent to fully emerge. (Note Sampras' seven month revolving door of coaches: first parting ways with Paul Annacone prior to the 2002 Australian Open, hiring and splitting with Tom Gullikson, hiring and splitting with Jose Higueras, and finally re-uniting with Annacone leading up to his unthinkable turnaround at the U.S. Open.)

Keep in mind that you cannot startle opponents with shot-making disguise if you're continually pressing and striving to bring your very best with every single shot. Good players will soon adjust and you'll have no place to go but downward, and the element of surprise will be most likely lost in a game with no time clock. Patiently pick the spots to elevate your game only when you really need them. Save the full weight of your shots, that little extra, for those moments when you've maneuvered your opponent out of position and have a particularly inviting ball in front of you, or have lulled them into complacency at a lesser pace. By moving the racket through the ball slightly faster than your norm without compromising ideal relaxation—approximately ten percent is more than enough—you'll get as big a piece of the ball as possible and achieve that precious little additional ball speed. The sudden explosiveness of your shot, in stealthy combination with your usual looking ball-striking demeanor, will be mostly unreadable and can penetrate an opponent in a flash, often making them late and unable to answer solidly, if at all.

When setting the stage, avoid laying all of your shot-making cards on the table while warming up. Hold back a little on those groundies, go easy, concentrate on good timing, and hit the ball at a very average pace. Even less than that here and there has merit until just prior to taking serves, when you should go ahead and nail a couple of balls for the sake of a little rehearsal at finding that particular feel. Then, get *their* rhythm locked onto a pace that, once play begins, is only aimed at keeping you in the point, negating them by absorbing whatever they throw at you, moving them around, and nothing more. As the match unfolds, go to your "cloaking device" when you can, but only when necessary—overkill is just that—in order to get the job done, claim enough of the big points, and eventually the match. Being totally in charge of orchestrating your own rhythm, and, at the very least overtly disrupting theirs, especially at crucial moments, to keep them off balance.

As always in any conflict or contest, don't let them see you coming. Smoke and mirrors—what they see may not be exactly what they get.

No Hurry, No Worry

You always take your tennis seriously. You've invested not only a great deal of time, but also a substantial amount of money, in the development of your game. You definitely do not like to lose, and you're very motivated to do that little extra to win. And just about every time that it's match day, whether it's playing on your USTA league team, in an area tournament, or in your own club championships, you not only get pumped up, but a little nervous, too.

After a two-month hiatus from the tour due to illness in his family, Andre Agassi surprisingly cruised to a 6-4, 6-2 first round win over Sweden's Thomas Johansson—a more than formidable opponent at the time—at the 2000 year-end event in Stuttgart for the world's top eight. "It's nice to feel nervous again; it's been a while," Agassi said, obviously pleased about what he was feeling inside. Nervousness is a normal and positive reaction for anyone who truly cares about their performance. Miles Davis once put it this way, "If you're not nervous, you ain't listenin'."

Other factors can also enter into the mix prior to playing matches that *are not* conducive to your best play. Eating too much of the wrong foods or drinking too little of the right fluids leading up to your start time is really asking for not only physical trouble, but also mental problems since your brain will not be functioning fully either. Not tapering off the day before, and instead involving yourself in a tough match or a grueling workout—usually undertaken with a crash course mindset— is also ill advised and can leave you flat and stale when it counts. Above all else, even among the most dedicated and well-intentioned, lack of sleep in combination with consuming a little too much spirits the night before will pretty much guarantee a less than stellar performance.

But what's almost never addressed, and is especially instrumental in undermining even a generally good preparation, is the club player's penchant—usually the very same ones that become particularly upset if they lose—for arriving for their matches either at the very last moment, or worse yet, outright late. The dreaded double whammy goes to those players who also arrive preoccupied by, or stressing over, something that's completely irrelevant to the tennis-only task at hand . . . talk about disruptive.

Besides doing all the right things in advance, an unhurried travel schedule—which absolutely includes smoothly accelerating and gradually braking your vehicle en route to set a tone—is crucial in calming your inner self and in also eliminating any distracting thoughts that might be bouncing around in your head. Even if life is relatively idyllic, the habit of leaving the house at the very last moment, and then having to drive under pressure to make up the time lost, will almost always adversely affect your play in a very big way.

Years ago, I would look forward to joining several other Boston-area club pros in a round robin singles shoot-out for beer money once a week. Although these guys were all ranked players, I felt that I had enough game to at least win on occasion, but I didn't. Each week I would finish my last lesson, jump in the car, and make the normally one-hour drive in forty-five minutes or less, weaving in and out of heavy traffic and passing every car in sight at breakneck speed in order to arrive on time. Eventually, after having grown weary of such a stressful routine, and still not winning, I came to my senses one night and decided to drive the speed limit, listen to some mellow music, relax, relish the time away from the daily routine, and accept the consequences of being late. Amazingly—actually, not so amazingly–I finally won our little event for the first time despite the handicap of an abbreviated warm-up. I then proceeded to win the next two weeks as well, in large part by smartening up a bit and changing my lesson schedule so that I could drive the speed limit and still be on time. I was cool, calm, and collected versus the hot-wired time bomb that arrived for all of the previous events. The change was remarkable: exact same skill level, but with a far different emotional climate and mindset, and very different results.

The choice of walking on the court exuding confidence versus insecurity, strength versus weakness, and tranquility versus irritability, is entirely yours. Travel writer Ed Hewitt, in the context of this day and age of global travel and geopolitical strife, believes that it's important for Americans to carry themselves in a very particular way—discreetly. A crossover cord is struck for tennis players entering the court when he states, "You only have thirty seconds when you encounter someone to make your impression. It's a matter of carriage, simple issues of appearance, what you say and do." In eulogizing the historic career of the late Althea Gibson—winner of two U.S. Nationals (as they were then known), two Wimbledons, one French, and the Jackie Robinson of the lily-white tennis of the '50s—Billie Jean King said, "She was imposing to begin with, and she had a swagger that added to that aura." So, if *your* game isn't exactly what you would like it to be, but you act like it is, you'll be surprised to find that you'll do better.

In a somewhat different light, current Pentagon official Admiral John Poindexter—best known for his dubious involvement in the Iran-contra episode—is so keen on the validity and relevance of body language he has spearheaded tax dollar financing for research projects at leading universities to develop methods of gait analysis to identify potential terrorists.

If you are indeed on top of your match preparation, but somehow it all goes wrong anyway and you arrive for your match in a somewhat frenzied state, then absolutely take the time to go for a nice slow walk before entering the site. Park down the street, if prudent, in order to avoid being rushed onto the court before you've taken the time to quiet your mind, and fully immerse your self in the present. Take a few deep breaths, inhaling through your nose and exhaling through your mouth, and smile at your good fortune in life to be a tennis player with yet another opportunity to enjoy such an incredible game.

In the title spirit of Richard Carlson's best selling self-help book, *Don't Sweat the Small Stuff,* don't sweat the small stuff. And never take for granted the steps that are always going to be necessary to avoid bringing that stuff on your self.

TEAM TENNIS

Two to Tango

The requirement of teamwork in doubles is absolutely essential in being successful. Lack of teamwork among four relative equals always spells disaster for the two players operating independently of each other. Understanding the dynamics of playing the net specifically represents *the* component of the game that can first trigger a brand of play that more closely resembles the way in which team tennis was meant to be played.

The non-stop attacking style of closing doubles played exclusively on the men's tour, and by veteran players worldwide, is not always attainable, or even practical, for the not nearly as fit or athletic average club player. However, playing the net like the pros when *already* positioned there is approachable, at the very least in part, and is the first step in genuinely experiencing real doubles, versus all the players on the court in partial or full singles mode.

The constantly changing role of the net man is, surprisingly, a complete mystery to many. In short, the player at the net must be continually shifting back and forth from an offensive to defensive position, or from striker to defender if you will, when their partners are staying back.

When stationed at the net on your partner's serve, always assume an aggressive initial position that is one to two steps forward from the approximate center of the service box. This allows you to be within poaching distance—both close enough to the net and far enough away from the singles sideline—should a weak return present itself, or if you're already committed to make a move. Players who defensively hug the alley, those too tentative to enter the fray and/or afraid of getting passed, are never in position to pose any kind of threat to cross and pick off a shot. They mostly leave their partners in the lurch to engage opponents single-handedly.

Conversely, the opposing net man on the receiving team is first positioned in close proximity to the "T," either just inside the service line or slightly behind it, depending upon the level of confidence in the partner's return game. From this area of the court, while facing or "square to" the net opponent, one has an equal chance to defend both the middle and the outside of the court against a poach created by a poor return.

Once the ball is served and successfully returned crosscourt—*always* the primary returning tactic—the unique challenge of dynamic doubles play begins. The net man on the service team, initially poised to cut off the return—and also responsible for protecting the line when necessary—must immediately shift back on a slight diagonal toward the defending position at the "T," now a couple feet *inside* the service line. At the same time, the net man on the receiving team, upon recognizing their partner's return passing over the net and safely away from the potential poach—by focusing directly on their net opposite during the return with the option of also glancing quickly back at their partner to get a feel for where their shot is going to be directed—then moves forward into the attacking position to ideally pick off any poorly struck or errant response.

With the ball now fully in play, and with both teams remaining in the classic one up and one back alignment so typical of club play—not at all unusual on the women's tour in the twenty-first century—each player at net then continues to alternate from offense to defense as the ball moves back and forth across the net. The players in the backcourt are engaged in a crosscourt duel aimed at simply drawing an error, creating a poachable ball for their partner to pounce on, pass an out of position net man, unleash a big groundie right at the net man, or force short ball replies to then come in behind. Joining their partner and taking control of the net ultimately puts big pressure on the other team to come up with a much better than average shot, and the fun begins.

During his call of the Ladies Doubles final at the 2003 Wimbledon Championships—a match that featured four of the tour's very best doubles specialists—Johnny Mac was in disbelief over the one up and one back alignment on display, on grass no less. He offered that old school forty-six-year-old (!) serve and volleyer, Martina Navratilova, "must be turning gray in the locker room" at the state of women's doubles while waiting to play her mixed final. One month later, in an interview just prior to the U.S. Open, Navratilova herself explained the apparent regression in tactics by citing the dilemma of facing the big hitters of today like the Williams sisters, "They don't volley as well as other players, and that's something you can exploit in a doubles match. But the hardest part is getting to that volley, because they hit such hard serves. They are so powerful it is also hard to get into a rally with them." Yet club pros all too often irresponsibly encourage immediate and indiscriminate net rushing.

The placement of the serve, often misunderstood, should ideally initiate the very first and usually best opportunity for the net man to contribute to the team. Remember, especially those of you who are consistent post-match complainers: it takes two to hold serve, it takes two to be broken, and it takes two players working together on the serve to be generally effective.

Assuming everyone is a righty, the server should place the ball up the "T" the majority of the time in the deuce court. The serving team net player, somewhat released from protecting the alley as a result, can now, with reduced risk, time their way into the middle to pick off the return and blast it through the feet of, or completely past, the defending net man. This is meat and potatoes time. Habitually serving out wide from the right court, as far too many club players insist upon, requires the partner at net to move toward the line, and at times even into the alley, in full defensive mode depending on the angle severity of the serve. What results is far fewer poaching possibilities—although it is possible to first "shut the line down" and then cut back to poach—not to mention that this serving strategy is right smack into the forehand strength of the average player. Is that the perspective that's responsible for why the deuce court is so often referred to as the "forehand side?" That stated, definitely go ahead and periodically make use of the "slider" out wide versus opponents attempting to protect their weak backhand by positioning themselves toward the center, and also more liberally on any court with a fast surface.

From the ad court, the server should continue to probe the receiver's backhand early on since it's usually the weaker and suspect side in clubland. Serving out wide, this time by design, to force opponents off the court where the crosscourt backhand return, especially at full stretch, makes returning serve effectively a demanding task for many. The net man once again moves from their initial centered aggressive position toward the alley, as in *all* situations when the action goes out wide, to cover any ambitious, desperate, or especially any potentially lucky late stab returns that can *only* go down the line. A well placed serve, especially a penetrating one well up in the box, can cough up floaters that are easy pickings for the net man and can easily be placed between the defenders or angled off for an easy point. On occasion, a serve up the "T" will not only keep the receiver from overprotecting a vulnerable backhand, but also free up your partner to take greater poaching liberties toward the center of the court, even versus a player with a strong forehand.

There is much more to the constantly-in-a-state-of-flux game of doubles. Becoming a properly positioned player when at the net will put you well on your way to experiencing the real fun of playing with a partner, being a team, opening up the court, covering any holes, and of course, learning the tango.

Choosing Sides

Opinions abound when doubles teams try and decide who should play the deuce or ad court. When first-time partners are quick to announce that "it doesn't matter," or that they "don't care" which side they prefer to play when asked, trouble is brewing just around the net post. How could your alignment possibly not matter, both individually and as a team?

Part of what is lost on them is a product of the club player's insistence upon referring to the deuce or right court as the forehand side, and the ad or left court as the backhand side. C'mon, let's get it right. (Yes, I'm *still* wondering where this stuff originated.) If the so-called "forehand side" right-handed player cannot handle the inside out backhand return of serve—regarded by most in the know as the most difficult shot in doubles—and they will absolutely have to against an accurate server, the match could well be over right there. If ever there was a misnomer! And what about the fact that a right-handed player in the ad-court can, with little risk, cheat on position well to the outside of the court, easily run around their backhand, and hit forehands all day long from the "backhand side?" Plus, let us not forget that playing with and against our left-handed friends changes those misperceptions further and flips the whole deal.

On the subject of lefties tweaking the mix, the Gullikson twins, Tom and Tim, were a very successful team in the 1980s whose record included, besides numerous top ten world rankings, a Wimbledon final. Lefty Tom played the ad court with righty Tim in the deuce court. John McEnroe and Peter Fleming, the stalwart Davis Cup tandem of the same era, also a lefty-righty combo, lined up the same way—I think you know who the left hander was. More recently, the Woodies, left-handed Mark Woodforde in the ad court, and right-handed Todd Woodbridge in the deuce court, were not the dominant team they ultimately became until they switched away from the old adage of "forehands to the middle." Yet, the new world's number one doubles team, righty Bob and lefty Mike Bryan, played their forehands to the middle in a convincing victory at the 2004 Davis Cup tie versus Austria. A few years ago at the Key Biscayne tour stop, well prior to their ascendancy to the top, I witnessed them change sides back to their losing first set alignment for the third and deciding set against Leander Paes and Justin Gimelstob after *winning* the second, very much at odds with the long standing Arthur Ashe axiom, "Never change a winning game; always change a losing game." During an impromptu lunch with their open, outgoing, and always energized teaching pro father, Wayne, immediately after their ultimate loss, I asked him why they changed sides at *that* juncture, to which he replied, "I don't know." Further, the now all-grown-up Bryans, after squeezing out a tight first set win over Jonas Bjorkman and Thomas Johannson in the Davis Cup encounter versus Sweden referred to earlier on, changed sides at the beginning of the second, which they then went on to dominate along with the match. Now try and go figure. I can only speculate that this penchant for changing sides at the completion of a set, won or lost, is intended to create a periodically altered conundrum for opponents facing an opposite-handed twin team who claim that they "know what each other is thinking."

However, since righty is typically teamed with another righty, the question is what the choice of side issues really are, especially at the club level where styles of play can be even beyond "contrasting," and partners without weaknesses uncommon. Here are some factors to consider.

Since all of the crucial swing points are played in the ad court—ad-in, ad-out, 40-30, 30-40—you might choose to have the strongest player, the one who usually performs best under this type of deciding pressure, playing these points. Carried further, the player with the seemingly less spectacular, but more reliable, return game can be most effective in the deuce court. These solid returners are able to regularly win a high percentage of first points, and also consistently put pressure on the server with tough returns. Not only do they allow their ad court partners more "score freedom" to go for their shots, but also provide them with the break point chances that these players typically relish and often convert.

But of course tennis is not an exact science, which I was reminded of while playing in a competitive charity event last year. In attempting to choose the appropriate side, I deferred to my partner's obvious superiority. The format consisted of a young stud pro teaming with one, to put it kindly, well into age group play. I suggested that he play the ad court in order to close out games and get us out of trouble if needed— at least that was the theory. We played a fairly solid match against a good team in our opening round, but *lost* too many of the pivotal points on unforced players, and came up a little short. On day two, now relegated to the consolation draw but still in the money, I suggested that *I* play the ad court since it was the side that I felt most comfortable on. Without objecting, my regularly-competing partner confessed that he had been playing the deuce court all season with a number of different partners. Now, playing our sides of choice, and throwing "logic" to the wind, we rolled to an easy win. The mixed team of Leander Paes and Martina Navratilova, the universal people's choice, do the same. Right-handed Paes, perhaps the best doubles player on the planet, plays deuce court, with the far less lethal left-handed Navratilova in the ad court.

Deciding what's best is even more difficult when teaming with players with mechanical weaknesses. The player with a suspect backhand, for example, should play the technically less demanding ad court. That's right, the ad court! As previously mentioned, the left court allows for considerable "cheating" on position well to the outside of the singles sideline in order to very effectively hide and protect the backhand, giving these individuals the opportunity to play almost exclusively to their forehand strength. Any serves or shots that do find the small opening are usually manageable for those with even marginal backhands without the added difficulty of reaching or having to hit on the run while going *away* from the court, and hitting crosscourt is then not nearly as much of a challenge.

The fun begins when enterprising opponents, seeing the "cheat," attempt to work the "T" when serving—a tactic that club players lacking in power, and especially in placement, typically fail to capitalize on. Once in the point, they also try to thread the needle up the middle, playing right into our player's loaded forehand. As an added bonus, the deuce side partner at the net, wise to the tactic, can also pick off any probes not perfectly directed up the middle *before* they could possibly spell trouble.

The positional risks of ad court "cheating" are surprisingly minimal. Since most club players hit at least an adequate running forehand, and can usually cover half the court going to their right when necessary, they are generally much more comfortable hustling back *into* the court to play their strength. When they play it "straight," and end up moving *off* the court far more often, their not-unusually weaker backhand is under considerably more pressure to make the crosscourt return.

The dilemma facing the deuce court player in attempting to cheat on position to play more forehands is inherent in the reality that any reasonably angled incoming shot—a serve out wide or a well-placed ball off the ground—will be going away from them in a big way. Leaving too much court open to the outside can be easily taken advantage of by even very average club players, making your typical crosscourt response—now *required* to be struck well in front in stark contrast to the ad court task—a demanding shot for even those with solid forehands. Once exploited, represented in too many late forehand errors gobbled up by the net man, one's court position has to be adjusted toward the singles line in order to take the angle away. Opponents are then able to hammer away at the difficult inside out backhand return of serve, and also even deliver a few groundstrokes into the backhand wing. So much, once in for all, for the "forehand side."

Obviously, there will most certainly be exceptions and anomalies. The still developing idiosyncratic games of club players, or even those who have unfortunately stopped developing, at times can somehow still get the job done against limited opponents who play doubles with no particular rhyme or reason. Typically, they are able to succeed to a certain extent through often ugly, but well managed inefficiencies, usually along with a good dose of raw athleticism. But beware, resigning yourself to always swimming upstream—because you're comfortable playing the game *your way*—will always result in a well-schooled doubles team playing you as if they're shooting fish in a barrel.

When you are struggling, and you're already aware of these basic issues, or even if you're early on in the realization phase, but your stubborn and generally-reluctant-to-change-anything partner is not up to speed, I can only suggest the "we-them" approach. Unless someone is a seasoned veteran with a secure ego—even then you don't know for sure—never suggest to a partner that *they* should do this, or that *they* should do that. The message, because of the implication that the team's problems are due to them, is most often not well received, and can be debilitating to them either through loss of confidence, over-consciousness, anger, or even ambivalence. Always employ the "we strategy"— "We might consider trying this," or, "We might do better against them doing that." Never risk the "you" word, even if you're playing well and have had very little to do with your team's difficulties. You are on the same team, aren't you?

Spanish Davis Cupper Juan Balcells offered his take on the demands of partnering after team star Alex Corretja was replaced by the lesser Alberto Martin in their losing effort versus Todd Martin and James Blake at the 2002 Houston tie when he said, "Changing partners didn't make a difference. We are accustomed to playing the same together, so there was no difference." Coincidentally, a *New York Times* photograph showed the American winners colliding at the net in order to cover the middle. Obviously, they were *not* thinking about who possessed the best forehand or backhand volley, as is so often offered by well-meaning club players when queried about who covers the middle.

Partnering in club doubles would be far less complicated if everyone, especially those competing in league play, would get on the same page and actually make an effort to really learn the game of doubles, primarily by attending coached practices—most often left as an option. But, unfortunately, some avoid the opportunity because they are afraid to grow, or already think they know it all. The greatest risk that you can take on the tennis court, and probably in life as well, is never taking a risk at all.

Practice matches, USTA league team clinics, or doubles match play sessions with your pro are the ideal time to experiment with switching sides and/or changing tactics. If it doesn't work out, no harm done— nothing ventured, nothing gained. Your club bragging rights are still intact since you weren't playing your usual side anyway, or you were just trying to learn how to play more aggressively, et cetera. So, you're off any potential hook. You will, however, at the very least, end up learning something more about the explosive dynamics of doubles, and your ability to actually expand your horizons. At the same time, you'll develop a greater understanding and appreciation of the difference in sides, and, hopefully, a preference for which one naturally brings out the best of both your particular ball-striking skills and your side mindset as well.

There is much to consider. Choose well. Be willing to change.

The One-Two Punch

If you're telling me that you're never going to be able to play high-level doubles because your serve—particularly your second serve—is not a weapon, you've probably got a point. Worse, the reality is that it's typically not only alarmingly unreliable and a constant liability, but it's also a kamikaze tactic to serve and volley against a capable returner. Okay, fair enough.

If it's any consolation, you're far from alone. Nonetheless, there are thousands of smart club players who, instead of attempting to go big time behind their undeveloped serve, wait for an inviting short ball before coming into the net, which is a perfectly good alternative if the serve-return match-up is not favorable. At least you're still getting in some of the time and are really attempting to play the game of doubles at the net when the opportunity presents itself. After all, most of those thousands previously preferred to hit their mid-court approaches, especially off the forehand, better than they serve anyway, so it represents a more viable way for so-so servers to effectively get in.

This strategy for closing can work very nicely since you have hit so many more forehands and backhands than serves in your tennis lifetime. It's only natural that you'll be more comfortable and confident coming in off the ground because you're that much more capable—always maximize the existing skills you already bring to the court. Until you're prepared to get some good coaching on serve mechanics, including how to apply them to the serve and volley tactic, and then put in the necessary practice time to become proficient, exploiting the short ball as a way to take the net makes perfect sense.

But this is not the main reason why you're not very likely to experience the feeling of tour-type dubs every now and then, even with your existing non-serve and volley game. Sadly, until most club players reach the 4.0-plus level—and sometimes not even then—they typically do not even recognize perfectly good opportunities to capitalize on, often getting opponents of equal skill in trouble only to then let them completely off the hook. It's very dead-end stuff when something really nice is ventured, and then nothing at all is gained. In terms of steady self-stifling improvement as a doubles player, this predicament represents being somewhere between the end of the line and the middle of nowhere.

The most glaring example of this shortcoming begins when aggressive opponents take the initiative to chip and charge, or "crush and rush" behind crosscourt returns, especially versus your second, since you're staying back on your serve. Your partner at the net will typically be neutralized by these tough returns. With no poaching opportunity, they'll properly retreat from their initial attacking net position back toward the "T" on the defense in the event that your response is poached by the opposing net man, or ends up too high and in the closer's volley wheelhouse.

But at times, you are able to crack a nice low laser beam response, or better yet, a bending topspin right at their shoelaces, one that the closing player will be forced to dig out with difficulty. After all, you are able to hit pretty well off the ground and you should be able to dial a number of these answers in. However, in this fleeting key moment your partner, who fails to recognize your success in handcuffing the net rusher and turning the tables, remains planted around the service line in still defensive mode. Now completely out of position, they fail to move back in to try and intercept the defensive volley. Your momentary advantage is lost. The other guys are not only still *in* the point but now can re-take control of it by being allowed, under no pressure from your partner, to freely float back a weak volley. As is often the case, you're now very possibly on your way *out* of the point in a game that can turn on a dime.

Obviously, this exact same scenario can also occur on your own return game when facing an opponent who *is* a comfortable serve and volleyer. A nice low return in and around their feet is produced, but, with a partner who never follows-up for a possible big time "one-two punch," you'll soon be thinking, "Houston, we have a problem."

"But I'm not fast enough to get in that quickly," these partners always plead at the post-match commiseration session. Baloney! It's not all that much about foot speed and explosive quickness in club play, although it's nice if you have both. It *is*, however, primarily about early recognition, and that's more about fast eyes making a quick read of the situation. Reading the quality of your partner's shots, or lack thereof, is the trigger to holding defensive net position when vulnerable, or closing in for the kill when the opportunity presents itself. I guarantee that you will be amazed at how much court you can cover, and how quickly it can happen, if you literally see the possibilities as they are unfolding instead of slightly after when it's already far too late.

Sure the game is mostly crosscourt, occasionally down the line, and sometimes up the middle, but only in part, and *that part* will only take you so far up the club double's ladder. The real deal has more to do with the net man constantly monitoring their partner's shot margins to the net, anticipating the opponent's ability or inability to respond, and then instantly taking full advantage of any resulting offensive openings, or dealing appropriately with any defensive necessities.

These same players, interestingly, almost always readily grasp the importance of adjustments in lateral positioning—when to move to the left or the right in order to cover the line, covering the middle when their partner is moved off the court, or taking away crosscourt angle opportunities out wide. But too many take far too long to understand the forward-back do's and don'ts of net play that are necessary to play doubles at a much higher and faster paced level. Some, strangely satisfied with their far-less-than-complete game, choose to keep their head firmly planted in the proverbial sand.

So, if the opposition has to play a low difficult volley, and you're initially at the service line net position in protect mode, get in and get after it! Follow the ball, move directly toward it, and be willing to cross a bit early if they have previously repeatedly escaped by angling their shot crosscourt. These balls are yours for the taking, and you'll get your fair share if you're aggressive. At the very least, even if they are not reachable, your effort will result in an imposing, attacking presence that will not only put added pressure on the volleyer, but will result in a surprising number of opponent errors over the course of the match—without even touching the ball.

Whether or not you ever develop a credible serve and volley game, you're at least going to get a taste of a common component of the pro game on a regular basis. Not only will you become a much greater threat at the net, but you'll also be perceived as such by others—always worth a few extra free points based upon nothing more than pure presence.

The Glass Half Full

"If I serve and volley, they'll just hit it at my feet. When I finally do try to poach, they always pass me down the alley. If I stay back, they chip it short or drop shot me. When I cover crosscourt, they go down the line. If I take away the line, they hit crosscourt. And whenever I attempt to come in, they lob over me," said the frustrated USTA league player with such a limited outlook.

Club doubles players with this kind of mindset, until their perception is drastically overhauled, are negative, reactive, and are generally afraid to fail. They tend to play "back" by standing in front of the baseline, or even in the middle of no man's land. They hug the alley when a partner is serving, position themselves permanently out of poaching range around the service line, and generally assume—subliminally or otherwise—that their opponents will most likely be successful and that they will most likely not. Being this afraid to play, to take a calculated risk and let it hang out, results in the glass never being able to be more than half-empty . . . very self-fulfilling stuff.

At the 2002 Winter Olympics, the United States women's alpine ski team was a disaster. Medal contender Caroline Lalive fell in all three of her races, prompting head coach Marjan Cernigoj to say, "The fear of failure overcame the desire for success."

Todd Martin, a multi-year veteran of the men's tennis tour with an outstanding career record and a superb all-around game, finally exorcised his long-standing Sampras demons by upsetting Pete, after thirteen straight losses, at the 2001 Australian Open. "Every time I've ever played Pete, I kept on making adjustments along the way rather than sticking to my guns and having a shootout with him. Today I finally stuck to my guns," Martin said. "I don't feel like I was very committed to doing it the right way before; and today, I did it the right way. If I would have lost, I still would have felt pretty good about it." All that time wasted despite being one of the world's best.

Similarly, Martina Navratilova's loss to Chris Evert in the 1985 French final—regarded by many as the very best of their eighty career meetings—led a disappointed Navratilova analysis of the outcome:"We (coach Mike Estep) went overboard on strategy and I didn't let my instincts play any role. I just kept reacting and didn't create."

The great curmudgeon, New York Yankees manager Casey Stengel, in one of his Stengelese classics (Who do you think taught Yogi Berra?) said, "Good pitching will always stop good hitting, and vice versa." Brilliant! Casey clearly understood the essence of the sporting contest—the eternal cat and mouse game—who can do it to whom best, and first. For every possible success one must accept, without trepidation, that the risk of failure is present. Nothing ventured, nothing gained, and so on.

Bode Miller, a two-time Olympic skiing silver medalist and also a very accomplished tennis player planning on playing in a few Satellite events after the 2003-2004 season, makes an encouraging and appropriate observation of the difference between risk and failure in tennis versus skiing: "I like the forgiveness of tennis the best. I like that you can make forty errors and still win the match. In skiing, you make one tiny mistake and it's over."

But misperceptions are common, particularly when opposing players who have been officially rated as relative equals are curiously able to somehow consistently come up big with incredible shot-making whenever our "half empty" friends coincidentally happen to face them across the net. The uncanny ability of these players to repeatedly hit perfect lobs, and put away all of their volleys, is especially remarkable: "They were just too good." Perception becomes reality.

The Zen philosopher Shunryu Suzuki knew a long time ago what Todd Martin finally figured out, "In the beginner's mind there are many possibilities, but in the expert's mind there are few." Shunryu's universal theme is perfectly applicable to the dynamic of the tennis contest since stress always thrives on indecision.

It's best to reduce the possibilities and simplify the task of playing good doubles, or singles for that matter, to a few simple guidelines:

1. Make placements before winners.
2. Good placements become winners.
3. Do not fear allowing opponents to play so that you can play, too.
4. Matching an opponent shot for shot is along the path to winning, not losing.
5. Play aggressively, but with realistic margins.
6. Attack all short balls and weak second serves.
7. Their return of serve will only be as good as your serve; your return will only be as good as the practice time put in.
8. Serve and volley when your serve matches up favorably against their return, and, minimally, periodically mix it up.
9. Your net game will only be as good as the shot you came in behind.
10. Their lob will only be as good as your ability to cover the court and handle overheads routinely.
11. First player to the ball in doubles takes the shot; there is no "my side, your side."
12. Never hog balls that are obviously your partner's because you think you're the better player.
13. Always know exactly what you want, and exactly what you expect.

Probably the least-filled glass of all is created by the fact that the lob in particular is so often feared at the club level. The biggest problem is that, by and large, no one is interested in practicing their overhead sufficiently enough to gain the timing necessary to be confident, and if ever there was a confidence shot, it definitely is the overhead. The lob itself is generally poorly read, or not read at all. Once a decent lob is recognized, late or not, far too many club players, in a surprisingly wide rating range, clumsily backpedal to the ball while facing the net. This practice results in very poor court coverage, and is especially dangerous among older players who run the risk of catching a heel and going down really hard. Many a fall-catching wrist has been broken this way, not to mention the occasional concussion if the fall is completely unbroken, especially on a hard court. Quickly pivoting away from the net to turn sideways will allow you to not only move more efficiently

laterally, but also safely. You can therefore ready your racket more naturally to pull the trigger on a timely basis, and prevent you from literally falling on your head.

While I'm on the subject, do not even begin to think that not taking any overheads in the pre-match warm-up is going to help your
cause that day or especially over the long haul. Would you believe that
I've been repeatedly told over the years that it's in order to prevent
opponents from "seeing how bad it is"? Well, it's never going to get any
better that way.

Unless an opponent possesses the ability to hit a disguised topspin
lob, a considerable shot-making skill for club mortals, there is absolutely no reason you shouldn't be able to anticipate a conventionally hit lob
that's about to be launched. If focused on the path of your own or your
partner's shot—totally locked onto the outgoing ball—whether you're
approaching the net or already there, you'll, through an attentive
peripheral vision, eventually become able to recognize an opponent's
distinct variation in swing path and see lobs coming a mile away. You'll
then be able to begin moving back earlier than ever before, resulting in
a big change for the better in both your skill at striking the overhead
through improved positioning, and also in correcting any previous
overestimations of other's true lobbing skills.

With improved visual dexterity—very much an acquired skill—
you'll recognize the difference between an opponent's normal fore-
hand-backhand striking technique versus the markedly different under
the ball golf-like stroke used routinely by the vast majority of clubbers
to lob with either slight underspin or nearly flat.

On the ever-simmering subject of how to best deal with the frustrating and annoying eccentricities of club doubles players, I recently
discovered that Albert Einstein, of all people—he must have had a court
in his Princeton backyard—clearly understood the mindset necessary to
succeed against all kinds of opponents in all kinds of situations, especially versus those proponents of truly ugly tennis, as outlined many
years ago in his "Three Rules of Work":

1. "Out of clutter, find simplicity."
2. "From discord, find harmony."
3   "In the middle of difficulty lies opportunity."

Now that's a glass a great deal more than half full.

The Art of Playing with Your Spouse and Others

Husband-wife doubles, and mixed doubles in general, are no doubt the most difficult and challenging match-ups in tennis. Whether you play them on a regular basis or only on occasion, you probably already know there is a great deal that can go wrong, especially if there is a disparity in playing skills. It is often referred to as "mixed troubles" among club pros across the globe for its potential volatility, and because it can truly bring out the worst in some otherwise perfectly nice people.

At a recent attempt at a *social* mixed doubles scramble, a certain player, normally a very agreeable fellow, became completely frustrated with his partner's double faults and openly exhibited a particularly negative demeanor. Fortunately for her, each round consisted of only four games, and she was able to move on, hopefully unscathed—I did make it a point to present her with a mental toughness award at the end of the season. Not surprisingly, the small group that I was sitting with nearby, all of whom knew this popular guy *and* his challenged partner—whose tossing arm had been permanently injured in an auto accident, leaving her forced to toss the ball with her grip hand—were dumbfounded at what they witnessed.

As a previous participant in USTA husband-wife tournaments, I have not only witnessed a few ugly scenes, but also know what it is like to have one of my own. It's a Kodak moment of my former spouse and myself, taken immediately after she had blown an easy put away in a very close match, that shows me glaring and clearly making her uncomfortable. Although filed away, now many years later, it's there to serve as a reminder of my boorish behavior that day. My actions could not possibly have helped her on any ensuing shots to be capitalized on, not to mention the climate created for the remainder of the contest . . . and well after.

Never, ever fail to unconditionally support a struggling partner! The game is tough enough without rolling your eyes, shrugging your shoulders in disgust, turning your back, barking instructions, or generally communicating to your opponents and anyone else in the vicinity that your partner is dragging your always perfectly wonderful game down. If that's your deal, you better watch out, because he who exalts himself shall be humbled—it's *always* just a matter of time.

Rod Laver, not someone you would expect to associate with this subject, once observed, "An otherwise happily married couple may turn a mixed doubles game into a scene from *Who's Afraid of Virginia Woolf.*" If you are paired with your spouse, always remember the two golden rules of husband-wife doubles: 1) Give as little advice as possible on the court; 2) Give as little advice as possible off the court. I guarantee that adhering to this policy will make going home at the match's end a much more pleasant experience, especially if you lost.

Another legend, Plato, put it this way: "You can discover more about a person in an hour of play, than in a year of conversation."

If you are undoubtedly the more accomplished and experienced player, male or female—I've seen it both ways—being both bossy and a ball hog is also unacceptable. Do not continuously tell your partner to "watch the alley" in order to get them out of your way and out of the point. Do not tell them to "switch" when they have the *up* position and are preparing to strike a ball that you could also easily cover. Do not run in front of your partner to take a shot that is clearly their ball, even if their backhand volley is lousy. And please, unless the bank is about to foreclose on your mortgage, do not ever say, "I'll take all the volleys in the middle," or especially, "I'll take all the overheads."

If you don't want them to participate in the g-a-m-e, then go play singles someplace else. Instead, get them involved, and keep them in it with a strategy that features the "anything you can reach is yours" prime directive. Always encourage them to get into the act, to be a part of the team. It's the *only* way they're ever going to become comfortable playing with you, and experience continued improvement each time out as well.

Some of the very worst mixed doubles behavior, or in any club doubles for that matter, occur when far better players repeatedly blast sitters right at and through much lesser players, a particularly pathetic tactic if the weaker player's protective skills are obviously not nearly sufficient enough to handle the assault. It's a complete mismatch. Don't be a jerk, and that especially goes for those small-minded club pros who I've witnessed deliberately humiliating amateur opponents—who've paid for the experience—in pro-am events for nothing more than glorified beer money. This is not good for the game—or the profession for that matter.

Anytime that you do find yourself in a situation where you're clearly the superior player, why not limit yourself to not embarrassing anyone by patiently working the point until they make an error, or a lucky winner? You can also intermittently engage and attempt to best the stronger, or equal opponent, head to head. Always strive to be a class act by giving back to the game on a personal level, i.e., person to person, especially when it's completely affordable with absolutely nothing to lose and everything that really matters to gain.

In the end, do not make winning at all costs your top priority, always at its very worst in berating your partner in a losing effort. Hopefully, your self-esteem does not hinge on the result of a weekend tennis match at a local club that means absolutely nothing in the grand scheme of things.

Most importantly, it is totally unreasonable to expect more of a giving-it-their-all spouse than you would of any other partner. Check those kinds of selfish expectations at the gate. I've yet to meet anyone who makes errors on purpose. Be positive with any partner making unforced errors, with supportive comments like: "no problem," "keep going for it," "good effort," "almost," "bad luck," "it's okay," and "let's go." You can be instrumental in helping them play their best, and in regaining their focus and composure when they get in trouble. Or you can literally join forces with the other team and add to *their* struggle.

Prior to his untimely death in December of 2000, Chris Antley, a winner of two Kentucky Derbys, explained his uncanny ability at getting the most out of mounts he had never ridden before with a brilliant mindset: "To make a horse my friend by the time I get to the starting gate." If he could successfully communicate like that with an unfamiliar horse at a racetrack, should it not be a given for you to be willing to at least try and coax the best out of another *human being*—especially one you're married to or friends with—on a tennis court?

So either commit to enjoying the experience of team tennis, win or lose, or it might just be more prudent to stick to singles and save yourself from all that aggravation with others.

GROWING YOUR GAME

On Being Coachable

One of the most important qualities necessary to be an effective teacher of the game is possessing an enormous amount of patience with regard to each and every student's learning curve. Without it, nothing very productive ever takes place, and even the best of intentions will not be enough to keep the process in sync and on track. After all, they learn only when they are truly ready to learn.

Conversely, the sure-fire quickest way for a lesson-taker to undermine a coach's best efforts is to constantly test that patience. Typically these aspiring higher individuals, in theory at least, are not conscious of their ways—although the level of one's net worth and accompanying lifestyle can at times seem to be clearly linked to being difficult—that ultimately are manifested in numerous forms.

Nonetheless, the result is, to the nth degree, cumulatively frustrating to a serious coach who is being overtly or covertly blocked from delivering on their end of the student-teacher contract. The unspoken agreement is a simple one: the teacher is expected to do the talking and the correcting or modifying; the student is committed to do the listening and the adjusting or adapting regarding their game. Even in the best of learning environments that is definitely not to say that one should ever be reluctant to ask questions since, of course, there is absolutely no such thing as a stupid one. On the other hand, what's the point in showing up primarily to engage in a form of mental gymnastics with an individual who, if you've hired the right person, knows infinitely more about the game, and what you need, than you do?

Whether in a group situation or in a one-on-one dynamic, a guaranteed "comes with the territory" frustration for club pros—I can confidently state that I speak for many—is without question represented in those individuals disguised as wanting to receive instruction, but who, in reality, want to *give* instruction. Many a hard working, well-intentioned tennis pro, the ones consistently offering prioritized solutions to the problems at hand—based upon years of experience and know how—can become totally derailed when they end up spending positive energy dealing with being constantly rebuffed. Why these players are compelled to repeatedly pronounce *their* analysis in typically ill-conceived attempts to reinforce their perception of, more or less, having an equal knowledge of the game is a mystery. In my most recent experience with this type, I remember, finally at wit's end, spontaneously saying with total sincerity, "Please, stop it. I'm begging you, please." The individual, probably offended, canceled the next appointment and the season ended shortly thereafter. Conclusion: uncoachable.

Then there are individuals who clearly want to be really good players, who regularly work with their pro, but, unwilling to change, fail to grow and ultimately plateau. Often they are very good athletes that unconsciously settle for a comparative mediocrity achieved primarily through their raw athleticism, of which they usually have plenty to spare. Trying to coach these types can actually do them harm since they are both reluctant and fearful of abandoning their already somewhat successful but woefully inefficient approach to the game. They are best left to their own devices. You hope that they don't sustain chronic injuries along the way, and that someday they might get it. Not. Again: uncoachable.

Another example occurs in the form of excuse makers. When reminded of precisely why they made a particular error, or when unable to execute the coach's instructional scenario, they've got a myriad of "reasons." The ball was dead, it was a bad feed, there's a soft spot in the court, they weren't ready, their racket feels funny, the lighting is bad, it's windy, or even, they forgot their sunglasses. One of the classics is a team member expressing a knee jerk brand of anger over not knowing what they were supposed to be attempting—even though a perfectly good explanation had been presented that everyone else in the group understood—because they weren't even paying attention. As a result, one moment later, they are compromised and embarrassed. An all-time favorite occurs when these underachievers have understood but completely ignored the advice being given, and proceed to repeat the same rookie unforced error over and over in practice. When queried, their telling response consistently goes like this: "Oh, I wouldn't do that in a real match." They are the kings and queens of classic displacement—it's never their fault. You guessed it, exacto-mundo: still uncoachable.

More is evident among those who constantly make references to how—inferring a better way, better place, better time—*their* old pro would teach it back in the day when they were (always the case) playing at a higher level. Or, in the instance of a clinic or team practice, how they did it at *their* club up north, down south, back east, or out west. Somehow these folks twist the old adage that a consultant (expert) must be a guy from out of town, concluding that if their new resident pro is *with them* at their new resort or club, one not of the five-star category, then he or she can't possibly be any good. Groucho Marx poked fun at this curious sense of self when he said, "I'd never belong to a club that would have me for a member." Yup, same old conclusion.

Then there's the individual just visiting, he who fancies himself as a good player and who *is* a good striker of the ball, wanting match play sessions. I can see my most recent example like it was yesterday. First comes the horrible "warm-up" predictably followed by losing game after game on an unforgiving slow clay court exclusively due to over-hitting and ridiculously high-risk, totally impatient first strike play. Then, while periodically making references to his former tour playing pro at home and *his* alleged strategic and tactical advice "on any surface," he continues on the same path to methodically defeat himself point after point. At 5-0 in the first, after diligently trying to get through to him on the changeovers with soft sell hints about righting himself, settling down, and playing within himself in order to play some quality tennis—I was only keeping the ball in play—I was thankfully able to offer a very specific observation. It was of the perfect proof-in-the-pudding variety delivered immediately after he finally got it right and won the kind of well-constructed, managed point I'd been alluding to all along. But, a moment later, I could readily see that *my* advice went in one ear and out the other at the speed of light, and he was on his way to handing me eighteen games in a row . . . the dreaded triple bagel. Chalk up another one.

And then there's the "pearl snatcher." This lesson taker has been around a long time, is reasonably cooperative, possesses decent mechanics, but is reluctant to take the final step. Typically, they have to be weaned off the symptom syndrome and made to see the root-cause light, mostly a tedious task of reeducation. But, after a corrective progression finally reaches its solution moment, a sudden amnesia occurs—usually an ego-driven response to, "It couldn't be that simple, especially if it's a mental-emotional pearl."—and they are right back to reciting their irrelevant symptoms without causes. Uh-huh, tally it up.

The "back to the future" types exhibit their own special dysfunction. They are hard-pressed to stay in the present regarding one-at-a-time fixes being offered. They are not even listening and typically panic since their habit is instead to focus on anything and everything else that *will* mechanically break down. They cannot yet fathom the mental and emotional control necessary in shotmaking. Then they sincerely ask, "What am I doing wrong?" Yikes.

In a special category of their very own are two particular players I can readily recall. One, who informed me that the two-tone balls (one-half normal yellow and the other half orange) that I prefer to use for teaching—a great tool for getting players to actually see the spin that they have, or have not, imparted on the ball—were *distracting*. I'm still trying to figure out how any ball can be a distraction from the utmost task at hand in a ballgame like tennis. The other claimed that learning to breathe functionally during a point was not worthwhile because it was preventing them from playing their normal, breath-holding game. A clear case of nothing further said.

This leads me to two more common patterns of behavior—the last, I promise. First, there's the player who is so chronically hampered by one particular phase of their game that it drops their NTRP level from, let's say, 3.5+ to 3.0-. After fixing it in a mere forty-five minute session, much to their surprise, they immediately join their 3.5 to 4.0 friends on the next court in a game of "friendly" doubles. It is not uncommon, within fifteen minutes or so, for them, without even practicing their new and improved technique, to announce loudly after experiencing a first error that their "stroke" has been ruined. Right on cue, a member of the foursome all too often "consoles" them with the usual erroneous all-knowing statement, "You always get worse after a lesson." Need I say more?

If you do actually find yourself at a point where you genuinely feel, despite your best possible efforts, that your coaching situation is not a good fit for you—again, whether it's one-on-one or in a group—bail and *find a new coach*. Otherwise, you're wasting your time and your money, making life miserable for yourself and the pro, and most likely completely disrupting the opportunity for everyone else to benefit in a clinic or team format. Again, what's the point? Stop going.

Finally, just in case, if it's not unusual for you to be generally at odds in coaching situations, wherever and whenever others *are* willingly cooperative and coachable, perhaps some deep self-reflection might be in order.

Play Talking

It's Monday morning in clubville right after the Thanksgiving Day break. USTA league team players across the country have been either hosting family gatherings or away attending one, and have been off the court longer than they are accustomed to. The advanced group arriving for their coached weekly practice is a close one that's played together for years. Since they're tennis "sisters," the catch-up chatter begins with the very first ball and continues well into the warm-up, a component of the game that, as you well know by now, I believe needs to be constantly stressed as vital to a good performance. Realizing the spirit of the day, I acquiesce and instead of trying to quiet them down, I share the trick of "play talking" that pros teaching the game make use of all the time.

In an ideal world, no one but the coach should be speaking during a serious warm-up. Tennis, played well, is far too difficult to succeed at while simultaneously carrying on a conversation—unless you know how. Even then, it's hardly recommended and even, at best, a poor practice when attempting to dial in your A game.

Resigned to the fact that normally all business club players are occasionally going to find themselves engaging in this practice—usually to avoid being rude in response to another's query—learning how to talk and play, without completely disrupting your tennis, is probably a good thing to know.

The act of speaking, very much in conflict with simultaneously striking a tennis ball well, is, not so surprisingly, typically not recognized as disruptive to one's game. But from the very first ball struck in the warm-up, every shot should be accompanied by a well-timed exhalation. Once again, back to the breathing.

Unfortunately, when players are spontaneously more intent on yapping away than focusing on their warming up, especially when in the midst of a friendly hit, the tendency is for one's speech to end up truncated and in conflict with the moment of impact, leading to counterproductive breath-holding. What results is a predictable increase in muscle tension that interferes with one's ability to work precisely *with* the ball and actually can promote working *against* it instead. In short, you can't possibly approach your best level of play while talking a blue streak in the warm-up.

The play-talking trick is to enunciate a word, or just a syllable, in a slightly elevated tone right at impact to take the place of your usual pure exhalation. When absolutely necessary, as in the above-noted scenario, this practice will at least allow you to carry on a conversation without totally impeding your daily reinvention. This is of course closely related to Dr. Loehr's original technique of substituting the word "yes" in the place of a pure exhalation when first learning to breathe consistently—a method which ultimately would not quite suffice within even social confines of club tennis, and especially the competitive.

So if you must, although it's far better to finish up the chitchat *before* you begin to hit those first few balls, get your speech in sync with your ball-striking until some quiet is achieved and you can resume your normal exhalation pattern. I promise you that it will make a huge difference versus the alternative result if executed correctly, and you'll still be focusing your attention, albeit in a slightly altered way, on getting yourself ready to play *your* game and not the one of a poorly performing alter ego.

Purposeful Practice

There are a number of proven practice methods that can be utilized to improve your game quickly, especially if you're *not* into talking. None is more effective than the exquisitely simple one-on-one hitting routines that not only improve shot-making but, at the same time, methodically reduce the pressure of real play by building confidence through repetitive match play simulation.

Former U.S. top-tenner, Davis Cupper, and possessor of a Ph.D. in psychology, Allen Fox, in an article on Lleyton Hewitt's 2003 slide from the top, addressed the importance of the "confidence factor" in anyone's performance: "Confidence is not some sort of ephemeral, mystical phenomenon that your neighborhood shrink can talk you into. It is a subconscious and emotional 'expectation of success,' and we develop these expectations from an accumulation of past experiences."

During the 2003 Women's World Cup Soccer tournament, USA Coach April Heinrichs unabashedly praised rookie Abby Wambach's considerable contribution to the team because of a "competitiveness that did not waver in practice or against a weaker opponent."

Huge gains in both competitiveness and confidence can be realized in backcourt play, in singles or doubles, when one player practices hitting exclusively cross-court while the other must in turn respond repeatedly down the line. This is the only instance in which running around one's backhand—hopefully a tactic that you are now firmly committed to if you weren't already—is discouraged. This pattern of cooperation is aimed at allowing both players to anticipate freely while simultaneously striving for reliable placements on the run in sustained rallies. One learns very quickly, assuming that both players have relatively equal ball-striking skill, that the crosscourter enjoys a big advantage in not only exploiting the open court, but also in defending it. An argument can be easily made that this is the single most important hitting-off-the-ground, one-ball-in-play drill in tennis.

A variation on this theme positions both players a couple steps inside the "T" in order to practice reflex volleying. Again, one player is assigned the crosscourt angle, while the other volleys to the practice partner's down-the-line side. Cooperation remains the key: gradually stretching each other, slowly increasing the pace, yet easing up if you have your partner at your mercy in order to sustain the exchange. It's not about making winners, although occasionally letting loose is okay too.

The same drill pattern can also be linked to work on the volley and passing shot together. The player at the net places the ball either crosscourt or down the line. The backcourter responds by rehearsing the passing shot in the opposite direction. Since you already know where the ball is being hit, it's perfectly appropriate and often necessary to really turn it on and get going early to the other side. Again, do not lose sight of the fact that it's a co-op, not a contest.

When working together to practice the volley and the overhead simultaneously, play "half court" by utilizing the court space only from the singles sideline to the center service line—which is projected all the way back to the baseline. To foster some continuity, the player in the backcourt preferably initiates the exchange, first by making the net man play a volley, and then, on an alternating basis, throwing up mostly easily-hittable lobs. Both players will benefit from the rapid switching from attacking to defending: the net man striving to improve closing skills after delivering a playable smash, the backcourter driving the overhead right at or by the closer, and both having to operate aggressively in such a small court.

A more doubles-oriented variation of the same exercise is executed instead on a crosscourt basis while still honoring the same extended center service line, this time in order to create half court boundaries on the diagonal.

Overheads hit after allowing the ball to bounce, seldom necessary but demoralizing when missed, can be worked on with both players positioned in the back of the court. Player A consistently lobs deep while Player B returns the favor with penetrating overheads featuring, ideally, exceptional depth directed right back at, and preferably right through, the defending lobber in the same half court previously noted. Once again, crosscourt-specific targeting may be employed to add another option, and up the ante in a diagonally longer court.

"Alley Ball" represents another method of working on groundies while testing your mettle at the same time. This time, both players position themselves directly behind the alley and attempt to place every ball in the alley itself with either forehand, backhand, or the runaround by design. The work put in is particularly useful in gaining the skill to fight off the body shots that are inherent in this exercise, but also common on return of serve in actual match play. The added bonus of this drill can be extremely beneficial in becoming more comfortable in dealing with the considerable pressure of placing the ball on a dime, in any and all directions as applicable in real play, when absolutely necessary and under the gun.

Approach volleys can be practiced with each player positioned initially in no-man's land with the goal being to keep the ball in the air while both players gradually close in to the net in a cooperative, yet nonetheless, attacking mode. Once optimal net position is reached, the players then methodically retreat back to their starting points while simulating making "saving" volleys in a more defensive mindset. Placement assignments can be added to increase difficulty once a good rhythm is established: forehand-to-forehand, body-to-body, et cetera.

Naturally, the serve and return should never be omitted from any kind of practice session or workout. Regarding the serve, there is no excuse not to have a reliable serve—after all, you can practice it anytime you wish without the necessity of a partner. If you are alone, first warm up your serve exactly as you would prior to the start of a match. Always dutifully rehearse this incredibly important component of your game and then play one "service set" versus yourself. This exercise involves committing to a particular placement location that will "win" you these simulated points if delivered on target. If the ball is not right on the money, or at least reasonably close—you be the judge—the serve is counted as a fault even if it is in the box. You have two serves as always, and alternate serving from each side exactly as in match play. Simply, the point is yours if you deliver the goods. The point is against you if you fail to deliver as visualized. If you're not already able, eventually, by putting in the time, you'll be able to win this "set" against yourself easily, 6-0.

Still another option allows for the serve and the return to be practiced simultaneously when a sparring partner is available. In this instance, the server eliminates any internal scoring, points are not played out, and this practice is reduced to the game's two most important shots. On the receiving end, the player is working on three basic return placements versus both your first and second serve from each side: crosscourt, down the line, or right back at the server—ideally slightly on their crosscourt side—as applicable to specific singles or doubles needs. Rotations involving serving, receiving, and changing ends are entirely up to the player's needs and time constraints.

Since cooperation is always the key element of effective practicing, aspire to work *with* your fellow players, not against them. Long-term growth in staying power comes from indulging in long and extended exchanges to develop as near to total control over your shots as possible. Practicing ending rallies as soon as you can will result in quite the opposite. Any clean winners that do spontaneously occur—a direct result of taking the time to get into a deep groove—are fine, but should not then turn the practice session into a counterproductive first strike duel. It's always best to save any necessity for an immediate attacking strategy for match play.

With efficient practice habits, you'll build increased physical, mental and emotional strength. Even tactical gains will be subtly realized. Equally important, you'll enjoy a new comfort level in engaging opponents in extended rallies in matches, not only without the fear of losing, but also with an increased knowledge of precisely what it *really* takes to have the chance to succeed.

Leonardo da Vinci struck a similar chord centuries ago when he wrote, "Those who fall in love with practice without science are like a sailor who enters a ship without a helm or compass, and who can never be certain whither he is going."

Making some of this specific training part of your weekly regimen will ensure that you'll not only be well on your way to an increased fitness level—an inherent bonus *never* to be underestimated in the sport of tennis—but also experience a vastly improved ability in shot-making.

If you become frustrated at any time in pursuit of a solid and complete all-court game, or in developing any specific shots that you know you'll need long-term, keep in mind the advice that Paul Annacone gave to a slightly late blooming Pete Sampras early in his career: "I told Pete, who was ranked about 70 in the world at the time, not to worry that he was lagging a little behind Andre and Michael (Chang). I told him that he shouldn't get discouraged, or second-guess his rate of progress, because the scope of those other guy's games was a lot smaller. Pete had so many weapons in his arsenal, that the hard part for him would be the emotional education of how to exercise his options and when to deploy all those weapons." Pretty good advice that's so applicable in competing with, and catching up to, any one-dimensional wonders on your own tour that you've set your sights on.

Speaking of Agassi, his coach, Darren Cahill, in commenting on his charge's spectacular 2003 season including going into the French with a 23-2 record, said, "The main reason he's still competing at this level is because he never trains to maintain, he trains to improve."

More good advice comes from Agassi's better half, Steffi Graf, who said in a 2004 career retrospective, "I was constantly working on trying to get better and trying to perfect my game. I didn't take it serious[ly] to win. I was more driven by the way I was playing, rather than with the results of the tournaments. I think that gave me an edge in terms of not feeling the pressure that I had to win rather than my own pressure of competing well."

If it's inspiration that you need to believe that improvement is *always* possible, look no further than Hall-of-Famer Jimmy Connors who, at nearly forty-six years young while still headlining the Nuveen Senior Tour in 1998, said, "I think I can strike the ball better now than I could fifteen years ago. And I think I anticipate better than I did in the past."

Still not convinced that *you* can keep improving? Try this one on. It will startle you. Sampras himself, on the subject of his own development and career, said it best in 2004, after sufficient time to reflect had passed, "Honestly, I think the best tennis I played was when I was older. I was ten times the player as I got older than when I was really dominating."

Like Sampras, don't exclusively measure your progress in wins and losses. There is much else to factor in—like practice time, match play time, level of competition, periodic lesson tune-ups, fitness level, injuries—especially in clubland.

Playing by Yourself

As someone who has spent an entire adult life playing, teaching, and coaching tennis, I must admit that I have always been envious of golf's natural predisposition to practicing alone. Tennis' mano a mano challenge, versus golf's man against the course, has never invited solitary practice time.

Although my golf game needs decades of work, I have enjoyed being able to occasionally go to the practice area, and the putting green as well, to quietly try and dial in some king of swing rhythm or putting stroke—all by myself. Because I'm such a hacker, I especially appreciate the lack of on course pressure—foursomes breathing down your neck—which affords me a relaxed opportunity to work on my mechanics, such as they are.

Although not obvious at first glance, the same opportunity is available to tennis players at just about every level of club play. All you need is a reliable ball machine, or even just a hopper of decent balls. The emphasis is on *decent* because you should never waste time practicing with dead balls unless you find yourself in a Third World country with no choice. You will only be reinforcing false muscle memory, which will become painfully obvious when you do pop open a new can and immediately experience a complete loss of control and not being able to find the court.

I've never been adverse to working on my game alone—without the, at times, unwelcome responsibility to a practice partner—especially after an extended layoff away from the court, or anytime that I feel the need to reclaim a shot that I've lost some feel for.

A good routine is to start by placing the ball machine immediately behind the baseline to best simulate a typical incoming shot. Initially, as in any warm-up, the machine settings for ball speed and shot interval should be at the low end in order to bring your game to life gradually from a position in and around no-man's land. Then, after a few minutes, or whenever you feel ready, begin slowly backing up along with incrementally elevating the settings, either during pick-up or sooner, to increase shot pace, time between shots, and ultimately depth as well.

A key component in this progression is to take your time. If your primary goal in practicing is to get it over with, why bother? The single worst thing that you can do is start right off blasting balls at full court with high expectations. Both your mechanics *and* your body—particularly if you get out of bed in the morning somewhat less flexible and energized than you once did—will surely suffer despite all the best intentions in the world. Since you have no one else to be concerned about, take at least a full half-hour to reach a reasonably solid level of play, particularly regarding shot pace, but without ever sacrificing consistency. You should even be playing within yourself when you're by yourself—a never ending pursuit if there ever was one.

After completing the warm-up phase, set the machine to feed balls that allow you to build upon whatever part of your game that needs the most work. Whether it's playing the net, working on your approach game, the lob, overhead, drop shots, whatever: first find a nice groove on your groundies. By taking the time to adjust the machine just the way that you want it, and getting help to achieve the right settings whenever necessary, you'll enable yourself to then effectively put in whatever additional practice is necessary. With only your groundstrokes up to speed, always briefly revert back to a warm-up level of intensity anytime that you're moving on to something else to focus on.

If a ball machine is not available, or you're just not into it that day, a great deal can also be achieved in the muscle memory department by simply "teeing-up" balls right out of a hopper. Tossing up shots for yourself, coupled with a specific striking task—a high-bouncing short ball forehand approach, for example—can be very productive in creating a greater shot-making comfort level, not to mention the resulting increase in confidence, *always* an incredibly important intangible.

Hitting on a backboard, currently dying a slow and unfortunate death in sell-sell-sell high-tech America—if it's more complicated it must be better—played a huge role in player development in simpler times. Today, both in private and public new court construction, as well as in capital improvement budgets of existing tennis complexes, the backboard has been mostly neglected and perceived as antiquated. It is generally not included as a simple cost-effective solution to both individual practice and future player development. In the distant past, all it took was an old racket and a used-up ball to ignite a real passion for the game in the right kid, or adult for that matter. I can still see a dozen kids at a time, with others waiting their turn, banging away at the huge backboard that's been brilliantly provided for eons at the Lake George Club in upstate New York!

A resourceful player that I regularly work with recently told me how much he's been getting out of a newly discovered three-wall outdoor racquetball court at the local community college, so I tried it myself. Once warmed up and in a good groove, it occurred to me that I was happily rallying not only with *myself* without any possible negative consequence—always a reality on the teaching court or when playing-in with members—but also able to positively tweak my dusty serve and strokes at the same time after a long season of so little time for my own game.

For Selima Sfar, a far-flung Tunisian—not exactly a hotbed of tennis activity—who achieved a ranking of eighty-second on the WTA computer at the start of the 2002 season, the backboard represented an important part of her development as a youngster. "There were no players, either boys or girls at all," she said, "so I used to play a lot against the wall." Say no more.

Should you actually have access to a by design tennis backboard, begin, as always, hitting very easily off one bounce while positioned fairly close to the wall. Once warmed up a bit, pace off the rough distance from the wall to an imaginary baseline—thirty-nine feet, or about thirteen "yardstick steps" for those of you without a tape measure in your racket bag—in order to approximate a normal backcourt position. Because the ball is colliding with the wall at net distance, you will be required to prepare a little earlier than usual compared with a ball being launched from the baseline by a ball machine. This is not a bad dilemma and is no different than responding to an opponent already positioned at the net. Playing the ball on the second bounce will always compensate for a particularly "dead" or "slow" wall to maintain the right distance.

Volleying up close against a backboard is not only beneficial in quickening reflexes, but also in digging out low volleys since a ninety-degree wall knocks the ball back downward every single time. Although not easy, this is time well spent.

In all these activities, be sure to always visualize where the ball should be landing on the wall—painted net line or not—to effectively rehearse net margins for projected depth while simultaneously factoring in the appropriate pace and spin for the type of shot being "seen."

You can put a good finish on a solo practice, and cool down at the same time, by serving a hopper of balls—you can never work on the serve enough or too much—beginning at no more than half speed, or even less if you prefer. Are you listening? Again, do not go big right away—I don't care how loose you think you are, or how good you think you are, especially you guys out there prone to ego-driven demonstrations of predictably uncontrollable power that's impressive to only those *not* in the know. You will not succeed at anything that has either a short- or long-term benefit. Regularly rehearse success, not failure, by building confidence through getting the ball in the box from the very first ball.

Last spring, while helping out at the local high school team practice, the number one player, immediately after I had both explained and demonstrated the benefits of warming up the serve deliberately, proceeded to rocket his first few serves of the day everywhere but in the box. After a second recommendation to slow down and get himself under some control first, he informed me that it wasn't necessary for him to warm up his serve in such fashion because he was "young and his tendons and ligaments can take it." A classic if I ever heard one! I hope that some day this young man figures it out, if he hasn't already, ideally prior to possibly injuring his young, resilient self and absolutely losing more than a few matches unnecessarily along the way.

While observing Lindsay Davenport practice with her longtime coach Robert Vant Hof at the 2001 Key Biscayne tour stop, she completed her workout by spending about fifteen to twenty minutes each on serving and receiving. Methodically, one by one, they covered all the options in both phases of the game—*the* all-important ones most often neglected in club tennis where it's needed that much more—in order to get her ready for the next day's match.

Once you are warmed up, work on a specific serve for a number of balls in a row. Keep it simple. If the thought of serving a hopper of balls is not anything that you're especially attracted to, use only about a dozen balls or so, going back and forth from end to end, to prevent boredom and/or impatience. You'll not only be more attentive and focused—after all, you're going to have to pick them up repeatedly—but also eliminate destructive "machine gunning" in order to empty a looming, large hopper as quickly as possible. When all is going well, and if you are still motivated and fresh, you could extend yourself by going ahead and serving that set against yourself as previously outlined.

Finally, never lose sight of the process. Always taking your time and going easy in the beginning will not only correct weaknesses and practice strengths completely on your own terms, but also trigger a greater appreciation of fully experiencing any solo time spent on your game.

Air Ball Plus

Learning a more offensive style of doubles can be surprisingly easy for just about any club player who is motivated to expand their game. Much more can be achieved, especially among those exclusively playing doubles—who unfortunately never take advantage of the get-in-a-groove benefits of playing singles—by avoiding the failing of so many who play match after match after match, minus any practice in between. The previously addressed role of the net players in one-up and one-back doubles ultimately should expand into all four players learning to become more comfortable with getting in as much as possible to take control of the net. This is how doubles tennis is supposed to be played, at its fast-paced best—in the air!

"Air ball" represents a training method that very naturally triggers truly aggressive play. The guidelines are simple. First and foremost, definitely do not keep score—it's an exercise, not a contest. Instead, have each player serve out four to six points, and rotate serve as usual. Once the ball is served into play and the return is made, every ball thereafter must be struck in the air. If the ball bounces on your side of the court before you are able to make your shot, the point is lost, and play halts immediately. No excuses—no ifs, ands, or buts.

Both teams will experience an immediate sense of heightened anticipation, first-step quickness, and a definitively more explosive movement *to* the approaching ball. Luckily, it can't be helped, even among the previously reluctant. With the server now serving and volleying every single time, the receiver must now make sure that their returns are nice and low, and—successful or not—move in immediately. The resulting dynamic is that both teams are now closing into the net in an attacking make-it or break-it mode. The team that controls the net, by being the first to create an especially inviting opportunity to take the ball cleanly in the air, is then in a position to dominate the point. The fun that results in playing the game this aggressively is an eye opener for first timers who would normally stay back, play completely reactionary tennis, and never know what they're missing.

Without a great deal of coaching, doubles players at any still-developing level get the hang of it in very short order. The server, now more aware of the necessity of a high first serve percentage, is intent on forcing a weak return to ideally get a great look at the first volley. Their partner, already positioned at the net, is more keen than ever to pick off the return and then split the defenders, or hit directly through their opposite at the net, or even angle the ball cleanly away.

The challenge for the receiver is to return the ball both crosscourt and down low to the serve and volleyer's feet in order to draw a defensive response. It's absolutely amazing how club players tune into this so much more immediately within the confines of air ball. The partner, recognizing the good return, moves in aggressively and directly toward the ball, crosses or covers the line as necessary, and is so much more apt to pick off the defensive low volley whenever possible, which can be often.

The rapidly increasing comfort level of all four players in this mode is surprising to all in a relatively short period of time. With everyone closing to take the ball in the air, recognizing when to attack or defend when back in normal play—seeing an opponent in a tough volley situation or conversely seeing an opponent with a high volley sitter—evolves into a conditioned response that eventually requires no thinking. Acquiring this ability requires a very quick read of the situation in order to employ the quick hands that we hear so much about, and, more importantly, the quick feet that we do not hear so much about. The ensuing byproduct is that now all four players actually *want* the ball without the all too common and typically reluctant-to-admit mindset of, "I hope it doesn't come to me."

Air ball can be played with or without the lob. Eliminating the lob triggers volley shootouts that can produce rapid-fire points that will put a smile on your face, win or lose. The lobbing option requires that the lobber must then close into the net in anticipation of the next shot. A short lob always places your partner at serious risk, but in this game you'll be far less cavalier about throwing up indiscriminate lobs since *you* could be the one to end up with the fuzz sandwich instead.

On occasion, because of the inflexible in-the-air requirement, a ball that could have been played more successfully with a half volley, or even with a slightly behind the service line ground stroke, is missed with a futile overextended stab volley. Nonetheless, despite any oddities, it's still great practice at learning which opportunity is which when in closing mode in real play.

Next time out, go ahead and give it a try. Play your usual first set, which will serve as a good warm-up for a more action-filled brand of air ball doubles in the second. I guarantee that you will not only get a better workout and have far more outstanding points, but also dramatically improve your closing skills, reflex volleying, overall doubles flexibility, and your all-court confidence in the process.

Other effective and related adversity training techniques for doubles or singles include:

1) modified air ball, allowing the server the option of playing one ball off the bounce before going "airborne";

2) limiting the server to one serve only to expose poor second servers and give the advantage to the receiver;

3) eliminating the alleys in doubles to encourage poaching and engaging opponents head on;

4) playing crosscourt-only singles—with air ball, with modified air ball, without air ball—to practice doubles by extending the center service line to the baseline with masking tape, a line in the clay, or by estimation;

5) one service return mulligan—a second chance after an error— per game taken at any time; and

6) one free point—without a point actually being played—per game taken at any time.

More Can Be Less

Players who do not play enough to fully develop their game, for whatever reason, never get to experience actually being in the zone, or someplace at least nearby. There can be no continuum without a routine of regular play. And, if they truly have the ability, they are usually cognizant of that shortcoming. On the other hand, players who play too much, and in time burn themselves out, are almost always unaware of *their* condition. Believing that more must always be better, they continually fuel the fire.

Playing the game to the best of one's ability requires that you be, simply put, fresh. Practicing or playing with intensity more than five times per week, and sometimes more, week in and week out without any let up, will eventually not only leave you drained physically—the obvious part—but mentally and emotionally as well.

Pete Sampras, during his 1998 quest for an unprecedented six consecutive years as the world's number one—an achievement that many believed he viewed as career affirming—played nonstop for the final two months of the year indoors in Europe in order to earn enough computer points to stave off a number of challengers hot on his heels. In the end, it was reported that—and one could apparently see for themselves on ESPN—he was so completely exhausted by such a sustained physical effort, coupled with the immense pressure of what he felt was at stake, clumps of his hair were falling out from the stress.

Highly respected tennis writer Steve Flink posed this question in a 1999 article on the considerable toll the game can take: "Is it inevitable the demands of this year-round game are too much for even the finest conditioned athletes?" The answer is, without carefully planned breaks, a resounding yes.

Sampras didn't have a choice if he was going to seize the moment, achieve the impossible, and six-peat. He, of course, knew that he would be setting a new standard, one that would most likely never again be approached, indeed ensuring, along with his slam record, a unique place in the history of the game.

You, unlike Sampras at that juncture, most certainly do have a choice, since you're in charge of your own schedule, and you can just say no. There are no event promoters whose financial success is dependent upon *your* presence, no requirements dictating how many events *you* must play, and no large chunks of money for just showing up to affect your better judgment. In reflecting on over ten years of educating players on how to take better care of themselves, Kathleen Stroia, the WTA's Director of Sport Sciences and Medicine, indicated that there had been progress when she explained, "The players (now) recognize the importance of periodization, which is the scheduling of tournaments so there is rest and recovery as well as peak performance." On the men's side, Ted Norris, the dean of ATP trainers, exhibited a less politically correct take on balancing one's amount of play with, "A lot of the guys have problems today because they don't schedule themselves the right way. They overextend themselves and don't really budget their time wisely. Sometimes it takes a generation or half a generation for the lesson to be learned, and then it is too late."

Overplaying will eventually break your body down, every single time. Your legs will get "heavy" and become unresponsive, your arm will go "dead"—Sampras' reason for dropping out of most of the very same season-ending indoor European tournaments at the end of the 2001 campaign—your finite motor control will suffer, and you will become very susceptible to injury. Burnout happens so incrementally when you unrelentingly play day in and day out without sufficient rest that you'll most likely not even notice the onset of diminished physical skills, but you *will* always end up consciously wondering why you're not playing, or progressing, as well as you think you should.

Besides the obvious physical harm, even more insidious is the damage to one's powers of concentration and emotional control, both crucially important in being a focused competitor. The negative effect of playing too much not only manifests itself over time, but in such a subtly cumulative way that club players are typically oblivious to its toll. The end result is spotty ball watching, poor shot selection, marked impatience, negative body language, emotional outbursts and/or whining, and a general lack of the mental clarity necessary for between-point problem solving compared to the rested norm.

Both body *and* mind need time to recover from the rigors of such a demanding and all-encompassing sport. Tennis is very physical of course, but it's also very much of a mental, emotional, and, depending upon how deep you immerse yourself in the game, a spiritual challenge as well. You've got to be firing on all eight cylinders, above and below the neck, and in your heart too if you're going to give yourself a chance to consistently perform well and continue to improve as the bar is continually raised around you.

Even the fittest tour players do not welcome the idea of having to dedicate more than four weeks in a row to their tennis—that's equivalent to a full month's work without weekends off. Usually it's necessitated by compact event scheduling leading up to a Slam, too many required upper tier events crammed into a relatively small part of the calendar, or the need to earn computer points to insure one's seeding status. Factor in time zone-crossing air travel and you can better understand why some of the very best look flat and very mortal at times, and also silently suffer nagging injuries. For the more successful players, that's playing singles matches on average a little less than every other day while still practicing diligently on their off day. For the few top players who continue to play both singles and doubles and win, along with the somewhat less successful journeymen who need to play both events just to survive financially, the load can be enormous. There are no guaranteed contracts in tennis; if you don't win, the bills do not get paid.

I believe that it was Patrick McEnroe who, during an ESPN telecast, referred to Yevgeny Kafelnikov as the "human ATM machine" for his insatiable motivation to play every event in sight, amazingly injury-free, but with less than stellar results at times—the scent of tanking in the air.

After barely winning the year-end 2000 Chase Championships at Madison Square Garden over the pumped-up veteran Monica Seles, a still-young Martina Hingis said, "I was just so tired. It has been a long few weeks. I was playing doubles and singles all the time. I was just happy everything was done." At the original time of this writing, Hingis had just returned to the tour in the nick of time for the 2002 U.S. Open, after undergoing a serious ankle surgery, and extensive rehab on the other as well only to break down again shortly thereafter.

As a motivated and always-aspiring-higher club player, you definitely need to balance your schedule as effectively as possible by creating an inner checklist in order to keep yourself fresh, eager, hungry, and positive. Here's a good place to start:

1. Never ever play every single day.

2. Never play more than five days in a row.

3. Never play more than five days a week.

4. Consider three days on and one day off followed by two days on and one day off.

5. Always taper off with nothing more than a light hit the day before a big match if possible.

6. Take a day off whenever feeling tired.

7. Take time off when injured in order to heal.

8. Eat right, drink right, sleep right.

9. Listen to your body . . . it's smarter than you are.

If you're really interested in a consistently higher level of play, then paying closer attention to the quantity of your tennis through diligent monitoring—since too much will ultimately lower your level—will eventually evolve into a playing schedule that's exactly what *you* need to be at *your* best.

The Amazing Self-Righting Machine

If you've played tennis with a passion for a number of years, you've had injuries, all sorts of them, at one time or another. My own experience, spanning over forty years on court, includes always being vulnerable to being somewhat less than one hundred percent in one body part or another, which kicked in with a vengeance when I got a bit "older." But, you're just going have to accept that it's just part of the game if you're serious and consistently out there giving it your all in every point and exchange every day. In supporting slightly injured or completely out of action club members, I usually make it a point to share a certain perspective on the subject with an attempt at a little levity by telling them, "I got up one day about five years ago and absolutely nothing hurt."

The danger always begins when injuries that start out as seemingly minor become clinically chronic. Incredibly—it never ceases to amaze me—with patience and one's full attention, an injured body will almost always, over time, heal itself and the problem will eventually fade away . . . the amazing self-righting machine. Some breakdowns, the really unfortunate ones, are both sudden and serious in nature. Nonetheless, in all instances, regardless of the severity, your ability to play the game that you love is impaired. You don't like it one bit, and, without the tennis experience, life is not nearly as fulfilling. To the extreme, Boris Becker—although long since retired tennis' reigning existentialist—in a *Sports Illustrated* interview shared his own all-important relationship with, and clearly primal need for, playing the game in no uncertain terms by stating, "Tennis is sex, sex is tennis." The Wimbledon phenom still being Boris.

One of the biggest single causes of injury for club players is the cumulative effect of poor warm-up habits. Pushing your body before it's ready to be pushed, especially if you've been around long enough to remember the gas shortages of the 1970s, is really kind of dumb. World-class players, or heady players at any level, know that warming up slowly and methodically—especially early in the morning when the body's synovial fluid (joint oil) hasn't fully re-circulated after a night's sleep—not only prevents injury, but is also necessary to play the game both effortlessly and, as a direct result, as well as you possibly can.

Nonetheless, injuries do happen—sometimes inexplicably—to even finely-tuned athletes like a Pete Sampras who, while uneventfully moving into the net, pulled up lame versus Patrick Rafter in the 1998 U.S. Open final with a hip problem. Shoulder, elbow, wrist, lower back, hip, knee, ankle, foot, and a myriad of associated strains, pulls, and tears are all at risk in an athletic game like tennis. But, unless indulging injuries is part of your player profile, there are some make-sense solutions to staying healthy.

If you experience any type of reoccurring arm problems, and probably losing pace as well, then it's most certainly time to play with a "bigger" stick. Today's technology can not only ward off the ravages of time, i.e., too many balls hit, but also can specifically increase power, reduce effort, and decrease shock all at the same time with slightly longer, slightly thicker, and dramatically lighter rackets. Personally, when the time ultimately arrived—one's personal tennis doomsday—I had no choice but to resign myself to not being able to wield a "player's" thin beam, flexible, "swing from the heels" stick anymore. I didn't have the gas. Switching to a somewhat more powerful racket, one that was also substantially lighter and considerably more maneuverable, gave my hitting arm immediate relief, enhanced my racket speed, and also resulted in yet another extension to my physical tennis life while face-lifting my game in the process.

Slightly lower string tensions, five percent at most, in combination with the relatively new, more elastic "soft" strings in standard 16 gauge -17g cross strings add a nice touch—or natural gut if you've got the budget, can take the heat off of your existing stick at once. Forget about any 18g experiments since even touring pros seldom go there. The resulting increase in comfort is especially welcome if you're having trouble parting with an outdated clunker-war club, particularly any frame that has not been manufactured for years and cannot even be found at those hideous internet "retail" warehouses. Incidentally, these are same outfits that a steadily increasing number of club members everywhere purchase their new rackets from after reading a subjective review in a magazine, without even play testing it, to save chump change when their choice could very well undermine their game and their body. Support your pro who provides well-strung demos at your fingertips, who knows your game and your needs, and engage in a methodical demo process to ensure a choice that's right for you, albeit at a higher price. Isn't your tennis experience worth it?

If it's *your* elbow that's specifically doing you in, then a first step is experimenting with using the largest possible grip that you can still be comfortable with. Increase the size incrementally with one overgrip at a time in order for the change to become nearly imperceptible. Small grips, which so many club players are guilty of using, can contribute to an over-the-top death grip muscle tension that invariably triggers damaging sudden stroke deceleration, and which can also be responsible for last resort excessively wristy play. Regarding grip types, high-friction overgrips—which, if changed often, will help your game immeasurably—are especially important in allowing you to relax any potential stranglehold on the racket. If I had to make a choice between a string job that didn't fit my game, and a worn out, slippery, slimy grip, I would much rather deal with the string adversity. Nothing like a two hundred and fifty-dollar racket with a one-cent grip, yet, it's shockingly commonplace in club play.

If you have any type of chronic back injury, or any kind of leg problems, then you absolutely need to invest in the best shoes money can buy, ones that also match your specific foot type. Are you a pronator (wear will show on the inside edge of the sole), a supinator (wear will show on the outside edge), or relatively neutral (evenly worn)? Bringing a well-worn pair to a tennis footwear specialist—and I do not mean the kid working part-time at the Foot Locker—for an analysis of your specific needs might lead to some approximation of the "right" shoe. Properly sized high-quality footwear will not only absorb startling amounts of court shock and cushion your ride, but also provide needed support and flexibility in all the right places. Don't forget to make sure that they're not too small by trying them on in the afternoon, or immediately after you've played, when your feet have naturally swelled a little. Warning: repeated use of inexpensive or even high-quality shoes that are worn out—attention clay-courters who wear out the insole long before the outsole—will creep up on you and eventually break you down, physically discourage you, and eventually relegate you exclusively to the golf course. I recently came to the conclusion—the hard way of course—that I required a new pair of shoes once per month, or after approximately a hundred hours on the court, at a bare minimum. Rotating two pair, including removing the insoles after use to air out and dry out, will markedly extend the life of the shoe.

Concessions in playing style can sometimes be necessary too, particularly if you're a "lifer" and recognize names like Maureen Connolly and Chuck McKinley. At some point in time, you'll also recognize, hopefully before it's too late, when it's time to shelve the kick serve, and any other stroke that used to be pure energy but is now generally atrophied to the point that it's a shadow of its former self. You can also consider starting to hit the forehand "open," driving off of the back foot since your old classic textbook closed-stance version has worn out your "front" knee, and you're slower to the ball than you once were. And if your backhand has become user unfriendly, as is always painfully the case when the coffee cup becomes too difficult to lift, go to the two-hander so that your off-arm or top hand becomes the driving force. Or, you could commit to finally learning how to hit a one-hander properly, which so few ever make the effort to do—an approach that, if fully learned, is so much more flexible and resilient. If you choose to stick with the one-handed backhand, despite any current possible questionable mechanics, then develop to the fullest the physically less demanding slice, which, in the clubhouse, often gets an unfounded bad rap. However, if and when you've got a meatball right in the heart of your strike zone, go ahead and rip it with topspin as long as your elbow doesn't mind and you actually know how to technically get it done.

That covered, give both yourself and everyone else a physical break and do not drive up in your brand new BMW 7 Series only to offer your very used can of dead balls that you probably also store in your cold, damp garage. Always use new balls for any kind of match, or at least practically new (that means used only once the day or two before) if it's "just" a practice session and it's important for you to be "frugal."

Donate the rest of your used ball collection to your community or club's junior development program, where the arms are young and resilient, and the younger, smaller kids learn faster with low bouncing, non-responsive used up balls.

If it's at all possible, it's also a pretty good idea to stay on the clay, or better yet the grass if it's a Rolls that you drove up in. It also wouldn't hurt to lighten up a bit, drop the ego of an earlier vintage, and be able to say "nice shot," "too good," or "way too good," much more than you used to in order to come back another day . . . without the limp.

If all goes wrong and you do seriously injure yourself during play—DO NOT PLAY ON! Stop and begin icing immediately, right on the court or in the clubhouse *before* you go home, and even in the car if you have a long drive home. You can always stop at a convenience store and get more ice if necessary. The first few minutes and hours of treatment can make a huge difference in minimizing inflammation. Being macho, or "facho" if you will, will really do some damage, greatly extend recovery time, and risk more serious consequences. By the way, anyone that you're playing with who is without empathy, and worse yet put out by your decision to call it a day, is so completely selfish that they just don't get it. If playing the match out is more important to them than your health, they're probably not much of a friend anyway.

Whenever an injury is immediately severely inflamed and traumatized—painful, swollen, *and* warm to the touch—always follow the time tested RICE regimen. For the first twenty-four to seventy-two hours: rest (no body part physical activity); ice (the synthetic reusable packs that you can purchase from any good physical therapist are the best and make it much easier to take better care of yourself); compression (hand-wrapped ace bandages—the six-inch wide versions are the best in most instances—not applied too tight); and elevation (whenever possible). This is precisely when the name "Honey" should become sugar coated in your household.

When you are feeling good enough to come back, it's not a bad idea to start on the ball machine, or the backboard, or simply with ball hoppers—if you're really hurting—to drop and hit forehands and back-hands to, at first, initiate an "active recovery." You could also schedule a half-hour hit with your pro, who can not only tee shots up for you on the dime—better than a ball machine, I might add—but also offer any appropriate input to confirm that you are indeed recovered enough to call your pals and jump back into the fray.

Go ahead and baby yourself by either preheating the injured area in the shower before you play, or by icing it, *depending* on the type of injury. When in doubt, check with your sports-med professional—not your doubles partner—in order to do yourself a favor by going easy-easy-easy before you even think about putting the pedal to the metal again. You can also purchase a neoprene sleeve or Velcro wrap for any problem body part in order to keep the injured area extra warm during your comeback play, or all of the time for any area predisposed to chronic breakdowns. And, naturally, absolutely do not succumb to any happenstance peer pressure to be a fourth when simply dropping your racket off for restringing—"C'mon, it's just a little doubles" they always say—before you know for sure that you're physically ready.

Former world number three and Grand Slam winner, Mary Pierce, suffered for three years with rotator cuff, back, ankle, and weight problems—not to mention the Creatine rumors that circulated during her since-ended relationship with baseball star Roberto Alomar. In 2003, she mounted a nice little comeback, notably by reaching the fourth round at both Wimbledon and the U.S. Open. Yet, in the wake of all that physical baggage, she remains guarded: "Mentally I'm there. [But] my body is not following. There are still things I want to do and I'm still limited at times. That's where patience comes in."

If you're not into massage therapy—ideally on a regular basis, but especially when you're hurting—you should be. Finding an insightful therapist, one who is not only a knowledgeable technician, but also a genuine healer—yes, they really do exist—is *the* ticket. Preferably an avid tennis player, they will not be hell bent on some esoteric degree of self-directed "deep" tissue manipulation that is not only unpleasant at the time, but also leaves you, the one supposedly in need, feeling beat up and worse later on, much like a bad haircut. The relief that you'll experience from a true professional—not only from regular wear and tear, but particularly from any chronic injury episodes as well—is far greater than you could ever imagine. Please trust me.

If you're not into regular *post*-play stretching, especially when you're hurting or when just feeling a little stiffer than normal—probably a category that would include most club players with at least one gray hair—you should be. The benefit can be enormous. The emphasis is on *after* play—when your core body temperature is fully elevated after repeated muscle "burning"—to assist in alleviating an excessive build-up of the debilitating lactic acid (blood lactate level) left stagnating in one's muscles. Additionally, you cannot and should not attempt to stretch "cold" muscles without first taking the time to warm them up for stretching by, for example, jogging very slowly around the court or parking lot a few times. Jog, stretch (passively), play is a proper progression in order to play your best, although there are many who are healthy and successful who only stretch after play since they are extremely methodical in their on court warm-up.

Operating instructions for your amazing self-righting machine most importantly include first being realistic in your expectations relative to your fitness level, then paying close attention to your body's "talk" since it almost always warns you of impending danger if you're truly listening. Do not cross this "line" or you will surely pay the price sooner or later. No one, and I mean no one, knows your body better than you do, especially if you're keenly in touch with your physical self. At least learn to trust your own instincts and intuitions, and not someone else's amateur diagnosis.

After disposing of Roger Federer in straight sets at a warm-up event just prior to the 2004 Australian Open, Andre Agassi, at, for tour players, the ancient age of thirty-three, said, "As you get older, you have to make adjustments. You have to listen to your body a little clearer, which means pushing yourself when you're feeling like you can really make progress, and sort of being aware of where you need to give yourself the breaks."

Obviously, if you think that you've got a serious problem, you probably do. Absolutely consult a sports medicine specialist who is also an active participant in sports—again, preferably a tennis player—who can specifically relate to the considerable physical demands of the game on *both* a professional level and a personal one as well.

Afterword

Tennis is undoubtedly the greatest game on earth. Where else, but on a tennis court, can you connect so intimately with even a complete stranger? The continual juggling of one ball, it being smashed, caressed, and spun back and forth between two or four players on a court with dimensions proven timelessly perfect for the act. Muscles twitching, eyes keenly focused, heart pumping, fully engaged in its infinite currents. Then, lo and behold, anyone and everyone, fully trained or completely unschooled, nearly always experiences, at the very least, some inkling of the euphoria inherent in a perfectly struck shot—whether by design, good fortune, or blind luck—every single time out. Like the thirst quenching sensation of a cold glass of pure water, the belly filling satisfaction of a gourmet meal, or the full embrace of a lover, this ethereal game of tennis can, in an instant, transcend everything and more whenever you let go and allow it to be.

Its innate malleability is such that there exists no "right" way to play. You are totally free to both invent and reinvent yourself daily, and put your own signature squarely on each and every round ball struck, at best in a perfect synergy of the physical, mental, emotional, and even spiritual uniqueness of your being.

In sharing my passion for tennis, I hope that I have contributed, in at least some measure, to fueling your enthusiasm for a never ending pursuit of the true player within, and, best of all, to experiencing the pure joy of it all.

When the best athletes on the planet gathered in Greece—where sporting contests between men first began nearly 2,800 years ago—for the 2004 Athens Olympic Games, we were all fortuitously reminded of what Homer wrote in *The Odyssey*, "There is no greater glory for a man in all his life than what he wins [gains] with his own feet and hands."

Bibliography

Anderson, Dave. "It's Not Zen, It's the Zone for Rodriguez and His Performance Coach." *New York Times.* 21 April 2004, Sports Wednesday, p.C 27.

Annacone, Paul. "Charting a New Course." *USTA Magazine.* March/April 2002, p. 13.

Ask Mac. *Tennis Week.* 4 April 2002, p. 3.

Brown, Bruce Eamon. *Teaching Character Through Sport.* Coaches Choice, 2001.

Edomonds, David and John Eidinow. *Bobby Fischer Goes to War.* New York: Harper Collins, 2004.

Exley, Helen. *Tennis Quotations.* London: Exley Publications, 1996.

Fox, Allen. "Why Winning is Latent for Hewitt." *Tennis Week.* 21 October 2003, p. 23.

Jennings, Jay. *Tennis and the Meaning of Life.* New York: Harcourt Brace, 1995.

Jones, Charlie and Kim Doren. *Game, Set, Match.* Kansas City: Andrews McMeel Publishing, 2002.

Little, John. *Bruce Lee: Artist of Life.* Boston: Tuttle Publishing, 2001.

Millman, Dan. *The Warrior Athlete.* Walpole, New Hampshire: Stillpoint Publishing, 1979.

Nyad, Diana. "After the Scandals Have Played Out, Let the Games Begin." *New York Times.* 25 July 2004, Sports Sunday, p.10.

Phillips, Caryl. *The Right Set.* New York: Vintage Books, 1999.

Schiller, David. *The Little Zen Companion.* New York: Workman Publishing, 1994.

Wallace, David Foster. *A Supposedly Fun Thing I'll Never Do Again.* Boston: Little, Brown and Company, 1997.

Short quotes were gathered from the following publications: *The New York Times, USA Today, Time Magazine, USTA Magazine, USTA High Performance Coaching, Tennis Week, Tennis, Racquet, The New Yorker.*